Challenging Parental Alienation

This book addresses the concept of parental alienation – the belief that when a child of divorced parents avoids one parent, it may be because the preferred parent has persuaded the child to do this. It argues against the unquestioning use of parental alienation concepts in child custody conflicts.

Increasing use of this concept in family courts has led at times to placement of children with abusive or violent parents, damage to the lives of preferred parents, and the use of treatments that have not been shown to be safe or effective. The 13 chapters cover the history and theory of "parental alienation" principles and practices. Methodological and research issues are considered, and diagnostic and treatment methods associated with "parental alienation" beliefs as well as those recommended by research and ethical evidence are analyzed. The connections of "parental alienation" with gender and domestic violence issues are discussed as are the experiences of individuals who have experienced "parental alienation" treatments. The book argues that "parental alienation" principles and practices should be avoided by family courts, in the best interests of children in custody disputes.

This book will be useful reading for lawyers, judges, children's services workers including social workers, child protection court workers, and mental health professionals involved in child custody decisions.

Jean Mercer is Professor Emerita of Psychology at Stockton University in New Jersey, USA. She is a developmental psychologist with concerns about potentially harmful therapies that are used for children, including "holding therapy" and other coercive methods. She has published a number of articles critiquing theory and research on parental alienation allegations in child custody cases.

Margaret Drew is an Associate Professor of Law who teaches at the University of Massachusetts School of Law, USA, and has represented domestic abuse survivors in trial and appellate courts. Professor Drew's scholarship has focused primarily on intimate partner abuse and its impact on vulnerable populations. Some areas of interest are lawyer malpractice in domestic violence cases, the vulnerability of people living with HIV, the use of Collaborative Law in domestic violence cases, and bringing a human rights framework to legal remedies for survivors of abuse.

Challenging Parental Alienation

New Directions for Professionals and Parents

Edited by
Jean Mercer and Margaret Drew

Routledge
Taylor & Francis Group

LONDON AND NEW YORK

First published 2022
by Routledge
2 Park Square, Milton Park, Abingdon, Oxon OX14 4RN

and by Routledge
605 Third Avenue, New York, NY 10158

Routledge is an imprint of the Taylor & Francis Group, an informa business

British Library Cataloguing-in-Publication Data
A catalogue record for this book is available from the British Library

Library of Congress Cataloging-in-Publication Data
A catalog record has been requested for this book

ISBN: 978-0-367-55977-9 (hbk)
ISBN: 978-0-367-55976-2 (pbk)
ISBN: 978-1-003-09592-7 (ebk)

DOI: 10.4324/9781003095927

Typeset in Bembo
by codeMantra

Dedications

JM: To Scott Lilienfeld, Jeffrey Lohr, and Cathleen Mann, scholars of science and pseudoscience

MBD: To George
The Hammonds
and especially my clients

Contents

Contributors

Adrienne Barnett is Senior Lecturer in Law at Brunel University London, UK. Prior to commencing in full-time academia in January 2014, Adrienne practiced as a barrister in London for over 30 years specializing in Family Law. For over 20 years she has researched domestic abuse and, more recently, parental alienation, in private family law cases in England and Wales.

Kelly M. Champion (PhD ABPP) is Clinical and Forensic Psychologist in independent practice in Rockville, Maryland. She is board certified in clinical child and adolescent psychology and specializes in treating children and adolescents, child maltreatment, adult trauma, family assessment, court-involved families, and school bullying. Previous to her clinical career, she was Assistant Professor researching school bullying first at Gustavus Adolphus College and later at Arizona State University on the west campus.

Julie Doughty (PhD) is Senior Lecturer in Law, Cardiff University School of Law and Politics, UK. She has previously practiced as a solicitor in England and Wales, as a guardian ad litem panel manager, and for Cafcass (Children and Family Court Advisory and Support Service).

Margaret Drew (JD, LLM) is Associate Professor of law who teaches at the University of Massachusetts School of Law, USA. Since 1981 she has represented domestic abuse survivors in district, family, and appellate courts. She was recognized by the American Bar Association's Commission on Domestic and Sexual Abuse with their 20/20 Vision award that honored those who mobilized the legal profession against domestic and sexual violence since the enactment of the Violence against Women Act. Prof. Drew was in private practice for 25 years before joining academia.

Nancy S. Erickson is attorney and has a master's degree in Forensic Psychology. She acts as a consultant to attorneys and mental health professionals on issues relating to law and psychology, particularly child custody evaluations, domestic abuse, and the application of the Americans with Disabilities Act to litigants who need accommodations in court. For over ten years, she was Professor of law, teaching Family Law, Sex Discrimination Law, Constitutional Law, Women's Legal History and other subjects. She has also been a practicing attorney, primarily representing abused women. She has been honored for her pro bono work, has lectured to judges, attorneys, psychologists, battered women, and other audiences, and has written books and articles on many areas of family law, especially domestic violence and custody.

Stephen D. A. Hupp (PhD) is Licensed Clinical Psychologist and Professor of clinical psychology at Southern Illinois University, Edwardsville. He has over 50 publications related to child development and therapy.

Joan Meier is Professor at George Washington University Law School, where she directs the National Family Violence Law Center. She has published widely on domestic violence, custody, and social science and law, and has provided hundreds of trainings to judges, lawyers, legislators, mental health providers, and others. Between 2003 and 2019, she also founded and directed the Domestic Violence Legal Empowerment and Appeals Project (DV LEAP), handling appeals in state courts of appeal and the U.S. Supreme Court.

Jean Mercer (PhD) is Professor Emerita of Psychology at Stockton University in New Jersey, USA. She is a developmental psychologist with concerns about potentially harmful therapies that are used for children, including "holding therapy" and other coercive methods. She has published a number of articles critiquing theory and research on parental alienation allegations in child custody cases.

Madelyn Simring Milchman has practiced clinical and forensic psychology in New Jersey since 1986. Her expertise is in trauma, including child sexual and emotional abuse, incest survivors, domestic violence, rape, recovered memory, sexual harassment, PTSD, divorce/custody, parental alienation, and other types of trauma. She won the American Professional Society on the Abuse of Children 2019 Outstanding Frontline Professional Award for her work on the relationship between child abuse allegations and parental alienation allegations. She has served as an expert witness in child custody cases, relocation cases, reunification cases, criminal child sexual abuse cases, and psychological injury cases involving trauma-related issues. She has presented and published articles nationally and internationally in these and related areas including principles and methods for forensic evaluations and working with psychological experts. She serves as an evaluating expert, a scientific expert, a consulting expert, and a rebuttal expert.

Zoe Rathus (AM) is Senior Lecturer at the Griffith University Law School. She worked in private practice and at the Women's Legal Service for over

20 years prior to academia. She has advocated for legal system reform regarding violence against women for her entire career.

Arianna Riley is a writer from Seattle and a survivor of institutional child abuse and forced family separation. She has talked to various lawmakers in multiple states in the hopes of improving the safety of children and preventing court-ordered child trafficking. In her free time, you can probably find her at the beach enjoying life.

Sarah T. Trane (PhD ABPP LP) is Assistant Professor of Psychology with Board Certification in Clinical Child and Adolescent Psychology at the Mayo Clinic Health System in La Crosse, WI. Her clinical practice focuses on applying evidence-based methods to integrated behavioral health in primary care, including program development, training therapists, medical residents, and other medical staff in best practices for behavioral health of youth. Dr. Trane earned her doctoral degree in Clinical Child Psychology from the University of Kansas in 2000 followed by a postdoctoral fellowship in Pediatric and Family Psychology at the Mayo Clinic in Rochester, MN.

Suzanne Zaccour is a doctoral candidate in law at Oxford University, UK. She holds an LLM from the University of Cambridge, an LLM from the University of Toronto, and a double diploma in common law and civil law from McGill University. Her research mostly focuses on the use of parental alienation theory in the law, on domestic and sexual violence against women, and on inclusive language in French.

Foreword

In 1984, I began work as a prosecutor in Kentucky. I soon noticed that cases involving domestic violence played out differently from other cases. Witness/victims often did not appear for trial or recanted prior statements. Prosecutors and police became frustrated, and charges were often dismissed. I set out to learn what made domestic violence cases different.

I contacted our local domestic violence service center, and it was there that I was initially educated on the dynamics of domestic violence and the unusual considerations that victims of these crimes wrestled with, particularly when children were involved. I soon came to understand the counter-intuitive nature of some victims' responses to abuse. This learning assisted me in my career as a prosecutor and became invaluable when I was elected to the family court bench. I served on the Family Court for Jefferson County Kentucky for over 18 years. During that time, I heard thousands of cases involving domestic violence. I saw the dynamics of intimate partner abuse play out in my courtroom, including the attempt by abusers to manipulate the court. Mothers most often, but not exclusively, were the abused parties that came before me. Over the years of service, I observed anti-survivor tactics escalate, particularly in cases involving child custody and parenting time. Because I provide national and international training for judges and others, I heard firsthand of the allegations of "parental alienation".

I recognized that when allegations of alienation are raised in cases involving domestic abuse, the allegations were advanced to minimize any claims of abuse. I came to recognize, as well, that most lawyers and judges are not sufficiently educated on intimate partner abuse and how those dynamics play out in court. Some parents behave badly during divorce and separation and say unwarranted negative comments regarding the other parent's relationship and in the presence of the children. This behavior is unacceptable and the harm to the children must be addressed. In cases involving abuse, however, claims of alienation must be set aside with the court focusing on allegations of abuse by one parent and any trauma the family has endured. Typically, judges will find that when alienation claims are raised in cases involving abuse, the claim is a manipulative tool of the abuser being used to deflect attention from their abusive behaviors. This claim can come in many forms, whether it is called estrangement, enmeshment, resistance or other terms that essentially promote the alienation belief system. But all have the same goal in abuse cases – to minimize the court's focus on the abusive parent and the risk those parents pose to the children's well-being.

Because cases with competing claims of alienation and domestic abuse present polarized positions, judges, lawyers, and mental health providers must be competently trained in the multifaceted dynamics of domestic abuse to sort out abuser's tools of abuse from valid fears expressed by the targeted parent and their children.

Because courts tend to be reactive and not preventative, many children will suffer when placed with the abusive parent. Separating the children from their protective parent can lead to additional trauma to the children and the cycle of violent behavior continued. This book is important in showing ways for judges to prevent further harm in abuse cases where alienation claims are raised. Judges are then in a position to proactively prevent any further harm to the children and protective parent by considering their emotional, physical, and mental safety first in deciding custody cases.

Challenging Parental Alienation is critical reading for those involved in abuse/alienation cases to understand why alienation is best not entertained once abuse claims are asserted. To do otherwise is to further burden the survivor of abuse and the children. I am grateful that the authors have taken this topic on and explain the intricacies of how the parental alienation belief system can undermine justice for abuse survivors and their children, instead of supporting their protective gatekeeping from the abuser.

Judge Jerry Bowles (Ret.)

Chapter 1

Introduction to parental alienation concepts and practices

Jean Mercer and Margaret Drew

Allie was 17 and Merle 14 when they stated their strong preferences for living with their father and limiting their contacts with their mother and her boyfriend. The parents had been divorced for years and had managed to parent the girls successfully. But the presence of the boyfriend was a problem for the two girls, and when they stated this, their mother accused their father of having "alienated" them from her by manipulating their beliefs and emotions. After some litigation, a family court judge agreed that this must have happened and ordered Allie and Merle to be taken to another state to receive treatment for their attitudes. The girls were taken in handcuffs from the courtroom. Subsequently, Allie petitioned for emancipation and received it. Merle now lives in a different state with her mother and the boyfriend and does not see her father or Allie.

Elise's parents divorced before she entered her teens. They lived in the same town and Elise alternated living weeks with her mother and her father. When she was 17, she became tired of the weekly transfer routine and proposed that she should have a home at her mother's house and visit her father frequently. Her father did not accept this idea and declared that Elise's mother must have caused her to become alienated from him. He went to court and obtained a court order for Elise to be taken to a treatment program and prevented her from seeing her mother. Elise eventually managed to get back to her mother's house, but she was in her twenties before she saw her younger brother again, because he had been ordered to stay at the father's house.

Rob was in his early teens when his divorced father decided that Rob's reluctance to spend time with him was caused by his mother's persuasion. Rob's father went to court without notifying the mother and obtained custody of Rob on an "emergency" basis. A family court failed to investigate or listen to Rob's explanation that he was afraid of his father because of the domestic violence he had seen in their household. Instead, the court ordered that Rob enter a treatment program and prohibited him from having contact with his mother. As Rob got closer to his 18th birthday, he thought he might be able to see his mother again, but his father had him declared incompetent

DOI: 10.4324/9781003095927-1

and placed under the father's guardianship, despite Rob's successful school career and other abilities.

Siobhan was a high-functioning autistic girl in her mid-teens and living with her divorced mother when her father decided that she had developed negative attitudes toward him. In fact, Siobhan, who attended a special school, asked for time with her father, but he averred that if he saw her alone, she would claim he had molested her. Siobhan's father asked the family court for full custody of his daughter, on the grounds that her mother had harmed her by alienating her. He also said he would send her to boarding school when he had custody. The parents settled out of court after some negotiation about child support.

These anecdotes describe several different factors at work in child custody conflicts between separated parents. Boys, girls, mothers, fathers, and teenagers with different abilities and personalities, all are represented in these narratives. But the stories share a focus on a single idea, that children who reject contact with one parent are likely to have developed a negative attitude toward that parent because of the other parent's intentional or unconscious actions. The term frequently used for this concept is parental alienation, often abbreviated as "PA". The idea of parental alienation has been used with increasing and alarming frequency in child custody decisions since its introduction in the 1990s, despite a lack of evidence showing that the basic concept applies in more than a few cases. International and national psychological associations have refused to accept the proposal that a child's rejection of a parent is evidence of a psychological disorder. In this book, authors from various disciplines discuss principles, practices, and problems associated with the alienation concept and what happens when those with the power to determine custody accept the premises about parental alienation as reflections of frequent real events.

Terminology

Awkwardly and confusingly, ever since Richard Gardner (1985) introduced the idea of parental alienation, proponents of these concepts have used the term parental alienation to mean at least three different things: (1) the belief system that claims the preferred parent is the cause of a child's avoidance or rejection of the nonpreferred parent; (2) the avoidance or rejection itself; and (3) the posited behavior of the preferred parent that is said to cause the child's avoidance or rejection. Not only do these multiple uses of the term obscure what is being talked about, but the ambiguity of the language makes it too easy to imply that when one of these phenomena is referenced, one or more of the others must be present. This is especially a problem when a child is said to show avoidance of one parent, and this statement is also taken to suggest, without further evidence, that a parent's encouragement of the child's avoidance is present.

We are far from the first authors to note the ambiguities of the parental alienation terminology. As interested professionals and affected parents have struggled with creating a meaningful vocabulary, they have used terms like contact refusal, resist/refuse dynamic, parent–child relationship problems, contact problems, and alienating behaviors to try to discriminate between child avoidance of a parent and possible actions of the preferred parent that encourage such avoidance. People have often come back to "parental alienation" or "PA" as quick (though confusing) ways to speak of these phenomena. Nevertheless, readers of this book need to be aware of the various terminological efforts in order both to be able to follow what is said here and to compare it to previous published material.

In addition to confusing child behavior and parent behavior, "parental alienation" terminology tends to conflate behavior designed to inappropriately influence a child against the other parent with behaviors occurring for other reasons, as well as with various behaviors that do not necessarily involve a child's rejection of a parent. For example, using broad terms like "parental alienation" may equate this issue with rejection problems that are completely different. For example, a child's apparent rejection of a parent could be based on preference for contact with a parent away from the parent's house, or unhappiness with the location of a parent's house, or distancing from a stepparent or stepsiblings, in which cases, the issue is not the child's attitude toward the parent, but the child's feelings about other people or circumstances.

As there is now extensive literature arguing both for and against the parental alienation concept and its related terminology, we, the editors, and authors of this book, find ourselves in a difficult situation. We cannot abandon the term parental alienation, or we risk having no one understand the context of our discussion. A brand new vocabulary suggests that we are discussing a novel set of ideas—and we are not. But if we adopt the ambiguous multiple usages of past work by parental alienation proponents, we risk simply adding to the confusion and failing to make our own points. We can, however, decline to use "PA", however handy it might be, as the use of abbreviations tends to encourage reification of a concept, and this helps authors and readers to forget about the observable nature of the events under discussion. At this point, we are still without most of the needed empirical information about children's avoidance of a divorced or separated parent, and it would be counterproductive to yield to the temptation to think of children's behavior in terms of an abstraction that has yet to be derived from reliable data.

Therefore, we propose and will use a terminology that clearly disambiguates the three different phenomena that have in the past all been called parental alienation. For the system of ideas that relates a preferred parent's actions to a child's avoidance or rejection of the other parent, we will use the term parental alienation belief system. Supporters of this system's principles and practices will be called parental alienation proponents or advocates or authors.

Second, a child's avoidance of or rejection of one parent will be called child avoidant behavior, or child avoidance. This observable behavior can range from eye-rolling and muttering in resistance to everyday matters, to refusal to speak to or go near a parent, to emotional and physical collapse when forced to go near the parent. (It would not, however, include requests from the child to alter parenting time for the child's convenience, or to have a voice in decision-making.)

Third, observed events in which the preferred parent persuades, forces, or encourages the child to avoid the other parent will be called parent encouragement of child avoidant behavior, or parent encouragement. It should be noted that this third usage refers to an event that is often asserted but rarely proved by parental alienation proponents, who tend to infer the existence of parent encouragement when they observe child avoidance.

There are a few other terms commonly used by parental alienation proponents that also need to be replaced. When a child rejects contact with one of the separated parents and strongly prefers to live with the other parent, parental alienation proponents refer to the rejected parent as the targeted parent, implying that someone has intentionally caused the child's negative attitude toward that person. In this book, we will use the neutral term nonpreferred parent. Parental alienation proponents also refer to the parent favored by the child as the alienating parent, implying some certainty about the causal role of that parent's behavior in creating the child's resistance. Instead, we will use the neutral term preferred parent.

Some terminology used by parental alienation proponents involves psychological treatments proposed for correction of child avoidant behavior. These treatments may be referred to by their proprietary names (e.g., Family Bridges™) or in a general way as reunification therapies. The term reunification therapy is somewhat deceptive, as this term originally referenced treatment methods intended to help children who had been in foster care and needed to reunite successfully with their biological families. Treatments directed at changing children's attitudes toward a rejected separated parent are not necessarily comparable to those used to help children move out of the foster system. We will use the term parental alienation treatments to describe specific parental alienation-related methods intended to persuade a child to accept rather than reject a parent.

Finally, in our discussion of issues related to the parental alienation belief system, we need to choose a term to identify the parents who are involved in child custody conflicts. Many, but not all, have been legally married and divorced, while others are married but separated, and some were never married and may not even have lived together. For simplicity, we will refer to all these parents as divorced parents or separated parents.

Readers should note that the terminology associated with the parental alienation belief system changes frequently. Some interventions for children who avoid a parent have been called reunification therapies, although this term has historically referred to treatments for children returning from foster care to their biological families. Some authors now use the term reintegration therapies instead of reunification. The term enmeshment, descriptive of situations where family members are overly dependent on each other, is sometimes substituted for the phrase parental alienating behaviors in discussions of custody decisions. We expect that further terminological changes will occur and caution readers to be aware of the actual meaning of terms used in the discussion of children's avoidance of one parent and preference for the other.

About this book and its authors

This book is directed to an audience of psychologists, social workers, lawyers, judges, and others who may find themselves embroiled in child custody cases where one parent alleges that the other has alienated the children and encouraged them to reject the first parent, and thus caused the first parent to be rejected by a child and display child avoidant behavior. (Parents who are alleged to have alienated their children may also be interested in the material presented here.) Although most of these cases will begin with some evidence that a child has avoided contact with one parent, this will not necessarily be true of all of them.

Cases where parent encouragement of child avoidant behavior is alleged are often difficult and confusing for professionals as well as for the parents involved. The level of disagreement in these cases is stark, and there may be a history or even current events of domestic violence and child abuse. Both parents are likely to be angry or agitated and may be intransigent with respect to any compromises or negotiations. Financial issues are an important factor in parental alienation-related cases, not only with respect to property division and child support but also in terms of the expense to one or the other parent as payment for psychological treatments that may be ordered by a family court.

Professional journals in the fields of psychology, social work, and law have published many articles on issues of parent encouragement of child avoidant behavior, some written by parental alienation supporters, and others by authors who strongly oppose the parental alienation belief system. Several books present highly positive views of parental alienation-related thinking, but the present volume is the first book to bring together material that opposes the unquestioning use of parental alienation concepts in child custody cases. This book is intended to provide information that can be used in challenging unfounded allegations that a parent has encouraged a child's avoidance of the other parent. The authors and editors believe that the material offered here will counter misinformation that may be brought into the courtroom by proponents of the parental alienation belief system.

Discussion of parental alienation allegations can include an unusually wide range of topics, and no single discipline provides the training for addressing all factors. As the table of contents shows, this book examines the historical and theoretical background of parental alienation concepts, considers the scientific evidence that has been put forward to support parental alienation-related thinking and practice, and explores the roles of gender issues including domestic violence and other abuse in child avoidance cases. Two chapters examine issues of child custody evaluations and the related question of identification of children who avoid contact with a parent for reasons claimed to be a result of the other parent's encouragement or persuasion. The authors who have contributed chapters are professionals who have been engaged for years with child custody cases in which parent encouragement of child avoidant behavior is alleged; many have published important work on this topic in professional journals. Their chapters directed not only toward people in each author's own discipline, but toward other professionals who may benefit from understanding the roles played by professionals outside their fields in child custody proceedings where parent encouragement of child avoidance is claimed. For the benefit of all readers, Chapter 4 also includes material provided by people who have personally experienced parental alienation treatments.

The problems associated with the wide use of parental alienation concepts are interdisciplinary ones, and the solutions to these problems lie in interdisciplinary work combining the efforts of legal, mental health, and other professionals who are trained to work with families.

The authors of this book's chapters primarily live in the United States, Britain, Australia, and Canada but are in contact with concerned professionals and affected parents in many other countries. Although the origins of the parental alienation perspective appear to be in the United States, related ideas have spread through much of the world. A case in point is the situation in Brazil, where legislation some years ago criminalized conduct that was interpreted as parent encouragement of child avoidant behavior.

The problem of allegations against preferred parents

Why is the parental alienation perspective worth extended discussion? As human beings do many ill-considered and even despicable things, it appears more than possible that a few preferred parents do persuade their children that the other parent is dangerous or disgusting. Negative influencing of this kind could be expected to have deleterious effects on children and is certainly not fair to the maligned parent. Is it then inappropriate to include parental alienation views in child custody decisions? Or is the problem the fact that parent encouragement of child avoidance has been overemphasized and presented as a critical factor, when in fact there is no real rationale for this presentation theoretically or, often, factually?

There are several serious problems associated with the use of the parental alienation belief system in child custody work. One is the simple fact that there is no established method for discriminating between children who reject a parent for ample reason (e.g., experience of that parent as violent, physically, or emotionally abusive, or sexually predatory) and those whose rejection has been created or inappropriately influenced by the preferred parent. There has never been even a single published complete case study that would show how identification of a parental alienation case was accomplished. As a result, there are no data on incidence or prevalence of child avoidant behavior or of parent encouragement of such behavior. No information exists for determining how frequently there are false positive claims that actual encouragement of avoidant behavior has occurred, nor indeed how often there are false negative findings, the latter possibly meaning that children who have really been inappropriately persuaded are not identified and helped. Identification of inappropriate parental behaviors that have the goal of rejection of the other parent appears almost invariably to be an inference from the child's attitude and behavior rather than a matter of objective evidence that inappropriate persuasion has taken place. Children said to display rejecting behaviors are often not identified as having been subjected to inappropriate parental influence. Such children are hardly ever evaluated for real emotional disorders that could affect their behavior toward one or both parents. Yet parental alienation proponents may present arguments about child custody based on the assumption that their identification of parent encouragement of child avoidant behavior is correct.

A second and serious parental alienation-related problem involves the recommendations of parental alienation proponents testifying in child custody conflicts. These recommendations invariably include some form of parental alienation treatment, sometimes called reunification therapy, but such treatments do not usually stand alone. Children sent for some treatments are by court order transferred to the custody of the nonpreferred parent and prohibited from contact with the preferred parent, for periods of time that may begin with 90 days but may be extended for years. Some teenagers have reported adverse effects of programs they attended (see Chapter 4), and there is evidence that there is danger to some who are placed with abusive parents and prevented from having contact with the preferred parent or other family members who could monitor their well-being. The burden on the preferred parent is extraordinarily heavy. The anxiety and concerns of the preferred parent for the child are likely to be great, particularly if there is a history of domestic violence. But the arguments made by parental alienation proponents are even more problematic in their potential effects on preferred parents. Parental alienation advocates argue that a child who disagrees with all or part of a parenting plan is mentally ill, that the mental illness was caused by inappropriate parental influence, and that the preferred parent is thus by definition a child abuser and should not have contact with the child. If this argument is accepted by the court, the preferred parent is labeled as abusive, an event that may have the most serious repercussions socially and professionally, especially if the preferred parent works with families or children in any capacity.

When children are court-ordered to treatments, the preferred parents may be ordered to pay the costs of the treatment, which amounts to many thousands of dollars even for "workshops" lasting a few days. The preferred parents are also required to seek psychological treatment for themselves at their own cost as directed by parental alienation proponents. Treatment generally continues until such time as the preferred parents agree to acknowledge that they have been guilty of parent encouragement of child avoidant behavior, yet neither denial nor acknowledgment is accepted as the reason for renewed contact with the child.

Context and background of the problem

The focus of this book will be a detailed discussion and analysis of the parental alienation belief system and its effects on children and parents who come before family courts. We will include the impacts of gender issues, including domestic violence, as a factor in claims of parent encouragement of child avoidant behavior during child custody conflicts and litigation. First, however, this introductory chapter will discuss some of the factors that form the context within which parental alienation arguments and decision-making take place.

Child custody evaluations

Although readers of this book may not perform child custody evaluations themselves, they will find it helpful to understand how parental alienation-based allegations can influence the court in custody cases. This is particularly true when the reader understands some of the standards and recommendations for the performance of such evaluations. A brief discussion here will help prepare for references to custody evaluations in later chapters.

Custody evaluations are an important part of family court child custody decision-making. These evaluations may be done in somewhat different ways, depending on a child's age and particular needs; for example, evaluation of an infant and a teenager will have different concerns, and evaluation of a typically developing child will be different from that of a child with special medical or psychological problems. Nevertheless, there are general rules that evaluators are expected to follow, and these are often ignored when either parent encouragement of child avoidant behavior or domestic abuse is alleged.

The American Psychological Association (APA) posted guidelines for child custody evaluators ("Guidelines…" n.d.). The guidelines note that custody evaluations may be used in disputes over decision-making, caretaking, and access to contact with children when parents of dissolving families are in conflict. Such disputes occur only about 10% of the time during family dissolution, but when they do occur, the parents may be bitter and intransigent, and their emotions may be long-lasting. Information from custody evaluations can give the best guidance available to the court under these circumstances.

The APA guidelines emphasize the role of the evaluation in helping to determine the best psychological interests of the child and to provide an evaluation of those interests to be used by the court as a factor in determining custody and contact with a child. (The concept of the child's best interests is far from a simple one and will be discussed further along in this introductory chapter.) In a properly conducted evaluation, the child's welfare is considered to be of the highest importance and takes precedence over parental concerns. The evaluation should also examine the fit between the child's needs and parents' characteristics rather than considering child and parent as isolated entities or focusing on individual personalities.

The guidelines recommend use of some important factors in custody evaluation practice. Psychologists are directed to obtain informed consent for their investigations; this may involve communication at various levels of difficulty, depending on the abilities of the person being examined. Any report should include clear statements describing the people who will see the information and how the information may be used. Although it is not required that informed consent be given by people who give collateral information, such as teachers or neighbors, the guidelines suggest that this procedure is desirable. Multiple methods of information-gathering are encouraged by the guidelines, so that an evaluator may use standardized testing, interviews, and observation, but should also include items like documentation from schools or healthcare providers and from collateral sources such as extended family members whose statements can support or refute hypotheses about the best interest of the child.

The guidelines stress that interpretation of evaluation data should be in the context of the family dissolution and conflicts over children. Parents in these circumstances may respond differently to tests and interviews than they would in a less disturbing situation, and test results may thus be in some part a measure of their distress rather than an assessment of basic personality characteristics. The guidelines emphasize, as well, the necessity to evaluate both parents before formulating a recommendation. If this is not possible, the custody evaluation report needs to clearly state the information used and how it was collected. Professional and scientific standards for information must be met in child custody evaluation reports, and "unsupported beliefs" are to be avoided.

The APA guidelines just discussed contain no references to the parental alienation belief system or parental alienation treatments of various kinds. So far, the APA has not taken a clear position about the parental alienation belief system and has not considered child avoidant behavior as a disorder. However, the American Professional Society on Abuse of Children (APSAC) has moved to clarify its position on the role of parent encouragement of child avoidant behavior as a part of psychological maltreatment, which is a factor with an obvious role in child custody determinations. Although an earlier statement had sometimes been used to argue that APSAC officially considered unreasonable parental influence to be evidence of psychological maltreatment, the 2019 revision ("APSAC announces..." 2019) firmly states that APSAC does not include parental alienation-related allegations as evidence of psychological maltreatment of children. The announcement notes that claims of parental alienation are "too often made without careful evaluation of allegations of child maltreatment, intimate partner violence, and other parental bad acts, especially in custody disputes".

Both APA and APSAC have emphasized the importance of thorough, evidence-based examinations of all parties' claims in custody recommendations. As we will see in a later chapter of this book, parental alienation-based custody recommendations may fail to follow these guidelines.

Best interests of the child

The idea that child custody should be decided in a way that assures the best interests of the child is a relatively modern one, dating to the 1970s (Goldstein et al. 1973). Historically, children have been seen as chattel property, belonging to their fathers, with all decisions and authority legally the fathers' perquisites. From the 1880s, the roles of mothers in child-rearing received attention, culminating in the "tender years" doctrine that gave mothers custody for children from birth until about age seven and often led to continued maternal custody as the children got older; this doctrine was in part based on the idea that mothers did not work outside the home, were therefore available, and in addition had a peculiarly feminine capacity for childcare.

Goldstein et al. (1973) attempted to refocus custody decisions on children's individual needs and rights rather than on presumptive adult characteristics. They termed this focus "the best interests of the child" and noted that establishing the best interests of any given child involves examining the parents' characteristics and circumstances and the child's characteristics, all of which help to determine how the child's social and physical environment can support the best developmental outcome. Recognizing the difficulties children experience when separated parents are in conflict, these authors proposed that one parent be designated the custodial parent and have authority and responsibility for all decisions about the child, the custodial parent consulting with the noncustodial parent only as the former chose.

In the decades following the Goldstein et al. book, increasing interest in aspects of early emotional development led to discussion of attachment issues in children with separated parents. Some custody decisions—and some reversals of earlier decisions—were based on ideas about the psychology of emotional attachment but did not necessarily align with the psychological evidence about this aspect of emotional development. Lawyer arguments and judicial decision-making often failed to understand the nature of developmental change and to differentiate between young infant and adolescent development. This became a problem for custody decisions based on attachment arguments. Some decisions dramatically understated the importance of stable social relationships for very young children, and others overstated the importance of relationships with parents for older adolescents. Consequently, evaluators were (and are) asked to do "bonding and attachment" assessments, although there is no established protocol for such an evaluation, and the term "bonding" properly belongs to assessment of parental attitudes, not children's emotions.

Nonetheless, attempts to include attachment issues in custody evaluations led to a better understanding of the nature of child–parent relationships. These relationships were no longer seen as created by physical connections, genetic, or prenatal and birth factors. Instead, it became understood that children developed emotional attachments to a parent, and therefore could be distressed by separation at some points in development, as the result of a shift in the amount of time spent in social interaction with that parent. Social interactions between parent and child were often (almost always, in infancy) associated with care routines like feeding and bathing, so questions about the amount of time and caregiving each parent had provided to a child became part of evaluations. Some authors even proposed an "approximation rule" under which the proportion of time a child would be in the physical custody of a parent depended in part on that parent's caregiving history; the history became in a sense a proxy measure for attachment. Attachment concepts provided a fruitful approach to child custody decisions, although many jurists did not take into account the developmental changes in attachment shown by older children and adolescents.

Children's rights, parent rights, and shared parenting

The 1980s and 1990s were simultaneously a period of concern with children's rights and a time when fathers' rights (as well as parents' rights in general) began to be discussed intensively. As the rights, needs, and wishes of parents and children may be opposed to each other, and are clearly so in parental alienation-related cases, the increasing conflict between the two played out in contrary ways. While permanency planning was promoted for children in state custody, contested family court custody cases between parents became more common and resulted in protracted litigation that left the subject children in various states of uncertainty.

The 1989 United Nation Convention on the Rights of the Child proposed that children have rights that need consideration in addition to or even in opposition to their parents' human rights. Still unratified by the United States, this convention crystallized changes in the legal view of children, from their

earlier position as property to a new status as human beings with some limitations on their actions. Whether children should be considered as having rights
remains a question for some parental alienation advocates, who argue that
children and even adolescents are in fact injured by being given consideration
for their wishes. The precise nature of children's rights to self-determination
remains unclear. Indeed, these rights could hardly be stated clearly without
regard to individuals' age and developmental status, so the rights issue continues to play an unpredictable role in custody recommendations.

At about the same time that the increasing concern with children's rights
started, fathers' groups began to argue that they were unfairly treated by the
courts with respect to child custody and access, decision-making about children's medical and educational needs, and child support payments. Fathers
with these concerns coalesced into groups that formed a fathers' rights
movement and pressed for legislation and legal decisions that they felt would
provide redress for these alleged wrongs. Although it would be incorrect to
conflate fathers' rights advocates with parental alienation proponents, there is
no question that there is overlap between the groups. Fathers' rights groups
should not be confused with fatherhood initiatives that focus on fatherhood
responsibilities and promote healthy relationships between fathers and their
children. Fathers' rights groups are distinguished by their focus on perceived
legal injuries to, and victimizations of, fathers.

Although there are mothers who allege that their children's fathers have
unreasonably influenced the children against the mothers, the preponderance
of parental alienation cases involve fathers' accusations against mothers.

The conflict between children's rights and parents' (especially fathers')
rights has resulted in less frequent invocation of the idea of single-parent custody, once suggested by Goldstein et al. as in the best interests of the child.
This change has created presumptions about shared parenting and about
parenting plans that must be agreed on and fostered by both parents. Disagreements about formulation and implementation of parenting plans have
provided fraught situations in which parental alienation-related thinking may
be seen as providing a simple solution to a complex problem.

Adverse childhood experiences

The first two decades of the 21st century have seen increasing concern about
the impact on children's development of adverse childhood experiences
(ACEs). Arguments of both parental alienation advocates and their opponents
have included concerns about ACEs, and the ACEs concept is an important
part of the context of the parental alienation belief system.

As many readers will be aware, ACEs are intensely frightening or painful
events that occur during childhood, such as parental conflict and domestic
violence, abusive treatment, serious illness or injury, or civil disruption
and violence. Although every child experiences some adverse experiences,

research on ACEs has indicated that experience of many and serious adverse events is associated with medical issues such as heart problems in adulthood as well as with anxiety and other psychological reactions. Public health groups have emphasized prevention of ACEs as an important step toward improved health status in later life. When prevention is not possible, treatment of trauma in childhood is considered important both for the elimination of childhood issues such as post-traumatic stress disorder and for later health concerns.

Separation of parents may be associated with ACEs for the children. Exposure to parental conflict before, during, and after separation is a common experience for children, and may include interpersonal violence of various kinds, including abusive treatment of children by one or both parents. Changes of home, school, and daily routines are presumably less adverse events but can add to the effects of other ACEs.

Parental alienation proponents have argued that separation from one parent is an adverse experience, and that inappropriate parental influence, as carried out by the other parent, is an adverse experience that can be a cause of childhood mental illness. Identifying these events as ACEs, parental alienation advocates have equated separation experiences with other adverse events and proposed that parental alienation treatment is necessary to ward off the later results of adverse experiences as demonstrated through the unfortunately inadequate research of parental alienation proponents. Opponents of the parental alienation belief system, on the contrary, argue that parental alienation treatments may expose children to abusive parents, frighten and distress them by removing them from their familiar homes and caregivers, and cause them to experience adverse events before and during treatment.

In connection with ACEs, we should note that although historically psychological treatments have been thought of as benign and at the worst ineffective, attention has in recent decades been called to the potential for harm inherent in some psychotherapies (Lilienfeld 2007; Mercer 2017). Such harm may be either physical or mental, and it may be direct, as when an adverse event is experienced in the course of treatment, or indirect, as when family resources are expended on ineffective treatments. Linden (2013) argued that being made to cry or feel distressed or frightened in the course of a treatment should be considered an adverse event, although these unpleasant experiences might be considered acceptable if the treatment had been shown to be effective and if no other effective treatment were available. Treatments proposed by parental alienation advocates have been referred to as potentially harmful therapies for children (PHTCs; Mercer 2019a, 2019b), suggesting that at least some aspects of these treatments are ACEs that may be expected to cause ill effects.

Family courts

Over the past few decades, family courts have become increasingly reliant on the testimony of non-lawyer "neutrals", primarily mental health professionals. The role of these professionals has expanded until nearly every contested custody case includes a referral to a therapist or other mental health professional, whether they act as therapist, guardian ad litem, or custody evaluator. Judges are charged with making decisions that will affect families for decades. Often judges' dockets are far greater than they can handle thoughtfully on any given days. Unless an issue is the subject of a trial, judges rarely have enough time to hear significant evidence from the parties prior to the judge's decision-making. This is particularly true where the parties are self-represented. Some judges are pro-active, asking questions of the litigants to obtain enough testimony to make an informed decision. Others simply decide on the information provided, mistakenly assuming that it is not their role to inquire of the parties, particularly the self-represented ones.

Many judges welcomed the change to assigning investigations and evaluations to mental health professionals. Litigants display a variety of emotions in court. Custody of children is a high stakes challenge for judges. A misassessment of custody placement can result in serious harm to children. Incorporating mental health assessments into the custody process can give judges a greater sense of certainty when making custody and parenting time decisions. Relying on other presumably qualified professionals injected an appearance of legitimacy to custody decisions. This is not to say that judges knowingly affirm faulty recommendations made by mental health professionals, but in essence, family court judges have relinquished their decision-making authority to "neutrals" who legally should have only a limited role in determining the credibility of the parties. But parental alienation advocates often assign sinister intentions to mothers, thus discrediting the mother before she can have an opportunity to fully present her case to the court.

The increasing use of mental health professionals had several serious consequences for custody litigants, particularly for mothers in abusive relationships. Lawyers are trained investigators and factfinders. In the era when judges appointed lawyers as guardians ad litem and custody evaluators, reports were focused on substantiating assertions of the parties. Fact finding assisted the judges in assessing the parties' claims so then the judges could apply the applicable law. Recommendations typically were not within the purview of the attorney-investigators unless the parties requested them. A second critical change resulting from the introduction of mental health professionals into the family court was a de facto transfer of decision-making from the judge to the mental health evaluator. The difficulties that flow from this are multiple. Often non-lawyer investigators focus on resolution, not on investigating the truth of allegations. Consequently, allegations by mothers of abuse by the other parent may be only superficially investigated. Indeed, the truth of the allegations becomes secondary when the mental health professional interprets the survivor's insistence on child safety as obstructing resolution. Bias against abused mothers by mental health professionals soon became the norm.

This is not to say that bias against women began with the appointment of mental health professionals in family law matters. Women have long struggled with stereotypes that they lie, particularly in matters of gender violence. Family court, which inherently deals with cases that invoke gender stereotypes and gender roles, already entertained its own forms of bias against women. Mental health professionals, mediators, and other "neutrals" built upon that bias in a way that enhanced the stereotype of women lying and being obstructionist. This bias created the perfect pathway for the parental alienation belief system.

When the parental alienation view is presented by those who claim scientific credentials, courts will likely give credibility to their assertions, particularly when there is no expert to explain the false premises of the parental alienation belief system. Judges are not likely to demand a Daubert hearing to qualify an expert witness testifying about a child's avoidance of a parent. Typically, that is the role of the opposing counsel. If the mother is pro se or is represented by inadequate counsel, a Daubert hearing may never be held, thus depriving the court of essential scientific information. At this point in time, the parental alienation concept is so routinely raised in family court cases that many judges have accepted its premises as valid. Those judges who are predisposed to believe stereotypes of women as liars are not likely to be interested in exploring whether the parental alienation belief system is scientifically supported. But those judges who desire to make informed decisions are deprived of important information because there often is little support from "neutrals" to counter the claims of parental alienation advocates.

Forensic approaches to parental alienation-related child custody cases

When family courts hear child custody cases in which a child avoids contact with one parent, expert testimony often pits one mental health professional against another. Although the APA and APSAC guidelines about evaluation and custody recommendations stress the need for scientifically validated assessment methods and for systematic use of information to support a hypothesis about a child's needs, it is common for parental alienation proponents to make claims based on poorly validated tests and inferences derived from the child's rejection of the parent and no other information. Lawyers and judges are often ill-prepared to examine the scientific bases of such claims. Because testifying mental health professionals are more likely to support their own findings than to attack others' statements, judges are often swayed by parental alienation arguments, many not understanding the faulty basis for claims about parental encouragement of child avoidant behavior.

Lawyers and psychologists rarely put together cases challenging parental alienation-based claims based on their general acceptance in the field (the Frye standard) or the acceptability of the scientific evidence for the parental alienation belief system concepts (the Daubert standard). The recent statements of the APSAC, mentioned earlier, make it clear that a major organization rejects the parental alienation belief system and warns against its use in child custody decision-making, thus showing that such beliefs are not generally accepted in relevant professional fields.

The failure of parental alienation concepts to meet Daubert standards is a more complex issue, and it is unsurprising that few reported cases included Daubert hearings. The Daubert test requires evidence of a scientific nature to be supported by appropriate scientific work before the testimony or other evidence is determined to be admissible. Methods and standards of scientific evidence differ from one field to another. Techniques and analytical approaches are different in chemistry, for example, than they are in epidemiology. Lawyers who raise the Daubert standard in parental alienation cases must be schooled in the scientific standards applicable to mental health fields.

Since the 1990s, medicine and psychology have been concerned with evidence-based practices. The Cochrane Collaboration and the Campbell Collaboration provide easier access to information on evidence-based work. Evidenced based concerns have led to the concept of levels of evidence, differentiating between work that allows the conclusion that one factor has caused another, and simpler work that gives some information about a practice but does not allow the conclusion that the practice is safe or effective. To meet Daubert standards, psychological research must be at a high level of evidence that allows cause and effect to be demonstrated; practices that have been shown to be effective at such a level are called evidence-based treatments.

Evidence-based treatments (also called empirically supported treatments) in psychology are those that are supported by research involving randomized controlled trials or clinical controlled trials. The important characteristic shared by these methods is that they involve controls—comparisons built into the research design. At its simplest, this means that one group of participants undergoes a treatment of interest, and the other group does not. Comparisons are then made about the extent to which members of the treatment group change in some way from their pre-treatment to their post-treatment conditions; the same is done for the control group; finally, the amount of change seen in the treatment group is compared statistically to the amount of change seen in the control group. Only if a statistically significant difference in change between the groups is seen, and if the treatment group is superior, is it acceptable to claim that the treatment in question is an evidence-based treatment. (There are some other requirements as well—for example, the research must use established measurements of the characteristics that are treated—but space limits this discussion.)

If there is no control group, or if numbers of participants are too small to give the necessary statistical outcome, or if other problems exist, the treatment might be designated as "promising", but this is not the same as evidence-based status. At the time of this writing, no published research on parent alienation treatments shows that any of the methods is an evidence-based treatment. For that reason, it is correct to say that none of these treatments meets Daubert standards. A later chapter will consider this issue in more detail, but it will be helpful for readers to have this information as part of the context for understanding the parental alienation belief system.

References

American Professional Society on Abuse of Children. "APSAC Announces Revisions to its Definitions of Psychological Maltreatment." Accessed September 15, 2019. www.apsac.com/post/2019/08/16/apsac-announces-revisions-to-its-definitions-of-psychological-maltreatment-and-adds-a-cau

American Psychological Association. "Guidelines for Child Custody Evaluations in Family Law Proceedings." n.d. Accessed March 15, 2020. www.apa.org/practice/guidelines/child-custody.

Gardner, Richard. "Recent Trends in Divorce Litigation". Academy Forum 29 (2), 1985:3-7.

Goldstein, Joseph, Albert Solnit, Sonia Goldstein, and Anna Freud. *Beyond the Best Interests of the Child*. New York: Free Press, 1973.

Lilienfeld, Scott. "Psychological Treatments That Cause Harm." *Perspectives on Psychological Science* 2, 2007: 53–70.

Linden, Michael. "How to Define, Find, and Classify Side Effects in Psychotherapy from Unwanted Events to Adverse Treatment Reactions." *Clinical Psychology and Psychotherapy* 20, 2013: 286–296.

Mercer, Jean. "Evidence of Potentially Harmful Psychological Treatments for Children and Adolescents." *Child and Adolescent Social Work* 34, 2017: 107–125.

Mercer, Jean. "Are Parental Alienation Treatments Safe and Effective for Children and Adolescents?" *Journal of Child Custody* 16, 2019a: 67–111.

Mercer, Jean. "Examining Parental Alienation Treatments: Problems with Principles and Practices." *Child and Adolescent Social Work Journal* 36, 2019b: 351–363.

United Nations. "Convention on the Rights of the Child." 1989. Accessed March 20, 2020. www.ohchr.org/en/professionalinterest/pages/crc.aspx

When a child avoids a parent

Understanding the problem

Part 1

Chapter 2

History of the parental alienation belief system

Julie Doughty and Margaret Drew

This chapter sets out the history of the term 'parental alienation' and how the concept has been applied in family court disputes over the past four decades. The term was coined in the United States and most of this chapter therefore relates to developments in North America. More detail about other jurisdictions can be found in Chapter 3. The purpose of the present chapter is to set the concept in historical context: an extreme response to moral panic about divorce in the 1970s, when married women were attaining independence. While divorce has now been normalised in mainstream court proceedings, a difficulty arises when children resist or refuse contact with one parent.

Contributing factors to the rise of 'PAS' in the United States

The rise of child support enforcement

As noted, there was a significant rise in divorce rates in the United States during the 1970s. The Women's Liberation Movement developed and demanded equality and the right to decision-making independent of husbands (Burkett 2020). Both were core to the movement. Simultaneously, so-called 'no fault' divorce legislation was enacted, beginning in California in 1970 (UCR 1969). Generally, the legal term used was 'irretrievable breakdown of the marriage'. More and more women sought work outside the home. Many returned to study (Dartmouth 2016). Financial independence and education propelled women's autonomy and relationships that could not adapt to an expanded role for women often ended in divorce. Women married to controlling and otherwise abusive men were either prevented from leaving or were harassed by their former partners who threatened them with financial, psychological, physical, and other harm. Much of the harm was accomplished through failure to pay child support, or by obtaining court orders with inadequate financial obligations. Consequently, the need for public benefits surged and divorced women and children plunged into poverty (Pao 2015).

DOI: 10.4324/9781003095927-3

The difficulty in obtaining child support from abusive parents continues as a tactic of control.

To provide mothers and children with adequate revenue with the expected resulting decline in the need for public benefits, the collection of child support in the United States was formalised. In 1975, Part D was added to section IV of the Social Security Act. In an act unimaginable today, the amendment was passed by a unanimous Congressional vote. The Child Support Enforcement Program: A Legislative History (Congressional Research Service, Report March 21, 2016). The amendment provided for centralised collection of child support and encouraged the use of wage garnishment to assure payment. The so-called 'IV-D' agencies collected child support, disbursed it to the mother, and carried collection actions against non-paying parents. Previously, the states left the decision as to child support payment up to individual judges, which resulted in wildly different orders for similar situations. Child support enforcement stirred up the nascent 'Fathers' Rights' groups whose members often resisted paying child support particularly as states began hiring attorneys to enforce court orders of support and developed processes for enforcement and review (Office of Child Support Enforcement 1993).

But it was the implementation of child support guidelines that led to the increasingly aggressive paternal arguments for physical custody. In 1984, the U.S. federal government passed amendments that required states to adopt advisory guidelines for judges in ordering child support. The guidelines provided mechanisms for judges to deviate from them in making orders, but generally each state's child support orders became uniform based on the finances of the parties and the number of children in the family. One circumstance under which judges could deviate from the guidelines was when the parents had approximately equal time with the children—more commonly called shared physical custody. As is the case now, in non-abusive families, once parents' anger over the separation settled, those parents resolved their issues, including those involving the children. But when coercion was part of the family history, claims for shared physical custody of the children increased and resulted in fathers claiming that courts were biased in favour of mothers. For abusive parents and their organisations, the claims were and remain tactical. Fathers' rights groups did not recognise gender bias favouring fathers prior to child support guidelines when mothers received inadequate child support and had no easy mechanism for collection. Mothers usually had all the responsibility of child rearing often with few resources from the father. The correlation between increased child support orders and fathers' demands for physical custody cannot be ignored. Similarly, in the UK, reforms in child support legislation in 1991, championed by Margaret Thatcher, galvanised fathers' rights activism. In later decades, particularly in the 21st century, abusive fathers' demands accelerated to include sole physical custody, opening the door to another tactic, 'Parental Alienation'. The goal of abusive parents in asserting 'alienation' has progressed from a platform to avoid child support payments to eliminating the mother from any significant role in the child's life.

The use of mental health professionals custody disputes

Up until the later 1980s and early 1990s, most judges appointed lawyers to conduct investigations of claims in custody disputes. The shift to the use of mental health professionals in that role created support for abusive fathers, whether intentional or not. When lawyers were appointed, the court would instruct the lawyer what to investigate. While most lawyers are not trained in domestic violence, lawyers are well suited to be fact investigators. Instructions did not include making recommendations. With lawyer-appointed investigators, the court was informed of the facts of the parents' and children's situations and claims. Following the submission of the investigator's report on the facts, judges could incorporate the information into their findings, with judges solely responsible for the final decision-making. Lawyer investigators made errors, but when the report was factual without recommendations, interpretation of the findings could be argued by litigants and counsel with the judge ultimately making the custody decision.

By the 1990s, judges began appointing mental health professionals as 'neutral' investigators with the practice embedded in the family law system by the early 2000s. Judges assumed that mental health professionals could understand better the psychological and emotional components of separation and the ensuing disruption. But what court actors did not appreciate is that mental health professionals were no better trained in domestic abuse than their legal counterparts. Like law schools, schools of social work and psychology do not require training in domestic abuse. Yet judges view the mental health investigator as an 'expert' in psychological and emotional assessment even though few custody evaluators are subjected to the scrutiny that court testifying experts are (Shuman, 2002; see Chapter 5).

Over time, court practices changed, as well. Judges and counsel asked therapist custody evaluators and guardians to make recommendations to the court. And worse, judges believed that the mental health evaluators' recommendations were validated through psychological testing without understanding that testing does not rule in or out who is a victim and who is an abuser. Indeed, many psychological tests work against the interests of survivors who may exhibit symptoms of depression or anxiety while the abusive parent does not. Without an understanding of domestic abuse as the origins of any of the survivor's mental health concerns, the court actors ignored that the abusive parent (usually the father) was dangerous. Simultaneously, court actors, including custody evaluators, did not understand the sometimes counter-intuitive nature of survivors' decision-making, which were criticised by the evaluator who did not understand decisions that are safety-based. So began judges' relinquishing their essential duties to non-judicial actors.

Finally, an important development that worked against survivors was the court's expectation that a mental health professional would come up with a solution that was best for the family. Mental health guardians ad litem and evaluators expected the parties to work together toward resolution. When resolution is the concern, facts become less important as mental health professionals minimised evidence of abuse within the family. Many evaluators feel that 'assigning blame' is a hindrance to settlement. Yet in so doing, the court is deprived of valuable information that could result in a judgement that protects the children from abuse.

In abuse cases, settlement is often not feasible. One party seeks safety for the children and the other demands enforcement of parental rights. Because the abusive parent often presents well to (and sometimes pays for) the third party 'neutral', mental health evaluators can perceive the protective mother as the obstacle to settlement. This finding may be stated in the evaluator's report. And when allegations of 'parental alienation' are raised, the confluence of misinterpreted test results, along with an appearance of obstructiveness, a misunderstanding of the dangers and dynamics of domestic abuse, and the minimisation of abuse often results in recommendations that disfavour and sometimes exclude the survivor/mother from parenting and fail to protect the children from the abuser/father (see Chapter 5).

Origins of 'Parental alienation'

The origin of the phrase 'parental alienation syndrome' (PAS) is a rare instance of consensus amongst commentators on the topic. As explained below, the concept of an aligned child was introduced by Wallerstein and Kelly in the mid-1970s (Wallerstein and Kelly 1976), with additional influence from Johnston and colleagues in the mid-1980s (Johnston et al. 1984) This took a dramatic turn with Gardner's notion of children being 'brainwashed' by a parent into suffering a mental disorder. Gardner claimed that he could diagnose a child of divorced parents who was suffering from what he coined as 'parental alienation syndrome', widely known as PAS. This was later rebranded as 'parental alienation' when PAS failed to garner recognition amongst professional societies.

The aligned child concept

From 1970, Judith Wallerstein and Joan Kelly, psychologists, conducted a longitudinal 'children of divorce' study of 131 children in North California. In 1976, they published a paper focusing on the emotions of 31 children of school age, taken from their larger sample of children across age ranges. Amongst the findings on these children's responses to their parents' divorce, Wallerstein and Kelly described two types of adaptation in child-parent relationships, namely: empathy and alignment. Whereas some children developed a more caring attitude toward both of their parents and their siblings following the family breakup (empathy), an aligned child was one who formed a relationship with one parent, specifically aimed at the exclusion of the other. The researchers claimed that this alignment was encouraged by 'the embattled parent' who felt 'aggrieved, deserted, exploited, or betrayed by the divorcing spouse' (Wallerstein and Kelly 1976, 266). Their research methods included analysis of parents' behaviour as well as that of their children, so it can be assumed that the clinicians who engaged directly with parents came up with these descriptions. The extent to which the researchers' negative views of parents' behaviour were based on work with the children or the adults is not made clear. Their observations were alarmingly judgemental of the abandoned spouse who allegedly was directly harming their children:

> The angers which the parent and the child shared soon became the basis for complexly organized strategies aimed at hurting and harassing the former spouse, sometimes with the intent of shaming him or her into returning to the marriage. More often the aim was vengeance.
> (Wallerstein and Kelly 1976, 266)

Overall, however, their research focused more on children's feelings and alignment than on parents' intentional behaviour. The authors did give the children some agency and attributed their alignment primarily to their own distress about the circumstances surrounding the separation, and the ways in which they coped with the fallout from divorce proceedings.

Wallerstein has since been described as having initiated the modern academic debate on divorce with this study, and as one of the foremost acknowledged experts on divorce in the popular media and many legal institutions. Coltrane and Adams (2003) saw her publications as strongly pro-marriage and anti-divorce, which they say led to her findings on the adverse effects on the children in her sample being exploited by moral crusaders in subsequent decades. On this reading, the concept of the 'aligned child' may have been one aspect of the powerful symbolism often used by conservative and religious groups of endangered childhood, under threat when society abandons its traditional values.

As Joan Meier (2009) later explained, although Wallerstein and Kelly's work was influential at the time, the aligned child construct did not immediately catch anyone's attention in court proceedings. Over the longer term, Kelly worked with Janet Johnston who, in 1985, published a paper about their project with 44 children, aged six to twelve, who had been subject to custody disputes arising from divorce (Johnston, Campbell, and Mayes 1985). This sample of children was from lower middle income, economically stressed, racially diverse families in the San Francisco Bay area. The study described children's attitudes to their parents in six categories, including 'strong alliance' and 'aligned'. At this stage, 'alignment' was defined as a moderate preference for one parent but a desire not to upset the other, whereas a strong alliance was one where a child presented 'a strong, consistent, overt (publicly stated) verbal and behavioural preference for one parent together with rejection and denigration of the other... accompanied by affect that is hostile, negative and unambivalent' (Johnston, Campbell and Mayes 1985, 569). Of the 44 children, only 7 (16%) were in strong alliances, with 19 (43%) aligned, and the remainder in other categories such as no preference, conflicted loyalties, or rejection of both parents. The researchers concluded that older children tended to become involved in their parents' acrimony, with the result that one parent might become excluded or relegated, but that both parents contributed to the alliances and alignments that the children made. The article warned of harm to children's moral development and to their suffering anxiety, tension, depression, and psychosomatic illness as they assumed strategies to cope with the conflicts between their parents. Although these outcomes varied between the classifications identified in the study, there was no emphasis on the seven 'allied' children as being objects of greater concern than the others. So, this empirical study in the early 1980s identified the possibility of allied children as one small component of a complex phenomenon of children affected by divorce.

The parental alienation belief system

As Meier (2009) noted, conflict that included denigration of one parent by the other was long perceived as a transient, mutual problem amongst adversarial parents, not one that was central to children's best interests and parents' rights. It was only when Richard A. Gardner (1985) created and marketed PAS, as a means of refuting mothers' claims of child abuse, that courts began to take notice.

PAS differed from earlier observations on alignment or alliance because Gardner argued, in florid language, that children who rejected one parent during or after divorce had been coerced into doing so by the other parent, and consequently the child suffered from a syndrome exhibited by a combination of behaviours by the preferred parent and the child. Language in Cold War propaganda about brainwashing and mind control in communist regimes that had caught the public imagination in the 1950s was appropriated to enliven his idea that some mothers induced false memories and beliefs in their children. Gardner postulated that PAS directly caused children to grow into dysfunctional, criminal adults and was the cause of much that was wrong in American society. He died in 2003 and remains a controversial figure, respected by current proponents of parental alienation (see for example Richard Warshak's hosting of Gardner's papers on his own website) but dismissed as a misogynistic ideologue by others, for example, Clemente and Padilla-Racero (2016).

Gardner was a psychiatrist and psychoanalyst who self-published several books about divorce from the 1970s onward. It appears that he was medically trained and worked at one time as an army psychiatrist, but he mainly practised in a private capacity. There are continuing doubts as to whether he held any academic or research posts during his career. For example, a position he stated he held at Columbia Medical School was a voluntary one and not a professorship. Nevertheless, he was called on to give expert evidence in many court cases, his speciality being the denial of sexual abuse allegations by children and attribution of any resistance to seeing a parent to PAS. Gardner stated that he could diagnose PAS when a child presented with the following eight behaviours:

1 Denigration
2 Frivolous rationalisation
3 Lack of ambivalence
4 Independent thinker
5 Automatic or reflexive support
6 Absence of guilt
7 Borrowed scenarios.
8 Spread of animosity.

Gardner's recommended treatment of PAS was removing the child from the alleged malign influence of the alienating parent, with no regard to the child's own views or any distress such a step would have on them. It appears that he was unable to accept a straightforward explanation that a child resisting contact with a parent might be doing so because of something that parent had done. Instead, his only conclusion could be that the child was suffering a mental disorder, induced by the other parent. Kathleen Faller, a social work academic, published an influential paper in 1998, focusing on PAS as a purported explanation of reports of child sexual abuse when parents are divorcing. She concluded that the fundamental flaw in Gardner's reasoning was that it precluded any alternative explanation for such allegations, other than they must be false, whereas a more likely explanation was that the allegation might be true or that the mother might have made an honest mistake (Faller 1998). Faller's paper was relied on in the leading case in the England and Wales Court of Appeal, Re L, V, M and H (children) [2000] EWCA Civ 194 (see Chapter 3).

A number of extreme aspects of Gardner's premise, not least its focus on vengeful mothers, led to polarisation between those who saw it as a solution and those who rejected it as junk science. There were some attempts to drop the 'syndrome' suffix (for example, Darnall 1998) but it was not until 2000 that a concerted effort was made to address the flaws in PAS theory and practice with a view to making it more respectable.

The reformulation of PAS into parental alienation

In May 2000, the Association of Family and Conciliation Courts (AFCC) held an annual conference in New Orleans under the name Alienation, Access, and Attachment. Kelly and Johnston are referred to in the advertisements for this event as members of a 'Northern California Task Force on the Alienated Child', who would be presenting a reformulation of PAS. The

AFCC published journal, Family Court Review, ran a special issue in July 2001 comprising six articles based on the conference papers. This was edited by Kelly and Johnston under the title, 'Alienated Children in Divorce'. Thus, the concept remained one largely based on research with families who had been through Californian divorce courts.

The stated aim was 'to reject the adversarial framework the PAS label supports' (Kelly and Johnston 2001, 243). They argued that their version treated alienation as 'a very real and very tragic consequence of divorce for some children' and maintained that a child who was irrationally alienated from one parent was undoubtedly at risk of harm. They were anxious to disassociate themselves from Gardner, while at the same time paying tribute to him for bringing the problem of alienation to public attention. They identified the following criticisms that had been made of Gardner's premise.

First, PAS focused almost exclusively on the alienating parent. Second, the lack of a 'commonly recognized, or empirically verified pathogenesis, course, familial pattern, or treatment selection' of the problem meant that it could not be considered a diagnostic syndrome as defined within psychiatry. It was the use of the terminology of a medical syndrome that had created controversy amongst mental health professionals and fuelled the continual debate on the validity of PAS. Finally, there was hardly any empirical or research support for the reliable identification of PAS, apart from Gardner's own clinical experience and expert testimony, nor for the efficacy of the drastic solutions he recommended. Kelly and Johnston were unhappy about the extent of misinformation about PAS in the media and on the internet and the gendered nature of much of the controversy. However, they also believed that there were many family disputes where questions of alienation arose and had to be examined and understood, in order to recommend the best legal and psychological interventions. Their solution was to drop the 'syndrome' but keep 'parental alienation'.

One of the important points on which Kelly and Johnston differed from Gardner was that they accepted that some older children estranged from parents were agents in their own rational and self-protective decisions and that these decisions were often misinterpreted as parental alienation. They stated that the most common age range of the alienated child was from 9 to 15. Younger children did not possess the adaptive capacity to absorb and reproduce alienating strategies. The core feature of alienated children was extreme disproportion between the child's perception and beliefs about the rejected parent and the actual history of the relationship. Exploring the reasons for this had to take a wide range of family-based and external factors into account, including the influence of the adversarial process, lawyers, and therapists.

In their 'reformulation' of PAS, an alienated child was defined as:

> one who expresses, freely and persistently, unreasonable negative feelings and beliefs (such as anger, hatred, rejection, and/or fear) toward a parent

that are significantly disproportionate to the child's actual experience with that parent. From this viewpoint, the pernicious behaviours of a 'programming' parent are no longer the starting point. Rather, the problem of the alienated child begins with a primary focus on the child, his or her observable behaviours, and parent-child relationships.

(Kelly and Johnston 2001, 251)

This shift toward a more child-centred approach and the differentiation between rational and irrational estrangement was an important and, on the face of it, welcome development. The extra nuance and complexity of the reformulated model however introduced other difficulties into identifying and resolving alienation. This multi-factorial model requires resource-intensive professional input across legal and behavioural science disciplines and, therefore, is available only to wealthy parents. Again, the question arises as to how generalisable the study of families in California was to the wider population, who might not have access to specialist lawyers, expert witnesses, and therapists.

Johnston, Walters, and Friedlander (2001) also wrote in the same journal issue that, where parental alienation was identified, court orders would need to specify the roles of all the professionals, lines of communication, limits of confidentiality, and decision-making authority, in order to ensure a coordinated, rule-governed process for managing ongoing family conflict and implementing therapeutic intervention. They wrote about a 'contract' to be agreed between the parents and the court. All of this presupposes parents who are able and willing to cooperate with a time-consuming, expensive, and probably quite uncomfortable series of meetings, and allow or persuade the children to participate. A template for such a contract is appended to the article, which states that to ensure each parent assumes responsibility for the resolution of the family conflict, each parent should pay for their own individual therapy sessions, for half of each joint session, and for half of the children's sessions (Johnston, Walters, and Friedlander 2001, 331).

Kelly and Johnston's reformulation was strongly refuted by Gardner as condescending and wrong (Gardner 2004). Their response to him (Johnston and Kelly 2004) repeated that there was no convincing evidence to support his one-dimensional PAS premise—that an alienating parent is primarily responsible for a child's alienation. The authors explained further their concern that the term PAS flourished in a traditional adversarial legal system because it promised clear-cut answers as to who was right and wrong:

If in any way substantiated, PAS sanctifies the rejected parent as an innocent victim and indicts the aligned parent as the malignant perpetrator. There is less willingness to concede that real abuse, abiding mistrust, and blaming between parents jointly contribute to extremely negative views of one another and undermine any capacity they have to coparent.

(Johnston and Kelly 2004, 626)

They also emphasised their strong disagreement with Gardner's recommendations for drastic legal and mental health interventions. The exchange had come to an end at this point, as Gardner had died in 2003.

Although this period saw a rejection, or at least a moderation of the more troubling aspects, of Gardner's invention, there were two associated drawbacks. The complexity of Kelly and Johnston's model did not have the same appeal to busy professionals, including judges, or anxious parents as the simplistic PAS model, and the amount of time and money needed to apply it effectively was prohibitive. In retrospect, it may have been a mistake to retain even the 'PA' in PAS; the AFCC and its advisers might have more successfully shed Gardner if they had introduced a new descriptor altogether.

Growth in popularity of parental alienation despite lack of scientific or evidentiary basis

Shortly after the reformulation efforts, another influential academic article, this one by a lawyer, Carol S Bruch, was published in U.S. and British journals (Bruch 2002). She summarised the flaws in the PAS premise that made it 'pseudoscience', with very detailed references to U.S. cases and research, but was not convinced the Kelly and Johnston reformulation had sufficiently countered this. She accused the authors of going 'far beyond their data [to] craft recommendations for extended, coercive, highly intrusive judicial responses' (2002, 385) and pointed out that the remedies discussed were untested and very expensive. Bruch referred to conversations with Wallerstein and that the latter had reported that children's alignments were transient, mostly within one or two years. Wallerstein warned in a retrospective study against overzealous interventions to break alliances (Wallerstein, Lewis, and Blakelee 2002). In the absence of scientific recognition of PAS (or any new theory), its potential value should be tested rigorously before it is applied to decisions about children.

The pseudoscience critique continued. Spanish academics, Clemente and Padillia-Requero, were involved in a serial argument about PAS, which included a demand from William Bernet that an article by them on the veracity of children's testimony be retracted. In their final article in the debate, Clemente and Padilia-Requero concluded that PAS was gobbledegook, unethical, and a travesty of justice (Clemente and Padillia-Requero 2016). Interestingly, in a more recent critique of this Spanish study, Bernet (2020) is explicit that there is no reason to distinguish between PAS, alienation, or any other term for alliance and non-justified rejection.

Bernet is a professor of psychiatry at Vanderbilt University, Nashville, Tennessee, United States, who has been arguing for more than ten years that parental alienation is a classifiable mental disorder and, as noted above, continues to advance the Gardner checklist. In retrospect, the condemnatory tone taken by Kelly and Johnston is striking, if Gardner has since been restored to respectability by current alienation proponents.

Judges and lawyers are not in a position to evaluate the scientific rigour of evidence given about parental alienation as a concept. To assess whether expert testimony is admissible in court, most states in the United States apply either of what are known as the Frye or the Daubert test, or a combination of the two. The Frye test is whether the principle or method used by the expert is generally accepted in the relevant scientific community. The Daubert test is one of reliability, whether there are: a way to test the theory; peer-reviewed publications supporting it; standards for controlling or maintaining it; and known or potential error rates. Although it has occasionally been claimed that PAS has met these tests (Hobbs 2002), an analysis by Jennifer Hoult in 2006 found that there had been only 64 higher court judgements (i.e., those that set precedent) that referenced PAS. Of these, only two considered its admissibility—and both concluded it was not. She described a 20-year run of PAS in American courts as 'embarrassing' and suggested that legal professionals and courts may have found PAS attractive because it claimed to 'reduce complex, time-consuming, and wrenching evidentiary investigations to medical diagnoses'. Despite the Kelly and Johnston reformulation, Hoult was still finding 'syndrome' cases where PAS was put forward as a simplistic answer to complex human problems.

Meier (2009) has attempted to explain how a concept that had been rejected by scientists came to be accepted by family courts. She suggested a range of possible reasons, two of which that stand out as the most generalisable in other jurisdictions. Firstly, it is difficult for court professionals to come to terms with the prevalence of domestic abuse in society, whether that society is heavily patriarchal or one that is more liberal. As recent research and reports (for example, in England and Wales, Ministry of Justice 2020) continue to demonstrate, courts appear to find it easier to accept an allegation of parental alienation than an allegation of domestic or child abuse. The trope of the vengeful 'woman scorned' is pervasive, whereas the extent of intimate partner violence and coercion is still minimised. Although there has been considerable progress in raising professional awareness of the adverse effects of domestic abuse on children since the 1980s when PAS was invented by Gardner, there are still constant complaints about a lack of judicial training in these issues (Ministry of Justice 2020).

Second, as Meier expressed it, this is 'an article of faith' of most family courts and the psychologists who report to them that children need frequent and regular contact with both parents for optimal psychological health. Meier was writing about U.S. courts, but this observation is equally true in other jurisdictions where legislation has been repeatedly amended to promote shared parenting (see Chapter 3). This mind-set was described in the Ministry of Justice report (2020) on the safety of women and children in family courts in England and Wales as a 'culture of contact at any cost'.

Recent large empirical studies by Meier in the United States and by Neilson in Canada have confirmed the tendency for courts to accept claims of parental alienation more easily than the lack of a scientific and evidentiary basis would suggest was plausible (Meier et al. 2019; Neilson 2018).

The rise of the reunification industry

As this chronology of parental alienation in the United States shows, there was a close association and interdependence between the courts and mental health professionals who found alienation occurring in separated families. Courts needed psychologists to identify the problem and recommend a solution; psychologists needed courts to identify the families that they could then diagnose and/or treat. In other words, parental alienation did not exist outside court proceedings—and perhaps not far beyond wealthy divorcing couples and their children. Presumably, there have been court cases where parental alienation was identified, but remedies were not ordered or not implemented, and applying the label did not directly affect the outcome. There may have been some cases where judges decided that it was not in the best interests for an 'alienated' child to be subjected to a transfer of custody, a period of no contact with the 'alienating' parent, or therapy. There will also be cases that fell away through attrition. However, interest in parental alienation may have faded if there were no resources available that claimed to repair and restore pre-existing good relationships through court orders. In the US, this resource is known as reunification therapy.

The burgeoning of a reunification industry came to the fore around 2010, again highlighted by the *Family Court Review* journal publishing another special issue, based around a long article by Richard Warshak, on the reunification business Family Bridges. Warshak states on his website that he is qualified both as a psychologist and a psychiatrist, has trained with Family Bridges, and is the author of a guide to parents entitled *Divorce Poison, How to Protect Your Family from Bad-mouthing and Brainwashing* (Warshak 2011). Family Bridges had been founded by Dr Randy Rand in 1991, originally as a method of helping children who had been abducted to resettle with their parents and was later extended to children alienated through divorce (Warshak 2010). Warshak's article in the journal analysed his own work with the organisation, with 23 children, between 2005 and 2010.

Kelly (2010) observed that Family Bridges held promise but was very expensive and favoured the 'alienated' parent; she called for an evaluation of that, and other educational and therapeutic interventions designed to help alienated children repair and strengthen balanced relationships with both parents. She pointed out that parents who accessed Family Bridges had to pay psychologists' fees for four days, travel, accommodation, and follow-up contacts or consultations, as well as legal fees. They also had to obtain specific court orders transferring the child's custody and restricting contact.

Another programme was Overcoming Barriers, developed by an inter-disciplinary group including lawyers. This programme was also expensive, charging $7,500 per family, in the 2000s. Families who attended the pro-gramme by court order were said to feel anger, resistance, and frustration, which needed working through and limited the time available for more positive interaction (Sullivan et al. 2010).

Recently, some reunification programmes do not necessarily involve transfer of residence, but weekly therapy sessions and enforced contact. Some intensive alienation treatments continue (Mercer 2019). They are contro-versial, particularly because they are not regulated. Treatment for parental alienation is classified as psycho-educational, not as medical treatment, and is therefore not covered by health insurance schemes in the US. Mainstream news media have featured young adults who were traumatised as children by the consequences of court orders that they be removed from home and trans-ported without explanation (Tabachnik 2017; see Chapter 4).

Parental alienation across the globe

As discussed above, findings that some children of divorcees in California appeared to react unreasonably and disproportionately in rejecting one of their parents during and after separation have, over the decades, become the basis for widely held beliefs in parental alienation as a diagnosable condition and a burgeoning industry for expert witnesses and providers of therapeutic services in the U.S. family courts. Despite some early reluctance in other jurisdictions (see Chapter 3), the concept has caught the imagination of pres-sure groups and campaigners in other countries, with different cultures and systems. The U.S. literature still seems preoccupied with divorce, but in other jurisdictions, parenting problems tend not to be seen in terms of failed mar-riage but as occurring across a range of diverse family forms. Another North American feature is greater cultural acceptance of and access to therapeutic treatment for children.

Linda C. Neilson has described a virtual explosion of claims and court findings associated with parental alienation since 2002 in Canada (Neilson 2018). She identified cases which were commissioning reports from promi-nent U.S. self-described experts.

It is perhaps inevitable that, as awareness grows in most countries of the extent and harm caused by domestic abuse and coercive control, that more attention is also going to be paid to the more simplistic notion of the avenging mother. At the time of writing this chapter, there have been recent confer-ences, legislation, and other actions supportive of belief in parental alienation have occurred in Brazil, Croatia, Israel, and Italy, as well as in the countries discussed in chapters in this book. But recently some progress has been made. Spain outlawed the use of Parental Alienation Syndrome (Bolitín Official 2021). A recent decision by the Italian Supreme Court rejected the use of parental alienation finding it, amongst other reasons, prejudiced against mothers based on gender characteristics (Repubblica Italiana, 2021).

Attempts to have parental alienation classified as a disease

The *Diagnostic and Statistical Manual of Mental Disorders* (*DSM*; American Psychiatric Association 2013) is a standard classification of mental disorders used by mental health professionals, developed by the American Psychiatric Association (APA). Its current iteration is *DSM*-5, published in 2013. Given the flurry of activity by the AFCC and the lengthy publications generated by Warshak and others around 2010, it is not surprising that this period saw campaigns to have 'parental alienation disorder' recognised in the revised *DSM*. Bernet et al. (2010, 186) proposed these 'Diagnostic Criteria for Parental Alienation Disorder':

The child—usually one whose parents are engaged in a high-conflict divorce—allies himself or herself strongly with one parent and rejects a relationship with the other, alienated parent without legitimate justification. The child resists or refuses contact or parenting time with the alienated parent.

1   The child manifests the following behaviours:

   a   persistent rejection or denigration of a parent that reaches the level of a campaign.
   b   weak, frivolous, and absurd rationalisations for the child's persistent criticism of the rejected parent

2   The child manifests two or more of the following six attitudes and behaviours:

   A   lack of ambivalence
   c   independent-thinker phenomenon
   d   reflexive support of one parent against the other
   e   absence of guilt over exploitation of the rejected parent
   f   presence of borrowed scenarios
   g   spread of the animosity to the extended family of the rejected parent

3   The duration of the disturbance is at least two months.
4   The disturbance causes clinically significant distress or impairment in social, academic (occupational), or other important areas of functioning.
5   The child's refusal to have contact with the rejected parent is without legitimate justification. That is, parental alienation disorder is not diagnosed if the rejected parent maltreated the child.

As noted by Doughty, Maxwell, and Slater (2018) there is a vast amount of literature about defining parental alienation, which makes it impossible to quantify its prevalence, and is unhelpful when trying to balance arguments that it is endemic or that it is non-existent. Bernet's criteria above raise more questions than answers in this regard. The APA had previously advised against use of alienation terminology (APA 2008) and the 'disorder' was not included in the *DSM* in 2013.

Clemente, Miguel and Dolores Padilla-Racero. 2016. "When courts accept what science rejects: Custody issues concerning the alleged 'parental alienation syndrome'". *Journal of Child Custody* 13, 126–133. doi:10.1080/15379418.2016.1219245

Coltrane, Scott and Michele Adams. 2003. "The social construction of the divorce 'problem': morality, child victims, and the politics of gender". *Family Relations* 52, 363–372. doi:10.1111/j.1741-3729.2003.00363.x

Congressional Research Service. *EveryCRSReport.com*, March 21, 2016. https://www.everycrsreport.com/files/20160321_R44423_7c7c042b8038f53dcc732f-b77538a7924e1cfe14.pdf

Dartmouth Census. *History, Women, Marriage, Education, and Occupation in the United States from 1940–2000*, November 3, 2016. https://journeys.dartmouth.edu/censushistory/2016/11/03/women-marriage-and-education-in-the-united-states-from-1940-2000/

Doughty, Julie, Nina Maxwell and Tom Slater. 2018. *Review of Research and Case Law on Parental Alienation*. Cardiff: Welsh Government. http://orca.cf.ac.uk/112511/

Faller, Kathleen. 1998. "The parental alienation syndrome: what is it and what data support it?" *Child Maltreatment* 3, 100–115. doi:10.1177/1077559598003002005

Gardner, Richard. 1985. "Recent trends in divorce litigation". *Academy Forum* 29(2), 3–7.

Gardner, Richard. 2004. "Commentary on Kelly and Johnston's 'The alienated child: a reformulation of parental alienation syndrome'". *Family Court Review* 42(4), 611–621. doi:10.1111/j.174-1617.2004.tb01327.x

Hobbs, Tony. 2002. "Parental alienation syndrome and the UK family courts". *Family Law* 32, 182–189.

Hoult, Jennifer. 2006. "The evidentiary admissibility of parental alienation syndrome: science, law, and policy". *Children's Legal Rights Journal* 26, 1–61. https://ssrn.com/abstract=910267

Johnston, Janet R., Linda Campbell and Sharon S Mayes. 1985. "Latency children in post-separation and divorce disputes". *Journal of the American Academy of Child Psychiatry* 24, 563–574. doi:10.1016/S0002–7138(09)60057-1

Johnston, Janet R. and Joan B. Kelly. 2004. "Rejoinder to Gardner's 'Commentary on Kelly and Johnston's 'The alienated child: a reformulation of parental alienation syndrome'". *Family Court Review* 42, 611–621. doi:10.1111/j.174-1617.2004.tb01328.x

Johnston, Janet R., Marjorie Gans Walters, and Steven Friedlander. 2001. "Therapeutic work with alienated children and their families". *Family Court Review* 39, 316–333. doi:10.1111/j.174-1617.2001.tb00613.x

Kelly, Joan B. 2010. "Commentary on 'Family Bridges: using insights from social science to reconnect parents and alienated children' (Warshak, 2010)". *Family Court Review* 48, 81–90. doi:10.1111/j.1744-1617.2009.01289.x

Kelly, Joan B. and Janet R. Johnston. 2001. "The alienated child: a reformulation of parental alienation syndrome". *Family Court Review* 39, 249–266. doi:10.1111/j.174-1617.2001.tb00609.x

Meier, Joan S. 2009. "A historical perspective on parental alienation syndrome and parental alienation". *Journal of Child Custody* 6, 232–257. doi:10.1080/15379410903084681

Meier, Joan S., Sean Dickson, Chris O'Sullivan, Leora Rosen and Jeffrey Hayes. 2019. "Child custody outcomes in cases involving parental alienation and abuse allegations". *GWU Law School Public Law Research Paper No. 2019–56*. doi:10.2139/ssrn.3448062

Mercer, Jean. 2019. "Are intensive parental alienation treatments effective and safe for children and adolescents?" *Journal of Child Custody* 16, 67–113. doi:10.1080/15379418.2018.1557578

Milchman, Madelyn. 2020a. "Seeking a bridge between child sexual abuse and parental alienation experts". *APSAC Advisor* 32(1), 23–27.

Milchman, Madelyn. 2020b. "Is critique of parental alienation syndrome/parental alienation disorder (PAS/PAD) timely? A response to Sandoval and Geffner". *APSAC Advisor* 32(1), 43–47.

Ministry of Justice. 2020. *Assessing Risk of Harm to Children and Parents in Private Law Children Cases: Final Report*. London: Ministry of Justice https://www.gov.uk/government/consultations/assessing-risk-of-harm-to-children-and-parents-in-private-law-children-cases

Neilson, Linda C. 2018. *Parental Alienation Empirical Analysis: Child Best Interests or Parental Rights? Fredericton: Muriel McQueen Fergusson Centre for Family Violence Research and Vancouver: The FREDA Centre for Research on Violence Against Women and Children.*

Neilson, Linda C. 2019. *Collective Memo of Concern to World Health Organisation.* http://www.learningtoendabuse.ca

Office of Child Support Enforcement, U.S. Department of Health and Human Services. 1993. *Role of the IV-D Agency and its Staff in Delivering Services*. IM-93-03, July 23, 1993. https://www.acf.hhs.gov/archive/css/policy-guidance/role-iv-d-agency-and-its-staff-delivering-services

Pao, Maureen. 2015. *How America's Child Support System Failed to Keep Up with the Times.* https://www.npr.org/2015/11/19/456632896/how-u-s-parents-racked-up-113-billion-in-child-support-debt

Repubblica Italiana. *Las Corte Suprema Di Cassazione*, 2021, No. 13217/2021.

Sandoval-Norton, Aileen, and Robert Geffner. 2020. "Can there be a bridge between interpersonal violence/abuse and parental alienation proponents: a response to Milchman". *APSAC Advisor* 32(1), 39–42.

Shuman, Daniel W. 2002. "The role of mental health experts in custody decisions: science". *Psychological Tests, and Clinical Judgment Family Law Quarterly* 36(1). https://www.jstor.org/stable/25740372?seq=1

Sullivan, Matthew J., Peggie A. Ward and Robin M. Deutsch. 2010. "Overcoming Barriers family camp: a program for high-conflict divorced families where a child is resisting contact with a parent". *Family Court Review* 48, 116–135. doi:10.1111/j.1744-1617.2009.01293.x

Tabachnik, Clara. 2017. '*They Were Taken from Their Mom to Rebond with Their Dad. It didn't go Well*'. Washington Post. May 11, 2017. https://www.washingtonpost.com/lifestyle/magazine/a-divorced-father-his-estranged-kids-and-a-controversial-program-to-bring-them-together/2017/05/09/b50ac6f6-204c-11e7-ad74-3a742a6e93a7_story.html

UCR. 1969. "Reagan signs first major divorce law". *Desert Sun* 43(29). https://cdnc.ucr.edu/?a=d&d=DS19690906.2.59&e=-------en--20--1--txt-txIN--------1

Wallerstein, Judith S. and Joan B. Kelly. 1976. "The effects of parental divorce: Experiences of the child in later latency". *American Journal of Orthopsychiatry* 46, 256–269. doi:10.1111/j.1939-0025.1976.tb00926.x

Wallerstein, Judith S., Julia M. Lewis and Sandra Blakeslee. 2002. *The Unexpected Legacy of Divorce: A 25 Year Landmark Study.* New York: Hyperion Books.

Warshak, Richard A. 2010. "Family Bridges: using insights from social science to reconnect parents and alienated children". *Family Court Review* 48, 48–80. doi:10.1111/j.1744-1617.2009.01288.x

Warshak, Richard A. 2011. *Divorce Poison: How to Protect Your Family from Bad-mouthing and Brainwashing.* New York: William Morrow.

Chapter 3

The international expansion of the parental alienation belief system through the UK and Australian experiences

Julie Doughty and Zoe Rathus

This chapter explains the contemporary position of parental alienation in the family court systems in Australia and in the UK, primarily England and Wales. England (with Wales) and Australia are common law jurisdictions where the law about post-separation arrangements for children is found in legislation and interpreted by the higher courts. There is no reference to "parental alienation" in any of our statutes and both jurisdictions encourage ongoing post-separation involvement of parents with their children. Discretion is given to judges, with the "welfare" (UK) or "best interests" (Australia) of children being the paramount consideration.

A common factor in the jurisdictions is that many parents have no access to independent legal advice or other authoritative providers, so tend to consult family, friends, and sources via the internet. They are therefore influenced by informal, unregulated commentary and search engines that return myriad entries, much of which relate to courts in the US (Crowe et al. 2019). In this way, concepts and discussions originating in American courts (such as popular use of the phrase "custody battle") become pervasive internationally but are potentially misleading, given that family law and procedure differ amongst cultures and countries.

We have employed separate processes to track the trajectory of parental alienation in our respective jurisdictions because social science literature has been cited more frequently in Australian courts than in the UK and many more Australian family law cases are publicly available. The sections on the UK tell the story through policy developments, practices, and key cases. The Australian sections compare and contrast the UK narrative, using published cases as an empirical backdrop. Finally, we reflect on the underlying reasons that the concept of parental alienation has survived in both jurisdictions despite its poor fit as an essentially North American concept.

The legal frameworks

Overview of UK law and practice

In England and Wales, continual attempts by government and judiciary to persuade separated parents to make their own arrangements about their

DOI: 10.4324/9781003095927-4

children have become a policy drive to reduce the number of court applications because the system cannot cope with an increased volume in the context of cuts in court budgets, legal aid, and community support. Despite this, many parents still see the family court as the default option to resolve disagreements. Applications may be made under section 8 of the Children Act 1989 for a "child arrangements" order (known as "residence" or "contact" orders between 1991 and 2014). The welfare of the child is the court's paramount consideration in making decisions, based on a presumption of continuing involvement with both parents.

Of those cases that do proceed, only a minority involve any investigation into the child's welfare. Where this is required by the court, the enquiries are undertaken by social workers in Cafcass (the Child and Family Court Advisory and Support Service) in England and Cafcass Cymru in Wales. These Cafcass officers have a similar role to custody evaluators in the US and family report writers in Australia, although Cafcass practitioners are social workers, not psychology or medical trained. Most parents will not have lawyers and in only a minority of complex cases will a child be represented.

Policies are being reviewed in 2021, following a report on children's safety that raised serious concerns about the quality of Cafcass reports and the minimisation of domestic abuse by the family courts (Ministry of Justice 2020). Further independent expert evidence is rarely commissioned in parents' disputes. The court has powers to appoint an independent expert witness, such as a psychologist, but this is discouraged because delay is presumed to be adverse to the child's welfare, under Children Act 1989, s 1(2). Despite efforts over the years by most judges, lawyers, and social workers to resist use of the "alienation" label for child avoidant behaviours, there is now a small number of "parental alienation experts" (psychologists and psychiatrists) who can be called on in more complex cases where the judge can be persuaded, this is necessary because Cafcass evidence is insufficient to evaluate the welfare factors. The position is not satisfactory because of confirmation bias, that is, these specialised experts will find what they are looking for.

There have been slightly different trajectories in Scotland and Northern Ireland, as we outline below.

Overview of Australian law and practice

As in the UK, Australian governments have been trying to keep people out of the courts since at least the 1990s. Under the governing legislation, the Family Law Act 1975 (Cth) (FLA) mediation, called "family dispute resolution" (FDR), had become largely mandatory before an application for a parenting order could be filed by the mid-2000s. Applications for "parenting" orders (also once known as "residence" and "contact" orders in Australia) may be made by parents, with decisions based on a presumption that equal shared parental responsibility (ESPR) is in the best interests of children.

Social science family assessments, called "family reports", and other expert opinions, play a regular role in parenting cases in Australia. Family reports are written by social workers or psychologists and are influential in out-of-court negotiations and legal aid eligibility decisions as well as in court (House of Representatives 2017). Despite their critical role, inquiries and research suggest mixed quality and genuine concerns about how family reports deal with family violence (Australian Law Reform Commission [ALRC] 2019; Jeffries 2016; Rathus 2019). Recent reports have made recommendations for better training, support, and clear accreditation for family report writers (House of Representatives 2017; ALRC 2019). If an independent children's lawyer (ICL) is appointed under Family Law Act 1975, s 68L in a contested parenting case, they are "best interests" lawyers who form their own view about children's best interests and advocate for that.

Australia has also experienced various cuts and reductions to legal aid funding over the decades and self-representing litigants are a ubiquitous feature of the family law landscape. Between 30% and 35% of parenting cases in the family courts involve unrepresented litigants (ALRC 2019, 98).

The contemporary place of "parental alienation"

The contemporary context of parental alienation in our jurisdictions emerges from a general reluctance in our family law communities to be drawn into the contested space of the "alienation" debate. Although the public discourse dropped the word "syndrome" (Silberg and Dallam 2019) and "alienation", "child resistance" or "parental rejection" were substituted, the issue continued to burn away in the courts – possibly more so in Australia. However, both places have experienced a recent upsurge in public attention following a range of media reports and public inquiries which have left no option but to deal with the issue.

Emergence of parental alienation since 2017 in the UK

Family justice practitioners and academics were startled to read a front-page story in the *Guardian* newspaper claiming that parents guilty of parental alienation were to have their children taken into state care (Hill 2017). It quickly transpired that the story was inaccurate (Transparency Project 2017), but the article either reflected or sparked a new phenomenon of alienation discussions in the mainstream, rather than on the fringes. The impetus for Hill's story is still uncertain, perhaps due to the murky gender politics involved.

Hill quoted a statistic of 11–15% of contact disputes featuring alienation, but this figure was taken from an article published in the US *Family Court Review* seven years earlier (Fidler and Bala 2010) and had no relevance to the UK. Neither Cafcass in England nor Cafcass Cymru in Wales quantified the incidence of alienation claims, then or since. Although there were mixed reports from Cafcass about the numbers of cases they dealt with that featured the problem, the rate in Wales was thought to be low. Nevertheless, both organisations were compelled to respond. In England, Cafcass embarked on a lengthy process of developing new practice guidance and in Wales, Cafcass Cymru commissioned a research review to provide an evidence base for practice (Doughty et al. 2018). Analysis by Cafcass Cymru of its most complex cases in 2017–2018 indicated almost none where parental alienation was the main or one of the main causes of concern. However, responding to campaigns was taking up a disproportionate amount of time and effort for Welsh Government. A number of petitions to the English and Welsh legislatures were organised by pressure groups during 2017–2018 to "recognise" parental alienation, including four to the UK parliament, calling for parental alienation to be made a criminal offence.

A lengthy petition taken by a fathers' rights group to the Welsh Parliament called for recognition of parental alienation as emotional abuse and funding of a national awareness campaign. Responses by the Welsh Minister for Children and the Children's Commissioner for Wales, who is charged with promoting children's rights, took note of the research review (Doughty et al. 2018) to reject these demands and to emphasise the strength of the current legal framework and their confidence in professional practice (Irranca Davies 2018). Although it was the scale of the campaign that appeared to be growing, rather than incidence of parental alienation in casework, heightened awareness led to engagement in stakeholder consultation, specialist training, and issuing new guidance (Cafcass Cymru 2019). A separate set of guidance, following stakeholder consultation, was issued in England (Cafcass 2018). These documents now provide the most comprehensive and accessible information about policy and the procedures a parent or professional might expect to encounter in court.

The three years since the splash in the *Guardian* have seen relentless promotion of the parental alienation belief system. The authors of the Ministry of Justice report acknowledged that "parental alienation" was a contested concept but because it had been widely referred to in submissions of evidence, they used the term in their report (Ministry of Justice 2020, 43). That report synthesises evidence submitted by more than 1,000 individuals, 87% of whom had personal experiences in the courts, and is peppered with references to courts using the term – to an extent that suggests it is now commonly encountered by family justice professionals.

In Australia – parliament pays attention

While in the UK, *Amelia* Hill startled the family law community with her 2017 article about the removal of children from alienating parents, two years earlier in Australia, *Jess* Hill had published an expose on the dangers of allegations of parental alienation for women and their children who had experienced family violence. She told harrowing stories of children removed from their parent of choice as part of her growing body of quality journalism on family law in Australia (Hill 2015).

But mention of parental alienation in official reports over recent years is uncommon. In the plethora of reports produced after the amendments in favour of shared parenting in 2006, only one mentioned parental alienation (Bagshaw 2010). Significant official reports (House of Representatives 2017; ALRC 2019) are silent on the topic, although both deal with the corollary to this concept – the idea that women make false allegations about family violence and child abuse (Rathus 2019). This is one of the insistent assertions of fathers' rights groups worldwide (Dragiewicz 2011). The silence was resoundingly shattered by the Interim Report of a Parliamentary Inquiry, published in October 2020 (Joint Select Committee on Australia's Family Law System (JSC) 2020). The Deputy Chair, and main instigator, of the Inquiry is well known for her view that women lie about violence to obtain advantage in parenting cases (MacMillan 2019). It was inevitable that parental alienation would be raised. The proportion of confidential submissions to this Inquiry is unusual, even for family law and, as with the UK Ministry of Justice report, makes public scrutiny difficult. Of the 1,523 individual submissions received, 93.5% are fully confidential.

The Committee was careful to make no firm comments about parental alienation in this Interim Report. It explained that "a polarised range of views on the extent to which a parent can be alienated from their children by another parent or family member" was put forward and acknowledged that the concept was contentious. The Committee declined to express a view on whether parental alienation is a recognisable disorder but noted that many submitters wrote to the committee of their experience (JSC 2020).

A final report will be published in early 2021 but the "polarised" views are now under scrutiny and, as in the UK, it is acknowledged that parental alienation is part of family law discourse in Australia.

How parental alienation terms first entered our courts

In the next sections, we explain how the terminology of parental alienation entered our courts. The initial 1995–2000 period relates to Australia. We then cover 2000–2010 in both jurisdictions. We also explain our methodology here.

Australia: 1995 to 2000 – parental alienation (syndrome) arrives

Methodology

Because of the availability of many family law trial and appellate decisions in Australia, we were able to conduct research using the search facilities of the

AUSTLII data base. We limited the searches by using only the terms "parental alienation" or "parental alienation syndrome". Although some cases that avoid these terms would be missed, this process revealed a rich source of information from more than 264 cases between 1995 and the end of 2020. We then scanned these cases to learn what literature and research had played a role in the courts, and how judges and other actors in the courts had responded to or approached allegations of a parental alienation in a case.

The chart below shows the total number of published cases in which the terms appear. This includes all trials and appeals. The courts included were the appellate court (the Full Court) and the various trial courts which have changed names and functions over the years – Family Court of Australia, Federal Magistrates Court, and Federal Circuit Court of Australia. It cannot be seen as a representation of the relative proportion of all cases heard in any year because publishing practices have changed, and many more decisions are now published (Rathus 2016). However, these are the published decisions that are available to judges, legal practitioners, family report writers, family dispute practitioners, and litigants themselves at the click of a mouse on a very user-friendly platform.

Discussion of events

Richard Gardner entered the family law *zeitgeist* in Australia in 1989 when Dr Kenneth Byrne, who had moved there from the US, wrote an article

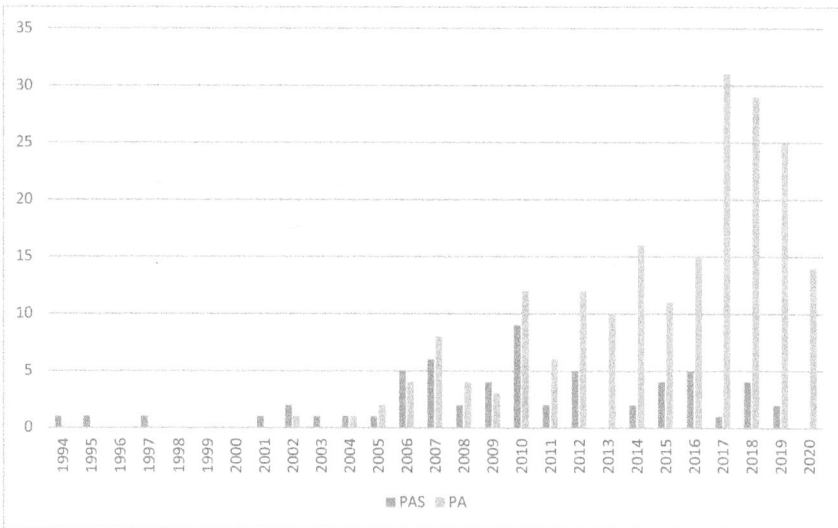

Figure 3.1 Published family law decisions where "parental alienation" only or "parental alienation syndrome" occur across all Australian family courts.

about parental alienation syndrome in *Australian Family Lawyer*, a journal circulated widely amongst family law practitioners – mainly lawyers – but also more broadly. Byrne adopted the most extreme views advocated by Gardner – that many, if not all, allegations of sexual abuse of children are false. He continued to write about his concerns regarding false allegations of child sexual abuse in family law litigation, publishing two further articles in *Australian Family Lawyer* (Byrne1991a, 1991b). These articles later sparked a *Reply* "in order to provide a more balanced view of the research in this area" (Cashmore et al. 1992). Byrne then replied to the *Reply* (Byrne 1992) – exemplifying the ever-twisting coils of contradictory research messages family law practitioners and other professionals and litigants face in the worlds of allegations of child sexual abuse and parental alienation.

The first time the term parental alienation (syndrome) occurs in a published family law case is at the end of 1994, not long after these exchanges were published. This was also when the first major amendments to the FLA legislated for a child's "right" to post-separation contact with both parents. Hesitation or reluctance by a child to see one of their parents was perceived as contradicting the new emphasis in family law. In the first three published cases, *M v D 1994*, *M v H 1996*, and *Johnson v Johnson 1997*, where this concept squarely entered the court, the phrase "parental alienation syndrome" was used, with the second two cases both relying on Dr Byrne. He was a witness in the 1996 case and his 1989 article was cited in the 1997 case, which, of the three, delved most deeply into parental alienation. This case is the first that records parents, particularly fathers, bringing articles that they have sourced themselves to lawyers and experts. It was an appeal by the father to recall an expert witness to be cross-examined about the syndrome, now that the father had "read extensively in relation to it" and because it "presented an explanation as to why the child was resisting contact with him" (Johnson v Johnson, 66–67). It is interesting to consider that in 1997 the internet was at a nascent stage, but the father in this case was a medical doctor. Within a few years, everyone had access to the same kind of information and many cases (for example, Grainger v Grainger 2019; Melsbach v Josephs 2019), where allegations of parental alienation are raised, record parents showering lawyers and witnesses with articles, blogs, and media reports of varying quality and reliability (Crowe 2019, Rathus 2018).

UK: 2000–2009-The Courts' initial responses

Because of the limitations in public access to family court records in the UK, the number of cases found to feature alienation is very low (Doughty et al. 2018). It was not until 2000 that the term parental alienation syndrome appeared in the law reports. The hot topic of whether contact with a parent who had abused the other was in a child's best interests was addressed in the leading case that consolidated four appeals, Re L, V, M and H (children)

2000. The Court of Appeal commissioned expert evidence from two child and adolescent psychiatrists, Claire Sturge and Danya Glaser. This was subsequently published in a popular practitioners' journal as "the experts' report" (Sturge and Glaser 2000). On the overall question of contact with a father who was abusive, the Court concluded that there was neither an evidential presumption for or against direct contact in such circumstances, but that factors such as the effects on the individual child, and the perpetrator's understanding of those effects, should be considered in a welfare analysis. These principles are now incorporated in the Family Procedure Rules 2010 Practice Direction 12 J. Only one of the four consolidated cases (the case called Re M), considered allegations of "parental alienation syndrome" made in the lower court, as diagnosed by Dr Ludwig Lowenstein.

Lowenstein was an educational psychologist who had lived in the US and trained in Australia and England. He apparently gave evidence on parental alienation in more than 50 court cases in the UK (Birkbeck 2013). He wrote more than 100 articles based on Gardner's premise, between 1998 and his death in 2013. The Re M judgement brought him to wider attention. The child was eight years old and had only ever had a relationship with his father through a supervised contact centre. This had ceased two years earlier, when he said he no longer wanted to see his father. The lower court had found that the constraints on contact may have hindered a positive relationship from developing, but Dr Lowenstein had attributed the boy's lack of interest to parental alienation syndrome. Butler-Sloss LJ noted that the experts' report stated that parental alienation syndrome was not recognised in either the American or international classifications of disorders nor generally recognised in psychiatric or allied child mental health specialities. (Baroness Elizabeth Butler-Sloss was the President of the Family Division of the High Court from 1995 to 2005). She would continue to be highly influential on these issues, as discussed later in this chapter.) She went on to say that it was accepted in family courts that some parents did alienate their children from the other parent, but this was a long way from a recognised syndrome requiring mental health professionals to play an expert role. She upheld the decision in the lower court that disapproved of Lowenstein identifying a condition that could be resolved by his own therapeutic programme.

The experts' report and these passages in the leading judgment on contact effectively curbed enthusiasm for the syndrome in the UK. Sturge and Glaser had relied primarily on Kathleen Faller's paper (1998) to refute parental alienation syndrome. They concluded that the sort of problems it was trying to address were better termed "implacable hostility", which could be caused by a range of factors: from fully justified fear of violence, through to what is now termed coercive control, to biased hostility. The other dampener was Carol S. Bruch's article published in a reputable UK academic journal shortly afterwards (Bruch 2002). She described Gardner's activities as "merchandising" and was excoriating about those who exploited his ideas. Parental alienation syndrome had provided "litigational advantages" to non-resident parents who could afford lawyers and expert witnesses who had "seized on a new revenue source". Lawyers had either willingly embraced a street myth or simply did not have the skills to evaluate new psychological theories. Either way, Bruch wrote, children's welfare was not their true concern.

Sturge and Glaser's principles were generally agreed in a judicially led public consultation on improving practice in contact disputes, "Making Contact Work" (Lord Chancellor's Department 2002). Some men's organisations disagreed, but the report concluded on this point that the label of "PAS" was irrelevant; it was barely mentioned. The combination of Re L, V, M, and H, the Sturge and Glaser report, the Bruch article and "Making Contact Work" left the concept of the implacably hostile parent (usually a mother) available as an argument, but parental alienation syndrome was off-limits.

Australia: 2000–2009 – the law reform agenda

By the beginning of the decade, dissatisfaction with the "right" to contact reforms of the mid-1990s meant that the "gender wars" of family law had clear battle lines (Kaye and Tolmie 1998, Graycar 2012). Fathers' rights groups lobbied tirelessly for 50:50 time with children post-separation as the default position, while many organisations that worked with women and children affected by domestic violence pushed for greater protection for these victims in family law.

These contradictory stances are reflected in what happened in the cases over this decade. Aligned with fathers' rights groups' claims of malicious mothers denying them contact with their children (Flood 2012), as the chart shows, Australian cases continued to demonstrate some use of alienation terminology in the early 2000s. But how the courts dealt with domestic violence was also receiving attention, with the English decision in Re L, V, M, and H (above) being cited 15 times in published cases between 2004 and 2009 in the context of direct links between domestic violence towards a parent and children's emotional well-being and safety.

As in the UK, Bruch was influential in bringing about a level of judicial scepticism after being cited in a 2002 appellate decision, in the marriage of R [Children's wishes]. In that case, the Full Court noted that orders transferring custody to the disfavoured parent "were not without their difficulties" [174]. A similar approach, and a level of judicial scepticism about parental alienation syndrome, was expressed by a number of trial judges subsequent to that case (for example, *Parker v Elliott* 2003, *C v C* 2004, and *Lane v Arthurs* 2006). In *C v C*, Moore J referenced the origins of the concept in the discredited work of Richard Gardner. Her Honour noted that parental alienation syndrome is a "descriptor unsuited to the discussion of complex dynamics involving at least three people and it is further unsuited because as a 'diagnosis' could lend itself to automatic or prescriptive treatments" [85]. She also observed that the expert witness who had opined that this was a parental alienation syndrome case, went on to acknowledge the lack of a scientific basis for the validity of the concept of a "syndrome" [83].

But while some Australian judges were applying the *Re L* principles, Australian policy making did not follow that path. Fathers' rights groups continuing demands for equality in the family law space created ongoing tensions (Rhoades 2010). While the English courts appear to have trimmed the excesses of parental alienation syndrome, although accepting that some parents were "obstructive", Australia launched the Inquiry that would lead to the presumption of equal shared parenting time being introduced into the FLA in 2006 (House of Representatives 2003). The presumption, which has a legislative link to orders for shared care or substantial contact time in FLA s 65DAA positioned mothers or children who were hesitant about contact with a father in direct conflict with the prevailing family law philosophy. The strong policy intent of the legislature was strengthened by the Full Court in *Goode v Goode 2006*, the first case to go on appeal after the amendments when it said.

> In our view, it can be fairly said there is a legislative intent evinced in favour of substantial involvement of both parents in their children's lives, both as to parental responsibility and as to time spent with children, subject to the need to protect children from harm, from abuse and family violence and provided it is in their best interests and reasonably practicable.
>
> [72]

These words cemented a culture of the importance of ongoing contact of children with their parents whenever possible within the judiciary and the family law system more generally. In our common law jurisdictions, some cases become beacons – and Goode did this. As is discussed in the next section, the words of Sir James Munby, five years later in England in Re C, had a similar impact. However, the amendments that Goode considered were controversial and became subject to serious review within three years (Chisholm 2009, Australian Law Reform Commission (2010).

As can be seen from Figure 3.1, in the second half of the decade, after the amendments, there was an increase in the mention of both "parental alienation" and "parental alienation syndrome" in published cases in Australia. After the negative Bruch article, the next scholar to be cited about parental alienation (other than Gardner) in a published case is Janet Johnston in 2005, just after she presented her more nuanced view on the many reasons for child rejection of a parent at the National Family Law Conference (Johnston 2004). In *Summers v Nathan 2005*, the judge relied on Johnston and "a large body of recent literature" to conclude that: "I am not persuaded immediately that 'P.A.S.' has been established irrevocably as being within a substantially established area of knowledge allowing for the receipt of expert evidence" [63].

The most frequently cited authors during this decade are Gardner ($n = 11$), often to state that his views have been discredited, and in a more positive light, Johnston, alone and with her various collaborators ($n = 14$). The first time an Australian appears to be cited in a published case is when the Full Court referred to Elspeth McInnes (2003) in *Braithwaite v Braithwaite 2007*. In that case, it seems that the Court itself introduced the article to confirm the mother's argument that there were significant problems with the idea of a "syndrome" – but then also found that there had been no diagnosis of this in the mother in any event. This is something of a recurring theme – mothers who feel that they have been accused of parental alienation spend time and money trying to disprove it for fear of a transfer of residence of the children, as in *Ralton v Ralton 2017*. This can divert attention away from what may be the real issues in a case.

2010–2020: conversations across the jurisdictions

In these sections we show how parental alienation travelled around the US, Canada, Australia, and the UK.

UK: 2010–2020

In England and Wales, there was resurgence of interest in parental alienation around 2010–2011 (at around the same time as the publication of the *Family Court Review* special issue), as is evident through the work of child and family psychiatrist, Dr Kirk Weir, well-respected as an independent expert witness in complex child protection cases, especially in issues of veracity of children's testimony of abuse. He was sceptical about the extent to which children's expressed wishes and feelings should be taken into account in parental disputes and wrote about a sample of 58 children in family proceedings who had declared their resistance or refusal to contact (Weir 2011). He was able to arrange what he termed "a good or reasonable visit" between 34 of these children and their non-resident parent and concluded that their ascertainable wishes and feelings were very unreliable. This drew him to American sources, especially Kelly and Johnston's reformulated definition of "parental alienation" (2001). He reported on only one meeting per child in the sample, whether successful or a failure, and did not claim to have resolved matters for all the families involved, but that, for some, it was a positive turning point. Unlike most U.S. literature, Weir did not appear to recommend therapy for the children, saying that although therapy was often considered to be helpful when cases were "stuck", in his experience it never was, and it caused harmful delay. Simply reintroducing the child (in an environment he rather jarringly described as "enforced contact") appeared to him to have broken down the barriers in the majority of cases.

Weir was invited to give talks and training sessions to judges and practitioners in England and Wales, and came to public prominence through a notorious case, *Re S (A Child) 2010*, where he reported the situation as one of alienation and "it is highly unlikely that any form of psychotherapy will lead to a change in [S's] response" [17]. He did not recommend a transfer of residence but such an order was made at one stage in the protracted proceedings. It is not possible to know, in retrospect, how influential Weir was, because the judgements in Re S were published at a time when allowing publicity on family cases by high court judges was rare. The judge, His Honour Judge Bellamy, was also unusual amongst his peers in citing research he had read (albeit having been supplied to him by Dr Weir from the 2010 special issue of the *Family Court Review*, including Fidler and Bala, later cited by Amelia Hill in 2017 (p. 63) and in *McGregor* (McGregor 2012).

At around the same time, wider interest can be seen in the fact of the Canadian legal academic, Nicholas Bala, being invited to speak in London by the Nuffield Foundation in 2011. Bala stated that alienation was common in high-conflict cases and was emotionally harmful to children in both the short and long term and that alienating parents did not always respond rationally to court orders. His presentation slides are still available online and provide a handy guide on the north American model that was being promoted to a UK audience (Bala 2011).

The family justice system was subject to a comprehensive review between 2011 and 2014, steered by a panel chaired by David Norgrove. The panel was, at an early stage, inclined to recommend a change in the law towards shared or equal parenting in dividing a child's time between separated parents. By the time its final report was published, the panel, largely influenced by evidence from Australia about the negative consequences of the presumption in Children Act 1989, had decided against pursuing that line (Family Justice Review 2011). Campaigns for a "50/50" presumption continued but, partly due to speeches by Baroness Butler-Sloss (by then a member of the parliamentary House of Lords), the draft Bill was amended to explicitly exclude any suggestion of prescribing fixed times. Instead, it introduced a presumption in the Children Act 1989, s 1(2)A and B that, unless the contrary is shown, the involvement of the applicant parent in the life of the child concerned will further the child's welfare. Richard Warshak, also prominent in parental alienation treatments, was an influential American advocate of "shared parenting" at the height of this debate in England and Wales, as was discussed in Chapter 2. It seems that disappointed fathers' rights activists in the UK reflected Warshak's thinking in a shift from imposing "equal" 50/50 time on children to enforcing contact against their wishes.

The 2014 reforms led to some improvements in procedure, including Family Procedure Rules 2010 Practice Direction 12J to be followed by family courts where safety issues were raised, based on the Re L principles.

At the time of writing, the presumption of continuing "involvement" is being reviewed by government in light of evidence in the Ministry of Justice 2020 report. However, it is probably not so much the 2014 amendment that imposes a heavy burden on anyone trying to argue against harmful contact as a long-embedded culture (Kaganas 2018). The senior judiciary have interpreted human rights law in this regard, as highlighted in this extract from a 2011 judgment in Re C, by a proactive former President of the Family Division, Sir James Munby, that has been cited in numerous cases:

- ...There is a positive obligation on the State, and therefore on the judge, to take measures to maintain and to reconstitute the relationship between parent and child, in short, to maintain or restore contact. The judge has a positive duty to attempt to promote contact. The judge must grapple with all the available alternatives before abandoning hope of achieving some contact.
- ... All that said, at the end of the day the welfare of the child is paramount; "the child's interest must have precedence over any other consideration" [49].

Although this analysis of the court's role concludes with the welfare principle, the positive obligations on the state to enforce the right to respect for family life under Article 8 of the European Convention on Human Rights appear to be at the forefront of judicial thinking. It has even been argued that fathers' Article 8 rights to respect for their family life are being promoted above women's and children's rights to be protected, under Article 3, from inhuman and degrading treatment at the hands of their abuser. Birchall and Choudhry (2018) examined concerns that were being raised about unsafe contact, including several disturbing examples of domestic abuse and child abuse being obscured by allegations of parental alienation against the non-abusive parent. They observed that, despite the scarcity of valid research, the perception of parental alienation was gaining traction in the family courts. Like fearful mothers in Australian cases, many of their interviewees were aware of theories that had a chilling effect and were anxious not to be seen as discouraging contact. It is remarkable that some interviewees referred to Gardner still being cited by the opposing party or lawyers, so many years after Johnston's revisions.

The Covid year of 2020–2021 has seen considerable debate on how family courts address domestic abuse, following the Ministry of Justice report (2000) but resolving the parental alienation controversy has hardly progressed.

Northern Ireland and Scotland

This section provides a brief overview of the two other jurisdictions in the UK.

Northern Ireland

The legal system in Northern Ireland is separate from but very similar to that of England and Wales and subject to the same human rights principles. Although parental alienation does not have a high profile in the family courts, this may change. New legislation, a Domestic Abuse and Family Proceedings Bill, is currently being debated by the Stormont Assembly and concerns have been raised that "parental alienation" was being mentioned by politicians across the political spectrum. There is no immediate change in the law, but these issues are to be taken up in ongoing work in relation to domestic violence and abuse. A factor to take into account here is the influence on the province of the Republic of Ireland, where parental alienation is being heavily promoted by a psychotherapist and a number of local county authorities have called on the Irish Parliament to "recognise parental alienation" in forthcoming family law reforms.

Scotland

Scots law is formally very different to the rest of the UK, but the principles of family law are similar. Recent reform of family law greatly increases the emphasis on children's participation in decision-making. This attracted some negative consultation submissions from fathers' rights groups who wanted less attention to be paid to the expressed views of children than was proposed. The Scottish Government (2019) made efforts to resist the terminology of alienation and was more concerned about the use of allegations by abusers to undermine victims' concerns and expose children to risk of harm. No changes in law to specifically address refusal or resistance to contact were introduced but left to the courts to determine within the new legal framework.

Australia 2010–2020

Two critical events occurred in 2012 that impacted on the family law system in Australia. First, the FLA was amended yet again – this time to better respond to allegations of domestic and family violence (House of Representatives 2010–2011, 1). Second, after a number of appeals from decisions in which trial judges cited social science literature – and maybe even relied on it to formulate their judgments, the Full Court decided *McGregor v McGregor 2012*, which largely suppressed the citation of social science in our courts thereafter (Kearney 2014, Bryant 2012).

The emphasis on responding better to family violence did not stop parental alienation being a live issue in Australian courts. "Parental alienation" is mentioned in 181 published cases over this period and "parental alienation syndrome" is mentioned in 34, starkly demonstrating the Australian preference for not mentioning the syndrome. The occurrence of the term "parental alienation" rose significantly over 2017–2018 – at the same time as the re-emergence of parental alienation discourse in the UK. One reason for this may be that, despite the family violence amendments, the fundamental structure of the legislation had not been changed so where children were reluctant to spend time with one parent – this offended the thrust of the FLA and provided an ideal seeding bed for allegations of parental alienation.

The period after the 2006 amendments represented the most intense use of social science literature by trial judges (Rathus 2016, Kearney 2014). Much of the literature referenced in Australian cases was about shared care and very young children (for example, McIntosh and Chisholm 2008, see Rathus 2016), but literature about parental alienation also made an appearance. Fidler and Bala (2010), as cited by Judge Bellamy in Re S, was central in *McGregor*. The trial judge referenced it in his judgement, and it then became apparent that he had used this article, and work of Warshak (2001) cited within, as a basis for questions from the bench during the trial, without stating this clearly to the parties. The Full Court was critical that he had gone beyond the evidence to determine that the children had been alienated in the sense described by Fidler and Bala.

While it is important that judges apply the law, and not social science, particularly when no notice is given (Rathus 2012; Kearney 2014), subsequent interpretation of McGregor brought in a peculiar silence and denial of reliance on research. The stark change wrought in judicial behaviour is evident in two cases heard by Judge Harman, a judicial officer with a genuine interest in and knowledge about the social sciences. In a 2010 case, *Udall v Oaks*, he cited seven different social science articles about parental alienation, including Bruch (2002), Kelly and Johnston (2001), and Fidler and Bala (2010). But six years later, in a complex case, *Proctor v Proctor 2016*, Judge Harman's discomfort is apparent when he explained why he had to resort to alienation terminology at times in his judgment. He clarified that he referred only to parental alienation terminology that had been used by the parties themselves and "that such terms have not been used in a 'loaded' way intended to import and impermissibly introduce such literature" [133].

After examining many cases where parental alienation is raised as an issue, it is suggested that the following presents a summary of the position of the Australian family courts:

- Parental alienation *syndrome* is not recognised as a diagnosis or concept which has scientific validity;
- It is recognised that some parents engage in behaviour intended to influence their children adversely in respect of the other parent. The terminology of parental alienation may be used in these cases, but other terminology is also employed;
- It is also recognised that there are many reasons why a child may be resistant to contact with one parent, and some of these may relate to the conduct of that parent towards that child or the other parent;

- There is some acknowledgement that once the issue of parental aliena-tion has been raised in a case, it can fill more litigation space than the facts suggest is proportionate.
- There is some reluctance to change the residence of a child against the expressed wishes of the child, and the court sometimes has concerns about the capacity of the disfavoured parent to deal safely with the tran-sition and the possible traumatic consequences, but changes of residence do occur – sometimes with a moratorium period of no contact for the "alienating" parent; and
- Sometimes the court reluctantly leaves a child with a resident parent, believing that they have been a part of the child's alienation from the other parent, but also believing that a change of residence would be too traumatic and would not be in the best interests of the child.

Although there are too few reported cases in the UK to make a full compar-ison, this approach is reflected in the totality of judgements that are available.

While the courts may be taking a somewhat nuanced view of parental al-ienation, actors in the family law system have been invited to an increasingly varied smorgasbord of events over the decade. Bala presented Australia with a version of his 2011 Nuffield speech the following year, neatly tailored for Australian audiences, and this is also still available on the Australian Institute of Family Studies (AIFS) website (Bala 2012). Judge Tom Altobelli (2006) presented a paper at the National Family Law Conference, which was later cited in the courts. Further into the decade, there were individual papers at conferences (Papaleo 2013) and local family law network events (for example, Hugall 2017).

Two national conferences devoted to the issue in 2018 included presenta-tions from influential American and Canadian figures in the parental aliena-tion world. One conference was organised by the Australian Chapter of the Association of Family and Conciliation Courts (AFCC). The other was or-ganised by a coalition of organisations including the University of Tasmania where a co-author of a new "Guide to Assessment and Intervention" (Haines et al. 2020) in parental alienation cases, Mandy Matthewson, is a senior lecturer in psychology.

COVID-19 adaptions have created a proliferation of presentations the topic for actors in the family system in 2020. At a Queensland practitioners' we-binar in September 2020, Dr Ben Jones remarked about parental alienation: "A lot of people talk about it and it's an 'oft thrown around phrase' – but it is 'an extremely rare' phenomenon" (Jones 2020). Despite this, during 2020, a number of webinars on parental alienation have been available to profes-sionals in the Australian family law system. This raises a concern that such a focus on this concept might lead family law professionals to see it where it doesn't exist – a form of confirmation bias. On the whole, no real critique is presented at these events, although there is usually some acknowledgement that parental alienation is controversial.

Dealing with the problems of parental alienation in our jurisdictions

It is no longer possible to ignore alienation terminology in the family courts in these jurisdictions. In this section, we argue that alleging parental alienation often results in obfuscation of abuse or poor parenting, and risks decisions which may harm children, turning the focus to the conduct of the alleged alienator.

Despite only a handful of reported cases in England and Wales and a general dearth of UK research (Doughty et al. 2018), scepticism of Gardner's unidirectional proposition has given way to the term being routinely raised when children resist or refuse contact. In Australia, the data show that the term parental alienation has been on a general increase in published cases over the decade from 2010 with 12 in that year to 29 in 2018, 25 in 2019, and 14 in 2020. Parental alienation syndrome, on the other hand, has declined in use from its highest point in 2010 of nine to two in 2019 and none in 2020.

The current President of the Family Division of the England and Wales High Court has expressed continued reluctance to apply what he described as a formal label of "Parental Alienation Syndrome" to cases that become mired in allegations and counter allegations but observed that alienation with a small a was normal in intractable contact disputes (McFarlane 2018, 8). His solution was an early fact-finding exercise by the court, as required in Practice Direction 12J, which applies to cases where there are allegations of domestic abuse but is rarely applied in the lower courts. Reasons include crowded court lists and backlogs; lack of legal representation; poor judicial training; and shortages of Cafcass officers (Ministry of Justice 2020).

No similar statement has been made in Australia but actors in the system rarely append the word "syndrome". As in the UK, a number of guidelines and procedures have been developed for cases where child abuse or family violence has been alleged, with alienation not directly mentioned. In 2009, the family courts produced a set of Family Violence Best Practice Principles. Initially directed at "decision makers", the latest version, published in 2016, states that the Principles provide "a checklist of matters to which judges, court staff, legal professionals, and litigants may wish to refer at each stage of the case management process in disputes involving children" (Family Court of Australia 2016). In discussing matters that may be considered where there have been findings of family violence or abuse (or risk of these issues Principles refer to the Sturge and Glaser (2000) report. They do not mention alienation. In theory, a "Notice of Risk" where safety issues have been raised flags up matters that should be dealt with expeditiously, but again the workload of the courts is punishing and there are delays in many parts of the system.

Second, almost all the academic and popular literature on parental alienation in our jurisdictions still emanates from the US – in a very different clinical, legal, and political environment to the UK and Australia. Gardner and Bruch were still being cited in England as recently as 2018, in Re D, and the diminished citations in Australian cases still largely involve the American authors. The Cafcass (England) guidance is heavily reliant on books published in the US by Amy Baker, which are unhelpful in promoting the diagnosis of a condition for which there is no cure. The most recent guide for social science practitioners in Australia has been produced by the Tasmanian group. Many of the references are to the American literature, including Bernet, Baker, and Warshak. Unfortunately, the authors state in the "legal" chapter that "relatively high rates of false accusations of violence and abuse in the context of parenting disputes is well known" (Haines et al. 2020, 230). This is simply not so (Moloney 2007, 31–33, and 47–48). They also encourage parents to bring contravention proceedings – which are often expensive and unsatisfactory for the parties. Their advice reads as tactical, rather than focused on the child. Although they acknowledge difficulties with contravention applications, they espouse the benefits of being able to "reshape the focus of the proceedings on the parent who has contravened and place considerable pressure on them and their lawyer". Contraventions were said to: "raise the prospect of the child being removed from" the other parent and amounted to "very helpful evidence for the other parent to take into a trial" (Haines et al. 2020, 234).

In the US, the parental alienation label may be envisaged by its proponents as a gateway to treatment, but this is rarely possible in the UK. Access to child and adolescent mental health services is highly rationed because they sit within the remit of the National Health Service (NHS), where resources are concentrated on physical illness. Treatment for psychological and mental health problems in adults and children remains a NHS responsibility, far down the list of priorities. Parents who are wealthy or desperate enough may pay for private treatment but in family court proceedings, if a child was assessed to be suffering emotional harm because of parents encouraging child avoidant behaviour, the expectation would be that the NHS would provide that therapy.

The parental alienation "industry" is not as extensive and obvious in Australia as in the US, but there seems to be a growing number of "treatment" programs as well as private practitioners who provide therapeutic services. Examples of orders for therapy and counselling can be identified in our data set of Australian cases – particularly where there is a change of residence of the children or other substantial changes to the parenting arrangements. Parents cannot be compelled to attend such programs, but failure to comply could lead to further litigation regarding arrangements for the children.

Conclusion

By writing this chapter collaboratively, we discovered fascinating patterns in the waxing and waning of the concept of parental alienation in our respective jurisdictions. While we both came from a position of scepticism about how this term has been deployed in our family law systems, we accept that some parents engage in unjustifiable behaviour adverse to the other parent's relationship with their children.

However problematically the law has evolved to enforce a normative presumption that children need their father, it is recognised in the United Nations Convention on the Rights of the Child that children have their own right to respect for a relationship with *both* parents. Our societies are based on a premise that a child's knowledge of their parents is essential to their identity. There is reluctance to simply accept that a child may not want to see one parent at a particular stage in their life but, equally, there is insufficient investment in the time and expertise that would be required to fully and effectively explain the child's reasons and work through a solution. In the absence of any satisfactory practical response to labelling individuals as "alienated" in Australia and the UK, we hope that energy can be redirected to more positive ways to support separated families.

Acknowledgement

We would like to thank our research assistant, Ruth Amdur, for her excellent work analysing Australian data.

Cases

Australia

Braithwaite v Braithwaite [2007] FamCA 468
C v C [2004] FamCA 708
Goode v Goode [2006] FamCA 1346
Grainger v Grainger [2019] FamCA 56
Johnson v Johnson [1997] FamCA 32
Lane v Arthurs [2006] FamCA 87.
M v D; Australian Capital Territory [1994] FamCA 179
M v H and Separate Representative [1996] FamCA 42
McGregor v McGregor [2012] FamCAFC 69
Melsbach v Josephs [2019] FCCA 2871.
Parker v Elliott [2003] FamCA 990
Proctor v Proctor [2016] FCCA 613
In the marriage of R [Children's wishes] [2002] FamCA 383
Ralton v Ralton [2017] FamCAFC 182
Summers v Nathan [2005] FamCA 1406
Udall v Oaks [2010] FMCAfam 1482

England and Wales

Re C (A child) [2011] EWCA Civ 521
Re D (A child–parental alienation) (Rev 1) [2018] EWFC B64
Re L, V, M and H (Children) [2000] EWCA Civ 194
Re S (A child) [2010] EWHC 192 (Fam); [2010] EWHC 3721 (Fam)

References

Altobelli, Tom. "'The Effective Use of Social Science Research in Family Law in Australia'". Paper presented *at 12th National Family Law Conference*, Perth, 2006.

Australian Law Reform Commission. *Family Law for the Future: An Inquiry into the Family Law System – Final Report*. Commonwealth of Australia, 2019.

Bagshaw, Dale. *Family Violence and Family Law in Australia: The Experiences and Views of Children and Adults from Families Who Separated Post-1995 and Post 2006*. Melbourne: Monash University, 2010.

Bala, Nicholas. "Parental Alienation and the Child's Voice in Family Proceedings". Nuffield Foundation. Paper presented 13 July 2011. https://www.nuffieldfoundation.org/sites/default/files/files/Alienation%20UK%20July%2013%202011%20Bala%20Presentation.pdf

Bala Nicholas. "Parental Alienation, Contact Problems and the Family Justice System". AIFS. Presented 20 February 2012. https://aifs.gov.au/events/webinars-seminars/parental-alienation-contact-problems-family-justice-system

Birchall, Jenny and Shazia Choudhry. *What about My Right Not to Be Abused? Domestic Abuse, Human Rights and the Family Courts*. London: Women's Aid Federation for England, 2018. https://www.womensaid.org.uk/research-and-publications/domestic-abuse-human-rights-and-the-family-courts/.

Birkbeck, University of London. 2013. Obituary, Accessed February 1, 2021. http://www.bbk.ac.uk/about-us/obituaries/dr-l-f-lowenstein

Bruch, Carol S. "Parental Alienation Syndrome and Alienated Children – Getting It Wrong in Child Custody Cases". *Child and Family Law Quarterly* 35, 2002: 381–407.

Bryant, Diana. "The Use of Extrinsic Materials – With Particular Reference to Social Science and Family Law Decision-Making" Conference Paper. *Judicial Conference of Australia Colloquium*, Fremantle Western Australia, 2012.

Byrne, Ken. "Brainwashing in Custody Cases: The Parental Alienation Syndrome". *Australian Family Lawyer* 4(3), 1989: 1–7.

Byrne, Ken. "Allegations of Child Sexual Abuse and the Expert Witness: Common Problems – Part 1". *Australian Family Lawyer* 6(4), 1991a: 14–17.

Byrne, Ken. "Allegations of Child Sexual Abuse and the Expert Witness: Common Problems – Part 2". *Australian Family Lawyer* 7(1), 1991b: 5–9.

Byrne, Ken. "Sexual Abuse Allegations & the Expert Witness: A Reply to Cashmore, Chisholm & Waters". *Australian Family Lawyer* 8(1), 1992: 15–20.

Cafcass. *Child Impact Assessment Framework*, 2018. https://www.cafcass.gov.uk/grown-ups/professionals/ciaf/

Cafcass Cymru. *Children's Resistance or Refusal to Spend Time with a Parent: Practice Guidance*, 2019, https://gov.wales/childrens-resistance-or-refusal-spend-time-parent-cafcass-cymru-practice-guidance

Cashmore, Judy, Richard Chisholm, and Brent Waters. "Sexual Abuse Allegations and Child Placement: A Reply to Ken Byrne". *Australian Family Lawyer* 7(3), 1992: 32–36.

Chisholm, Richard. *Family Courts Violence Review*, 2009. Canberra: Attorney-General's Department.

Crowe, Jonathan, Rachael Field, Lisa Toohey, Helen Partridge and Lynn McAllister. "I'll Just Google That!" Online Searches and the Post-Separation Family Law Information, 2019.

Experience". *Alternative Law Journal* 2019. doi:10.1177/1037969X19827450

Doughty, Julie, Nina Maxwell and Tom Slater. *Review of Research and Case Law on Parental Alienation*. Cardiff: Welsh Government, 2018.

Dragiewicz, Molly. *Equality With a Vengeance: Men's Rights Groups, Battered Women, and Antifeminist Backlash*. Boston: Northeastern University, USA, 2011.

Faller, Kathleen. "The Parental Alienation Syndrome: What Is It and What Data Support It?" *Child Maltreatment* 3, 1998: 100–115.

Family Court of Australia and Federal Circuit Court of Australia. *Family Violence Best Practice Principles* (4th ed.). Canberra: Commonwealth of Australia, 2016.

Family Justice Review. *Final Report*. London: Ministry of Justice, 2011.

Fidler, Barbara Jo and Nicholas Bala. "Children Resisting Postseparation Contact with a Parent: Concepts, Controversies, and Conundrums". *Family Court Review* 48, 2010: 10–47.

Flood, Michael. "Separated Fathers and the 'Fathers' Rights' Movement". *Journal of Family Studies* 18, 2012: 235–245.

Graycar, Regina. "Family Law Reform in Australia, or Frozen Chooks Revisited Again?" *Theoretical Inquiries in Law* 13(1), 2012: 241–269.

Haines, Janet, Mandy Matthewson and Marcus Turnbull. *Understanding and Managing Parental Alienation: A Guide to Assessment and Intervention*. London: Routledge, 2020.

Hill, Amelia. "Divorcing Parents Could Lose Children If They Try to Turn Them Against Partner". *The Guardian*, 2017, November, 17.

Hill, Jess. "Suffer the Children: Trouble in the Family Court". *The Monthly*, 2015, November.

House of Representatives. *Every Picture Tells a Story: Report on the Inquiry into Child Custody Arrangements in the Event of Family Separation*. Canberra: Parliament of the Commonwealth of Australia, 2003.

House of Representatives. *Explanatory Memorandum*. Family Law Legislation Amendment (Family Violence and Other Measures) Bill 2011. Canberra: Parliament of the Commonwealth of Australia, 2010–2011.

House of Representatives. *A Better Family Law System to Support and Protect Those Affected By Family Violence: Recommendations For An Accessible, Equitable and Responsive Family Law System Which Better Prioritises Safety of Those Affected By Family Violence*. Canberra: Parliament of the Commonwealth of Australia, 2017.

Hugall, David. *Parental Alienation: Childhood Alignment and Rejection*. Family Law Pathways Network, Gold Coast, 2017, February.

Irranca Davies, Huw. "Minister Sets Out Welsh Approach to Parental Alienation". 2018, May 1, https://gov.wales/minister-sets-out-welsh-governments-approach-parental-alienation-0

Jeffries, Samantha, Rachael Field, Helena Menih, and Zoe Rathus. "Good Evidence, Safe Outcomes in Parenting Matters Involving Domestic Violence?: Understanding Family Report Writing Practice from the Perspective of Professionals Working in the Family Law System". *University of New South Wales Law Journal* 39, 2016: 1355–1388.

Johnston, Janet. "Children of Divorce Who Reject a Parent and Refuse Visitation: Recent Research and Social Policy Implications for the Alienated Child". *11th National Family Law Conference*, Broadbeach, Queensland, 2004.

Joint Select Committee on Australia's Family Law System. *Improvements in Family Law Proceedings*. Canberra: Commonwealth of Australia, 2020.

Jones, Ben. "Parental Alienation: What Is It? How Do You Deal With It?" Family Law Practitioners Association (Qld), 2020, September 24.

Kaganas, Felicity. "Parental Involvement: A Discretionary Presumption". *Legal Studies* 38, 2018: 549–570.

Kaye, Miranda and Julia Tolmie. "Fathers' Rights Groups in Australia and Their Engagement With Issues in Family Law". *Australian Journal of Family Law* 12, 1998: 19–67.

Kearney, Michael. "The Scientists Are Coming: What Are the Courts to Do With Social Science Research?" In *Families, Policy and the Law: Selected Essays on Contemporary Issues for Australia*, edited by A. Hayes and D. Higgins, 275–281. Southbank: Australian Institute of Family Studies, 2014.

Kelly, Joan B. and Janet R. Johnston. "The Alienated Child: A Reformulation of Parental Alienation Syndrome". *Family Court Review* 39, 2001: 249–266.

Lord Chancellor's Department Advisory Board on Family Law, Children Act Sub-Committee. *Making Contact Work*. London: Lord Chancellor's Department, 2002.

MacMillan, Jade. "Family Law Inquiry Given Green Light by Senate as Rosie Batty Questions Pauline Hanson's Role". 2019. September 18. https://www.abc.net.au/news/2019-09-18/rosie-batty-family-law-inquiry-pauline-hanson-bias/11523914

McFarlane, Lord Justice. "Contact: A Point of View". London: NAGALRO Annual Conference Keynote Speech, 2018.

McInnes, Elspeth. "Parental Alienation Syndrome: A Paradigm for Child Abuse in Australian Family Law". In *Child Sexual Abuse: Justice Response or Alternative Resolution Conference May 2003*, 1–8. Adelaide: Australian Institute of Criminology, 2003.

McIntosh, Jennifer and Richard Chisholm. "Shared Care and Children's Best Interests in Conflicted Separation: A Cautionary Tale from Current Research". *Australian Family Lawyer* 20, 2007–2008: 3.

Ministry of Justice. *Assessing Risk of Harm to Children and Parents in Private Law Children Cases: Final Report*. London: Ministry of Justice, 2020.

Moloney, Lawrie, Bruce Smyth, Ruth Weston, Nicholas Richardson, Lixia Qu and Matthew Gray. *Allegations of Family Violence and Child Abuse in Family Law Children's Proceedings: A Pre-reform Exploratory Study* (Research Report No. 15). Melbourne: Australian Institute of Family Studies, 2007.

Papaleo, Vincent. "When Children Refuse Contact With a Parent – The Language of Conflict and the Reciprocal Relationship Between the Court and the Social Sciences". In *6th World Congress on Family Law and Children's Rights*, 1–18. Sydney, 2013.

Rathus, Zoe. "A Call for Clarity in the Use of Social Science Research in Family Law Decision-making." Australian Journal of Family Law 26, 2012:81-115.

Rathus, Zoe. "Mapping the Use of Social Science in Australian Courts: The Example of Family Law Children's Cases". *Griffith Law Review* 25, 2016: 352–382.

Rathus, Zoe. "'The Research Says' …: Perceptions on the Use of Social Science Research in the Family Law System." *Federal Law Review* 41 (6), 2018: 85.

Rathus, Zoe, Samantha Jeffries, Helena Menih, and Rachael Field. "'It's Like Standing on a Beach, Holding Your Children's Hands and Having a Tsunami Just Coming Towards You': Intimate Partner Violence and Expert Assessments in Australian Family Law". *Victims and Offenders* 14(3), 2019: 1–33.

Rhoades, Helen. "Children's Needs and 'Gender Wars': The Paradox of Parenting Law Reform". *Australian Journal of Family Law* 24(2), 2010: 160–175.

Scottish Government. *Review of Children (Scotland) Act 1995 Consultation: Analysis.* Edinburgh: Scottish Government, 2019.

Silberg, Joyanna and Stephanie Dallam. "Abusers Gaining Custody in Family Courts: A Case Series of Over-turned Decisions". *Journal of Child Custody* 16(2), 2019: 140–169.

Sturge, Claire and Glaser, Danya. "Contact and Domestic Violence – The Experts' Court Report". *Family Law* 30, 2000: 615–629.

Transparency Project. "'It Blew Up Too Soon For Us' – Cafcass Explain Their Position on Alienation". 2017, December 3. http://www.transparencyproject.org.uk/it-blew-up-too-soon-for-us-cafcass-explain-their-position-on-alienation/

Warshak, Richard A. "Current Controversies Regarding Parental Alienation Syndrome". *American Journal of Forensic Psychology* 19(3), 2001: 29–59.

Weir, Kirk. "High Conflict Contact Disputes: Evidence of the Extreme Unreliability of Some Children's Ascertainable Wishes and Feelings". *Family Court Review* 49, 2011: 788–800.

Chapter 4

Experiences of parental alienation interventions

Adrienne Barnett, Arianna Riley, and 'Katherine'

This chapter provides direct accounts of experiences of parental alienation interventions in North America and England and Wales. Parental alienation intervention is a significantly under-researched area. No objective data is available in either jurisdiction on the type, frequency, form, and providers of such interventions in the family court arena and there are very few independent evaluations of the effectiveness or effects of parental alienation interventions (see Chapter 7 for a review of existing interventions).

Absent from current knowledge and research are the highly problematic impacts of parental alienation interventions and 'treatments' on children and their preferred parents. These negative impacts are not apparent from the historical literature and legal analyses on parental alienation interventions. What is particularly unexplored are the lived experiences of the parents and children who are subjected to such interventions. This chapter provides a rare opportunity to hear directly from survivors of parental alienation interventions.

> Recently, accounts have been emerging from child participants in residential workshops run by *Family Bridges* in North America and they raise a concerning picture.
>
> I read a first-person account by a girl who said she'd grown suicidal and cut herself when she was taken to a Family Bridges workshop at age 15; she claimed that the psychologists had threatened to ship her off to a psychiatric hospital. A young woman told me that her little sister had suffered panic attacks during the workshop; when the older girl challenged the Family Bridges therapists, they kept saying the girls would need "extra help," which she understood to mean being sent to a wilderness camp for juvenile offenders. A teenage boy wrote that he is "still emotionally damaged from the program," and that he "has difficulty connecting to others because I feel I can't trust anyone." None of these children has a relationship with the parent who brought them to the program.
>
> (Hagerty, 2020)

DOI: 10.4324/9781003095927-5

The young woman whose sister had suffered the panic attacks is co-author of this chapter, Arianna Riley. Later in this chapter, her account of her experiences of *Family Bridges* is offered.

In England and Wales, the more recent case law indicates increasing recommendations for parental alienation 'therapeutic' interventions alongside transfers of care of the child to the 'alienated' parent. However, parents and children cannot be ordered to undertake 'treatment' or 'therapy'. One way in which it appears that 'therapeutic' intervention may be achieved is a hybrid arrangement whereby a court-appointed expert undertakes a discrete, time-limited segment of therapy for the purposes of their assessment. This can, however, lead to boundaries between assessment and therapy becoming blurred, particularly where the assessing expert is a psychotherapist (see, e.g., *Re H (Children)* [2019] EWHC 237; *Re S (Parental Alienation: Cult)* [2020] EWCA Civ 568; *Re T (Parental Alienation)* [2019] EWHC 3854 (Fam)). Additionally, 'therapeutic' intervention for a parent may be achieved by the parent agreeing to the intervention, particularly when it takes place during the course of proceedings. For the 'alienating' parent, however, such agreement may be driven by a fear of the consequences (such as losing care of, or not regaining contact with, their child) if they do not cooperate with the therapy (see, e.g., *Re T (Parental Alienation)* [2019] EWHC 3854 (Fam).

Little is known about what the therapeutic interventions recommended or undertaken in family court cases in England and Wales actually entail. Indeed, until recently, such interventions have rarely been specifically identified as 'parental alienation' or 'reunification' therapy. Parents may find themselves, as Katherine did, involved in parental alienation therapy without realizing that this was the underlying purpose of the intervention.

Katherine's account is written by Katherine herself, using a pseudonym. She has written it in the third person because she found the experience of writing in the first person harrowing and retraumatizing. Katherine's account raises all of the issues outlined above about parental alienation interventions in England and Wales.

Arianna Riley's Experience of Family Bridges

I will begin my story by saying, I had a fairly normal (early) childhood. I went to a neighborhood school, spent a lot of time with my family, and went to festivals and concerts every year. We took yearly family vacations and ate dinner together most nights of the week. Things seemed perfectly fine, up until they started to go wrong.

My parents separated in 2009, and almost immediately things started going wrong. My sister and I were fairly young at the time, and any disagreement that we had would often end up with my mom getting physical and hurting one of us. During this time, I was starting middle school across the city and there were a lot of scary changes happening; this meant, for me, intensifying emotional abuse. Things like being called a "slut" at age 11–12 repeatedly for dressing up in my own home and wearing things my mother had bought me, and at the time I didn't even know what the word slut meant. I just knew that it was meant to be hurtful, and it was hurtful to me, not the word but knowing that someone I loved was intentionally trying to inflict harm.

I dealt with this abusive behavior by going to live with my dad. My parents at the time had 50/50 custody, but it came to a point where my mother and I had been going to therapy and she continued to be abusive, so I went to live with my dad for a year or so. While I was living with my dad, I still talked to and actively saw my mother, including going to counseling with her. Things continued much like this for a few years. I would return to her house to live with her, she would break a promise or be violent repeatedly, I would leave and live with my dad so I could be safe, and on like that. Until she decided to completely disregard my feelings as well as those of my sister.

My mother had begun dating someone new around 2013, and in August of 2015 she decided that it was time to move him into the house, even though my sister and I were uncomfortable being around him due to his creepy behavior and I had told her repeatedly that I didn't want him in the house. She chose to move him in anyways, so I left for my dad's house. I had a car that I paid for fully with my money but that had been registered and titled to her because I was underage, and when I left, she tried to stop me by taking the car. She told me that if I wanted to live with my dad, I would have to give her the car. She only agreed to reimburse me for it after I begged repeatedly and accused her of stealing. However, she shorted me when I showed up for the reimbursement she had promised and expected me not to notice. However, as I had a job I was able to save up and buy another car.

One day in October, I was cooking with my friends and got a call from my sister. My sister chose to stay with my mom when the boyfriend was moved in, so she was calling from my mom's house saying that my mom and her boyfriend were escalating things, and last time this had happened they had trapped her in her room and screamed at her for hours. She told me that she thought this time they would become violent and she would be unable to leave. I immediately went round to get my sister and my friend agreed to wait at the house until we came back.

When I got to the house, I opened the door and started up the stairs toward my sister's room. My mom's boyfriend saw me and began physically attacking me as I was walking up the stairs, grabbing me, and trying to drag me down the stairs to prevent me from getting up to my sister's room. I just ignored him and kept going, filled with adrenaline. I could hear my mother was screaming at my sister in her room. I went to try to open the door to my sister's room, with my mom's boyfriend still pulling at me from the back, and my mom trying to shove the door closed from the front. My sister was very upset, crying, and saying that she just wants to leave and they can talk about this later after everyone has calmed down, meanwhile my mom was trying to attack my sister.

At this point, we managed to get down the stairs, and I assumed my sister was following right behind me, so I walked out and closed the door. I was wrong. I waited around 15–20 seconds before realizing that something must have gone wrong, and I opened the door to see my mother and her boyfriend physically restraining my sister from leaving. They tried to close the door, and I stuck my arm in the door so they couldn't close it, at which point my mother started beating on the part of my arm that was inside, trying to make me leave. This, fortunately, caused her to lose her balance when my sister moved, and my sister was able to escape when my mother let go of her backpack. After all this, we were safe, and we drove back to my dad's. My sister and I were shaken up, and my friends (who love my sister also) were very concerned and tried to offer their support in any way they could.

We stayed in contact with my mom but my sister was unwilling to go back because of the violence, and my mom refused to accept responsibility for anything. We called her once a week, I would have lunch with her, I even brought in a woman whose kids I took care of to have lunch with her and I together to try to smooth things over. Unfortunately, this did not work – the woman left shell-shocked and basically told me that she didn't have any further suggestions on how to improve things.

Then came January 2016. I had been living with my dad full time since August, and my sister had been living with him full time since November. During this time, he was still paying my mother child support with no complaints. Eventually my dad filed in court a motion to stop paying child support, since we were living with him full time. About two weeks after this, during our weekly call with my mother, she told me she didn't want to have lunch with me and didn't want to talk to me or have any interaction with me and she hung up on me. So I said, ok fine. What could I do when she told me not to talk to her?

I knew my parents had a custody hearing in court on my birthday. I knew that my mom had asked for that date because she thought I would be busy. Little did she know, I had enlisted my boyfriend at the time to go to the court proceedings to see what happened, as the court proceedings were public. Even after this, we still had no idea what was coming, unfortunately. We heard a slight inkling of a "program" and Richard Warshak, but we didn't know anything for sure. But just to be safe, the day before the decision on who I was to live with was announced (April 25, 2016), I went around to my employers and told them I may just disappear for two weeks, and they should make alternative plans. Fortunately, my employers were fairly understanding, all things considered.

On April 25, 2016, my sister and I were called to show up for the announcement of the decision. We arrived that morning with a contingent of friends and family, an assortment of people gathered over many years to support us no matter what happened. We all filed into the courtroom, and the judge asked my sister and me to stand and say a few words.

> Your honor, we don't feel safe living with my mother and her boyfriend since they are abusive, and she has even told me that she doesn't want to talk to me and doesn't want a relationship with me. In addition, there are many things that she is supposed to provide as a parent that she does not seem interested in providing, and it becomes neglectful. In conclusion, we should not be forced to live with them because we absolutely will not be safe.

The judge: "Well it sounds to me like you just have a very black and white view of the world, and not everything is black and white. Often, things are in shades of gray. I am ordering you guys to be sent to Family Bridges reunification therapy…" *audible gasps can be heard in the courtroom* and at that point I just tuned out. I handed my phone to my dad and gave him a hug, my sister did the same. I started hysterically crying and screaming. I said, "I'm not going, I refuse to go". The judge, at this point still in the courtroom said, "if you don't go, then they will send you to jail for 30 days." I said, "I don't care!" and continued hysterically screaming and crying while these strange people who had filed into the courtroom said, "come with me, you need to go with me."

At this point, I actually refused to go. I dropped on the ground and said, "I refuse. You can carry me and handcuff me but I will not go willingly." And they told me that if I didn't go with them they would put my dad in prison for 30 days. I got up real quick, because punishing me I could take, but jailing my father? And jeopardizing any safe housing I may have when I get out? That was completely unacceptable to me. After I got up, they took us out from the back and put us in a van and we began driving to the airport. At first, we refused to talk to these "transport agents". I had a plan. I had flown fairly frequently, so I was familiar with the rules at airports, and familiar with all of their "anti-trafficking" signage, which claims: "if you are being trafficked, just tell TSA and they will save you!" Well, I did. I told at least ten different TSA agents that I was being kidnapped. While they were checking my boarding pass, the nearest ones I could pull aside, TEN DIFFERENT AGENTS were told I was being kidnapped. NONE of them did anything besides laugh.

Then I felt extremely panicked. I asked the last agent for the police, but they weren't coming. I was trying to think fast, what's a surefire way to get police to come in an airport? Make a terrorist threat. So, in the middle of security, I loudly announced "I have a bomb in my shoe, I need you to come arrest me!" My trafficker meanwhile was busy trying to hustle me through the security machine, but the TSA agent had overheard me and, lo and behold, turns out if you make a terrorist threat they have to get the police and they are unable to allow you to fly anymore. My trafficker, sensing I am gaining the upper hand, begins trying to continue to hustle me through the machine, at which point I start to let out blood curdling screams. I do this for two minutes straight until the police come. Anything I can do to make a scene and get the police to interview me privately.

The police response: "they have a court order. So what's the issue?" Well, the issue is that I am being trafficked and forced to live with abusers. So I told the port police that I would like to make a report of the October incident of violence, so that I am not forced to go be abused more. He refused to take the report seriously, and then a bunch of other cops came, one of whom said that my sister and I needed to "stop complaining" because "parents have the right to discipline the way they want to". All the police ended up doing was helping the traffickers handcuff me, and then telling the traffickers they couldn't fly that day. And the no-fly decision wasn't even made by the cops, that was a decision made by the head of Alaska Airlines – if it had been up to the cops, they probably would have let them fly me in handcuffs.

After all this, we were to drive the 23 hours down to Ontario, California to start the Family Bridges workshop. After a few hours of driving, people were hungry and needed to use the facilities. The first time my sister had tried to use the bathroom on this trip, they went in the toilet stall with her to watch her which weirded her out. Again, when we stopped for food, they went into the bathroom with her. My sister let me know that this made her extremely uncomfortable and I thought it was gross behavior. During this long car ride, one of the transporters let slip that if children don't obey, she knows one that was sent to a wilderness camp and it's unknown when he gets to come back.

This is why the transporters are essential. They make the threats before you even get there. We told them that we didn't feel safe around my mother and her boyfriend, and they spent hours reassuring us that we wouldn't have to see them if we didn't want to.

When we "arrived" at the Sheraton, which was where Family Bridges was supposed to happen, we walked into a room with my mother and her boyfriend. We were SO upset. The transport agents had lied to us. The psychologists asked my sister and I if we wanted to say anything, and we said yes, we don't feel safe around them. They responded by informing us that we could no longer talk about the past (the implication also being don't mention our dad) and that we would have to cooperate to "pass the program".

What were the methods used?

We were stuck in the suite at the Sheraton for four days straight, trapped with my mother and her boyfriend with no ability to communicate with the outside world. Initially, there was a 90-day no contact order between us and my dad. The psychologists and Randy Rand came from 9am to 3pm every day. They started off by saying that we were not allowed to mention 'the past' aka my dad, and there was to be no reflection on any of my mother's past behavior as we were supposed to just move forward and love her like nothing had ever happened. We were told that we couldn't trust our memories because "there are two sides to every story" and that we should accept being abused because "the world isn't back and white". There is a lot that is implied, they showed us videos and then gave us sheets full of terms to define – not sure what the goal of that was, exactly. They do not explicitly threaten that "if you don't cooperate, we will send you to a wilderness program" but they do make threats that if you don't pass the program then you know what happens, you won't go home to see your dad. The biggest thing, one that they had us do multiple times daily and even after leaving, was the 'family meeting'. We had to start with positive things about our day/each other, then move on to the scheduled agenda, then make a decision.

My sister was very stressed out, and on one occasion where they had decided my sister wasn't being positive enough and repeatedly criticized and threatened her, my sister started hyperventilating. She was criticized again for needing a break and when we came back from the break, was again threatened with 'not passing the program' AKA years in a facility. Another rule was that we were not allowed to leave our mother's sight – this manifested in ways such as when we went out to dinner one night, I brought up my dad and my mom got angry. I asked to take a break, like was agreed that we should do when things got heated, and explained that I would be going to sit on the bench in front of the restaurant. My mother came outdoors screaming and threatening to call the police because I was out of her sight line, and then said that she had called Randy and he had advised her to come out there and threaten me with jail in order to get me to cooperate.

Progression and last day

Much of the torture sessions consisted of the psychologists showing us movies and short clips, and then asking us to define terms on a sheet of paper while threatening us. A short list of these clips includes:

Butterfly movie
Electric shock experiment [Milgram's obedience study]
Elizabeth Loftus – false memories talk
Swedish teddy bear sad movie
Desperate Housewives
Welcome Home Pluto
"Can you spot the gorilla"

While we were defining terms, there were rules on how our eye contact was supposed to be, and we were sometimes supposed to start off sentences a certain way – if we forgot, then we would be deemed "unco-operative" and threatened with "not passing the program". We also had to have mandatory family dinners and at the end a "reward" of a family vacation.

Running away/The Aftermath

When I was 17, we came back from Family Bridges on Cinco De Mayo [a Mexican holiday celebrated in the United States] 2016. Even though we were back home with my mother, there were still mandatory family meetings and we had to follow extra rules (such as being home for family dinner every day) that weren't in place ever before. Luckily, my employers at the time both took me back, but this was not so good for my home life. In high school, I had to do volunteer hours to graduate, and I had been working for a few years by that point. I had a boyfriend whom I had been dating for a while, and my mom did not let me see him until she had "briefed" him on what was and wasn't allowed. I was also barred from contact with my friends and family. They use this isolation method to try and keep kids from accessing help, and my mom was angry that I was out of the house so much because she wanted to keep me isolated (I pretty much was only leaving for school and work, and this was still an issue).

This very fragile isolation arrangement continued for 2 weeks or so, until I was informed of an incident that happened in the household that needed police involvement. I took my sister to the police station to try and report it, and the cop who took the report was very unhelpful. I was very upset and crying, telling him that I felt unsafe at home and that we really needed help, and he told me that I sounded hysterical and just needed some therapy. At this point, my mother and her boyfriend came and showed the cop the court order, and the cop forced us to go home with them and told them that he recommended therapy for me. I was supposed to work and volunteer that day, but when we got home, my mother said that I wasn't going to go, and there would be consequences. The biggest "consequence" for disobeying the Family Bridges program is being sent away to a wilderness camp or to a facility indefinitely, so later this day, I shut the door to my room and jumped out of my bedroom window.

I was considered "missing" for a bit before someone I was close to agreed to let me stay with her and tell my mom about it. This was working fine for a month or so, although the "fine" part is debatable since at this point my mom told me not to talk to my sister ever again. The final straw for me was my High School graduation, I specifically asked my mother not to invite certain people, told her I wasn't going to go if she invited those people, and she told me two days before that she had invited these people. The day of my graduation, I just didn't show up. I have zero regrets about this, I just told the friend I was staying with that I would be "missing" for the time being, and that was the last time I saw them until I was emancipated.

Researching options: first looking at CHINS petition

While I was living with other people and during the time that I was "missing", I was researching options that would allow me to legally live apart from my mother. If I couldn't get custody changed through family court, what could I do instead to help myself? This took a lot of time and effort, but the two options I found available were a CHINS petition and then emancipation. The CHINS petition stands for "Child in Need of Services", and basically transfers custody of the child to the state for the time being (even though you can live with family, for example). The problem with the CHINS petition was that it is very temporary, and you need to prove continued risk of harm, but initially, I didn't think that I would be able to get emancipated.

Throughout all of this, I was helped by an eclectic team of dedicated *pro bono* attorneys who spend many hours trying to help me. The first organization I consulted is called Team Child, and a lawyer there helped me go over the requirements for the CHINS petition and prepare that. Ultimately, we didn't end up going forward with that because of the temporary status and because since I was so close to being 18, emancipation made more sense. The Team Child organization recommended finding someone else to help me with my emancipation petition.

After some research, I was able to find another *pro bono* law firm helping children, and I arranged a meeting with a lawyer there. We met at a coffee shop downtown, and it was refreshing for me to hear from an actual lawyer that I had a real shot at emancipation. If I remember correctly, we prepared the full petition within two days of that first meeting.

How to get emancipated

Getting emancipated requires proving that you can live and survive on your own as a functioning adult. There is no set monetary standard for "you need to be making 3.5× rent in order for us to grant this", there is no set checklist of things that are guaranteed to work, it is really all done on a case-by-case basis. The court will accept living with a family as "survive on your own", which is what we ended up doing in my case. I got a second job, got letters from my employers stating that I was employed, and then I had letters from family stating that they would give me a place to stay upon emancipation. These were the things that the judge considered in her decision.

I also wrote to the emancipation judge on my reasons for needing emancipation – the kidnapping, the fact that my mother was preventing me from going to work, the isolation tactics. In the end, the judge read through what I wrote but said that the more important factors in her decision were my outpouring of family support and the fact that I had gainful employment. The only reason that I was able to gain emancipation and get free was because the court that does emancipations is different from family court, and as a result, I was assigned a different judge, one who didn't have a personal vendetta against me. This judge weighed her decision fairly based on the facts, and that day was one of celebration. Afterwards, my family took me out for ice cream and poke to celebrate, and then I immediately moved back in with my dad, that night.

The journey was far from over, because my sister was still not free, by this point my mom had told me repeatedly not to contact her, and the people who kidnapped me (Family Bridges and transport agents) were still in operation and seeing no ill effects.

Action on Family Bridges

When I first came back home, I called everyone I could think of. I called the FBI and the Ontario [California] police department to inform about the interstate child trafficking, but once they heard the words "family court" they told me they wouldn't do anything. I called and emailed my city council members, my federal representatives, you name it. Some of the city council people actually did respond and asked how they could help, but it turns out there wasn't much they could do in the end. From the beginning, I knew that I could file board complaints on the licenses of the psychologists involved, so I called the Board of Psychology in California and started to make official complaints about the unethical behavior of the psychologists involved in my case. A couple months later, I got an email that they were not going to investigate my complaint any further or take any more action. What I didn't know in all of this was that my dad had also been working behind the scenes to contact an even wider variety of people than I had.

My dad had been in contact with a lot of people in California, and one of them was Kathleen Russell, who is the Founding Executive Director of the Center for Judicial Excellence in Marin County, California (Center for Judicial Excellence, n.d.). Kathleen also founded and runs her own public affairs firm, Kathleen Russell Consulting. She tracks killings of kids in family court, lobbies the California state legislature, and helps to reach out to kids who have suffered from these programs. Kathleen has led many successful legislative campaigns including legislation in 2012 granting children of 14 and older the right to testify about their wishes in California family courts (Section 3042 Family Code – Fam). She also led the first audit of the California Commission on Judicial Performance in August 2016 to make transparent the operations of this "powerful state agency that is supposed to be disciplining our state's nearly 2,000 judges when they violate the canons of judicial ethics" (Center for Judicial Excellence, 2016).

One of the biggest things that Kathleen was focusing on at the time was trying to get the Board of Psychology to take action on numerous complaints relating to reunification therapy and the associated psychologists.

When I got the email from the Board of Psychology telling me that they weren't going to move forward on my complaint, we had to figure out next steps. The next step that we eventually figured out was bringing a large group of those negatively affected by family court psychologists to the Board of Psychology meeting and having us all sign up for public comment. Very few people normally show up at the Board of Psychology meetings, so when we showed up *en masse* to the California state capital, I think they were a bit shocked.

This mobilization was a fairly large undertaking, organizing this many people from all over the country to come to Sacramento at the same time, but we managed to successfully pull it off. Kathleen had also arranged a day of meetings with legislators at the Capitol, who were all very intrigued by our stories and all seemed genuinely concerned and willing to help.

In the end, thanks to putting continued pressure on the Board of Psychology, the psychologists in my case had other complaints against them and ended up losing their licenses. This means they can no longer practice psychology in the state of California. As for judges – they don't have much accountability, and often even when misconduct is reported, nothing is done. The only people who do truly hold power over judges are legislators – but they have to know that the problem exists and is widespread before they can do something about it. Lobbying legislatures is definitely useful. However, legislatures move slowly, and they are only one piece of the puzzle. If you are only focused on lobbying lawmakers, you will get nothing done.

This is where the importance of involving media and getting media attention comes in. Ultimately, reporters can force legislatures into action. However, journalists want to know how widespread a problem is so they can cover the most pressing issues affecting the most people but showing how widespread the problem is (and it is fairly widespread) proved difficult for us. The people involved in this program use fake data and the information had to be sourced out from people who don't want to talk. I'm sure there are many more people harmed who still haven't spoken publicly. The first article we got published was in the Washington Post, and that article only mentions my family and one other but started to ask the question, "just how widespread is this?" And that article was a start to a flood of more media.

In the beginning, we had to do the work reaching out to journalists ourselves. Now, there are multiple stories out where I have been interviewed, so the media can build on itself. My goal is for me personally to reach out to journalists for the first two years or so, get a good buildup of articles and then wait until the stories start feeding off one another and self-referencing so I can step back and let the media do their job. Laws trying to improve family court have been successfully passed in other states recently because the huge media attention has put the problem in the spotlight. So I found out from all this that the media is the biggest and best tool for effecting change at the government level.

Our work is not yet done. Family Bridges is still in operation. Although Randy Rand's license to practice as a psychologist is inactive, he still participates in interventions because Family Bridges is promoted as an 'educational' rather than a 'therapeutic' program (Hagerty, 2020).

Katherine's account

Katherine (a pseudonym) lives in England and has a daughter, Sophie (a pseudonym to preserve the child's anonymity), who was ten years old at the time that Katherine left a marriage that she describes as being physically and financially abusive and coercively controlling. Katherine's ex-husband warned her that if she attempted to apply to the family court for a financial remedy order, he would apply for a transfer of residence of their daughter. Over the next few years, Katherine experienced post-separation abuse and Sophie encountered incidents of physical abuse. Katherine's ex-husband was able to use the family court to support his threats to have the residency of their daughter changed. As Katherine kept raising domestic abuse in the family courts, she was met with the counter claim that she was alienating their daughter from her father. Katherine had not previously heard of the terms "alienation" or "parental alienation" but was told that she was at risk of losing her daughter if she continued to speak about the post-separation abuse that was continuing.

Several years after the first family court hearing, it was ordered that Sophie undergo a "flooding" treatment. Sophie was removed from Katherine for 10 days and placed with her father, with the hope that she would "love her father a bit more and her mother a bit less". Sophie returned to Katherine, looking pale and thinner, and clearly stated that she never wanted to see her father again. The treatment had failed but this was blamed on Katherine not supporting the treatment.

A few months later, Sophie was removed from Katherine's care. The family court judge refused an adjournment to enable Katherine to find legal representation for the hearing and instead directed that Katherine must hand over her house keys to the social worker who was also present. The social worker had previously never raised any concerns about Katherine's parenting but was now ordered to travel to Katherine's home and, unannounced, remove Sophie on the basis of parental alienation. The social worker called Katherine from inside her home and ordered her to tell Sophie that she needed to leave with the stranger and added that if he heard any signs of abuse, he would cut the call. Later the same evening the social worker called Katherine to tell her that he had seen evidence of child abuse because Sophie had asked to leave her bunny on mother's bed to look after her. The social worker explained that this amounted to child abuse as no child should have to worry about their parents. Katherine was permitted to see her daughter in a supervised capacity only and the contact would be stopped if she showed any signs of emotion.

Following a lengthy period of family court hearings, it was finally ordered that an established children's mental health center should be commissioned by a local authority, up to the total cost of £20,000, to re-establish a shared care arrangement. Katherine chose this center because the therapy center proposed by Sophie's father and social services would not allow Katherine any contact with Sophie for three months. However, Katherine was unaware of the treatment regime of the center she chose until the treatment had already started. Katherine was advised by her barrister that she should not appeal the court's decision but embrace the work that would be carried out at the center, as they would be able to independently recognize the domestic abuse and coercively and controlling behavior perpetrated on Katherine. However, Katherine explains that what transpired was the complete opposite and that Katherine and her daughter's experiences were discounted. Katherine attended the center sporadically for just under a year. During this time, she was told that if she did not change her behavior, then she would never be able to have Sophie returned to her and would only see her under supervised conditions until her 16th birthday. Sophie was also told that contact between herself and her mother would be suspended unless she stopped saying that she wanted to live with her mother.

Katherine was so afraid with what occurred at her first session that she began to secretly record the sessions, not only for her own mental well-being – as she could not believe what was happening – but also as evidence that something "wasn't quite right". Katherine disclosed that she had been doing this to the center's clinical director as part of a formal complaint to the center. During the 'treatment' at the center, it became clear to Katherine that her ex-husband was able to control what was being decided. On one occasion, during one of three joint sessions, where both parents were present, Katherine's ex-husband told the psychiatrist that he was unhappy that Katherine could not have eye contact with him. He said that he felt this was alienating behavior, and if this wasn't rectified then he felt Sophie could not return to her mother's care. The center immediately agreed with the father and did not try to understand why Katherine felt intimidated by her ex-husband.

After 11 months, the center admitted that it had failed in being able to achieve a shared care arrangement that they interpreted to be a 50/50 split of time. The center suggested that if the parents cannot come to an agreement about where Sophie should live, then the matter should be returned to court. However, the center did not seem to appreciate that this would involve starting a new set of proceedings because social services did not intend to extend the supervision order. They attributed this to Katherine being unable to change her view about the coercive control that she was still experiencing from her ex-husband, and Sophie's wish to still be with her mother. The center stated that they had £5,000 left from the total amount given to them by the local authority. In the summary of the last meeting, the psychiatrist reported that the remaining money could be used for ongoing therapy at the center but suggested that Katherine would prefer not to continue the work because trust had broken down. Katherine has no idea what eventually happened to the remaining £5,000.

Nearly three years later, Sophie continues to live with her father and to see Katherine for a minimal amount of time. Sophie is close to 16 years old and continues to say that she wants to live with her mother. Even though Sophie has been found to have attained a sufficient age and degree of maturity for her wishes and feelings to be taken seriously or even to be determinative (called "Gillick-competence" in England and Wales), her wishes and feelings have not been acted on because of the parental alienation accusations.

Below are excerpts taken from various sessions that Katherine attended at the center and the accompanying notes made by the therapists that were obtained by submitting a Subject Access Request to the center. Katherine describes how frightened she felt during the sessions and how coerced she felt into making sure she said what the therapists wanted her to say so that she would be able to see her daughter.

Katherine's experience of therapy

Session I

The first session at the center consisted of the psychiatrist, psychologist, and Katherine. After the session, Katherine was distressed and on returning home made some quick notes about her experience. Katherine remembers that questions were fired at her by the psychiatrist and before she was able to answer fully, another question was asked. The psychiatrist's main focus was on Katherine not being able to say anything positive about her ex-husband. He focused on Katherine being unable to normalize the abusive behavior that Sophie had witnessed and personally encountered. Katherine remembers trying to describe some of the coercive and controlling behavior, but the therapists told her that it did not matter what had happened in the past as the judge had ordered the center to try to find a shared care solution. Katherine was told that she was at risk of only ever seeing Sophie in supervised contact if she did not change her opinion of her ex-husband. Katherine was told that she needed to take responsibility for the alienation of Sophie and was told that even crying, as a response to the abuse, was emotionally abusive to Sophie. Katherine describes feeling like the session was a game of cat and mouse and she was being hunted by the psychiatrist, it felt psychologically unsafe, and she felt extremely vulnerable and frightened.

Summary of session by the therapist

Katherine was very tearful throughout the session and said that she feels that she was never heard and listened to. She feels victim in the situation and said that her ex-husband has manipulated the whole situation to get Sophie away from her. Even though the psychiatrist and I asked her to think about maybe one positive thing she may be able to say about her ex-husband, she could not think of anything positive to say about him. She kept on talking about how controlling he is and the fact that Sophie doesn't like him not because of her but because of the things he has done to her. She was not able to take any responsibility whatsoever for her own actions and ways in which she may have influenced Sophie.

Session 2

THERAPIST: With our work, it's basically what we're doing and what we did last week and what we are doing now to see whether you can see the part you played in Sophie becoming quite alienated from her father, actually and how you can reverse this.

THERAPIST: Sometimes a dad might be more aggressive with the child than the mother might want to be, that kind of thing.

[Later on]

THERAPIST: So what did you want to talk about last time? You said that you found it difficult.

KATHERINE: I just found it, yes, incredibly difficult. I just found it very, very hard and I came away feeling shocked and … Yes.

THERAPIST: What was it that shocked you?

KATHERINE: That I wasn't given time to answer a question and I felt like I was a, a rabbit and you two were foxes hunting me down and there's a lack of belief in what I'm saying and a lack of understanding. It felt to me, yes, I came away feeling very …

THERAPIST: Which is why it's not a good idea for us to be two clinicians which is why I'm seeing you on my own from now on because that can have that effect. I can see that. The thing is that because there's been a judgment and there's been findings, we can't really go against what's already been said, you know, what's been found. So we have to work with what the judge has said. Now we know that things have happened in the past, I'm not denying that, and Sophie did say yesterday that "My dad twisted my ankle and has also slapped me".

KATHERINE: Yes, he'd held her down on the bed and held her round her neck. I mean the findings against him, the physical and…

THERAPIST: Yes, absolutely but there is a sense of you either hold onto that and have her be very angry about that and be punitive about that which is not going to be helpful for Sophie or you can help Sophie to kind of move on and say, "Look…" What I was saying to Sophie is "I hear what you're saying, what I'm hearing is also that your father is regretting having done that and he understands that that's not right and he won't do that again". I think that's the message that needs to be given to Sophie now.

[Later on]

KATHERINE: So on Friday she said to me I don't want to see my daddy, I know I have to but daddy hurts me.

THERAPIST: The answer to that is, if you want to help move on is to say, "Daddy has hurt you in the past, but he won't do it anymore and he hasn't done it for a while".

KATHERINE: How can you as a mum?

THERAPIST: As a mum believe me, I mean I ...

KATHERINE: Yes, I know as a mother's it's so hard, isn't it?

THERAPIST: It's not that hard because my husband does things that I don't really agree with, he can be very hard with my girls, very harsh...

KATHERINE: But what about physical hurting, I mean it's wrong.

THERAPIST: Even physical hurting I would say, "Look, he lost control, I'm really sorry, he's really sorry, give him a chance to apologise and repair", and that was months ago, you know, and the fact that you're holding on to that isn't allowing Sophie to move on either.

Summary of session by the therapist

The therapist summarized Katherine's statements as follows: "I can see now how abusive he was; his control was always wrapped up in kindness ...."

She went on to say: "On [deleted] he raped me because I was ill and he felt that it was his right to sleep with me. He later admitted it and said that he didn't realise the impact". According to Katherine, she was [deleted] put a great strain on [her ex-husband] and on their marriage. "He couldn't control my illness and it made him nervous so he controlled me".

Session 3

THERAPIST: [Sophie] feels that she is not being loyal to you and I'm not saying that directly to her but you are giving off messages. What are you thinking? I'd like to hear what you are thinking. Sophie is literally repeating, word for word, things that you say and that's not right for a child. She needs to be able to have ...

KATHERINE: What is she saying, word for word, that I say?

THERAPIST: 'He's controlling'. That's a word that you use and now she uses that.

KATHERINE: I don't. I've never said that to her.

THERAPIST: It is a word that you've used and she's using it, so there are words that you do use.

KATHERINE: Do you think he – well, I don't use these. Sophie hasn't been with me for nearly a year now.

THERAPIST: I know but a year is nothing and she very much ...

KATHERINE: A year is a very long time.

THERAPIST: She was very much, I'd like to say brainwashed by you before that and there's a certain....

KATHERINE: I'm sorry – I'm very …

THERAPIST: I'm sorry, but this is, in all the reports, it's there. You have …

KATHERINE: You haven't read all of the reports.

THERAPIST: I have. I've read most of the reports.

KATHERINE: You said that you hadn't read the reports last time.

THERAPIST: I have. I've read most of the reports and they all say the same thing, which is why Sophie has now been taken away from you and put with her father, which is very unusual.

KATHERINE: I haven't brainwashed my daughter.

THERAPIST: Well, the report talks about parental alienation and so do the experts, and that's what we see because we see …

KATHERINE: There has been one expert and I wasn't allowed to challenge him.

THERAPIST: I know but all the evidence shows us, this is our expertise, that Sophie has been alienated because as a child she can't remember a single good memory with her father has been alienated because that's just impossible.

[Later in the session]

THERAPIST: So supervised contact under what – why? Because he held her down once?

KATHERINE: He didn't just hold her down once.

THERAPIST: I really do think that these are things that you've made mountains out of little things.

KATHERINE: I'm sorry?

THERAPIST: I've read the reports and I've read what the police have said and I've read everything, and it's not – you know, that thing with her leg, she was kicking him and held her ankles. So what, is my – because you have so much – because he's been abusive to you and controlling to you, you are putting that onto Sophie. He's not the same with Sophie as he is with you. He's a different father….

This isn't just [the father's] doing. This is your doing as well, you calling the police, you constantly saying to people that she didn't mean that. You're doing this, you're doing this – this is your animosity with him. It's not just [the father]. [The father] has made mistakes, yes. He's made more mistakes to you, obviously, than he has with Sophie. With Sophie, it's been two incidents and they're not really big. You know, every parent can lose it and hold someone down or shout in their face or do something. It's not the end of the world, but you made it the end of the world.

Summary of session by the therapist

Katherine was low today and said that she was really struggling with not having her daughter with her and spoke about contact sessions which were cancelled because social services couldn't supervise….. I did reiterate how important it is that she gives Sophie encouragement to be happy with her father and really to catch every comment Sophie makes and say something positive about [her father]. Katherine insisted that this is what she has always done but I continued to challenge her on this ...

2nd Joint Session with Katherine and Sophie

The center decided that they would allow unsupervised contact between Katherine and Sophie. However, before this could occur, Katherine would have to explain the family court judgment to Sophie in front of the psychotherapist.

Katherine had to explain to Sophie that she wanted to have a shared care arrangement with her father and apologize for everything that had happened. Katherine felt coerced into doing this but realized that this way, the only way that she would be able to see her daughter unsupervised.

THERAPIST [TALKING TO SOPHIE]: It's been hard it was really hard for your dad and when you were saying, when you were saying I don't want to see you, I don't like you, that was really painful for him. I'm an... and I think he realised that he had made some mistakes to make you a bit scared of him, yep? [inaudible] ... getting any better and it wasn't getting any better and I think the judge really thought, well, the only way to get Sophie to get to know her father and to know that he's actually a lovely dad is to have her live with him. And I think, I think your mum was a bit worried at first and she thought, oh my God she's living with her dad, how's that going to go? But I think she realised that he's a good dad you know, he maybe wasn't a good husband to her but he's a really good dad to you and he's going to get better and better the more he gets to know you. So, I think your mum's kind of saying, I'm really glad that Sophie is liking her dad I think it's really nice I think she's really reassured by that.

Summary of session by the therapist

The therapist summarized the session like this: Katherine started off by talking to Sophie about why the judge had decided that Sophie needed to live with her father in order to allow them to bond more and to get to know one another without the interference of the conflicts between her parents. She then said how important it is for Sophie to feel that she can love both of her parents and she apologised to Sophie for putting her through so much pain. I did not insist on Katherine telling Sophie that the judge found that she had alienated her from her father; I felt that Katherine saying that Sophie needed to bond with her father without the interference of the parents' conflict was enough.

Session 9

After being able to spend time alone with Katherine, Sophie continues to express her wish to live with her mother. The therapists have not seen Sophie for months. It is now suggested that Sophie hears the judgment again.

THERAPIST: But that's the problem you see. When you say she's not living with her dad, forever, it gives her this hope that I'm coming back.

KATHERINE: I'm not telling her that though. I'm telling you that.

THERAPIST: Well, I don't think you are directly, but I think you are in your attitude, and I think that's what she's thinking, that if I push hard enough and if I have tantrums enough, and if I write letters enough then, and she doesn't seem to understand, of course she doesn't know why she is, why she was taken away because she's asking in the letter, while I was there taken away from my Mama? So we think in the team with [the psychiatrist] that we should share the judgement, that we make a child-friendly version of the judgement for her so she understands why she was taken away from you. She needs to know the truth, otherwise she's going to be very confused for the rest of her life.

KATHERINE: Well, I'm sorry, the truth about what though?

THERAPIST: The judgment. You remember the judgment?

KATHERINE: Yes, and I disagreed with it completely.

THERAPIST: Well, you can disagree with it if you want to, but it is a fact finding and it is a …

KATHERINE: But it wasn't right, I mean as we've said before.

THERAPIST: Well, you see, that's concerning to me because if you are still saying it wasn't right and it's not true and all of that …

KATHERINE: Of course. Of course, I am.

THERAPIST: Well, then I don't foresee the future where she can be living with you I'm afraid because this judgement, I'm going to write a child friendly judgement with the help of [the psychiatrist] to her and she needs to know everything that the judge is saying. She needs to understand why she was taken away from you. Of course, we wouldn't give her the judgement like this because that's too violent for her, but she needs to know that the judge found that you had manipulated her.

[Later on]

The therapist shows Katherine a letter that Sophie has written to her father. The therapist accuses Katherine of manipulating Sophie.

THERAPIST: What do you think when you read the letter?

KATHERINE: I think it's sad.

THERAPIST: What do you think is sad about it?

KATHERINE: That she feels that she needs to write it. She is [age deleted]. I think it is sad. It's just awful.

THERAPIST: Well, I think what's sad is the fact that you can't see your responsibility in her sadness. I find that very concerning. You can't see any responsibility for her situation, because this is down to you. Her situation is down to you, Katherine, and I'm sorry. It's not down to me. It's not down to the judge. It's not down to the social worker. It's not down to [your ex-husband]. It's down to how you presented the father to her. [Your ex-husband] has made certain mistakes and he's apologised for them, but the rest is you.

KATHERINE: He hasn't apologised for them. I'm sorry but he hasn't. I'm being honest with you now, he hasn't apologised to me, not me.

THERAPIST: He said he had indeed because I asked him. He said that he had apologised to you.

KATHERINE: He never apologised.

THERAPIST: Well, maybe that's something he should do, but I do think that this is a situation where she is adamant that she doesn't want to stay with her father, and that whole situation when she was taken away from you, was caused by you. It wasn't caused by anyone else.

[Later on]

THERAPIST: But I'm saying what the Dr and I saw in that first session. Since then, you've changed, but in that first session you couldn't think of one positive thing about [the father] and one reason why Sophie should see her father. You could not think of one reason, Katherine, you couldn't.

KATHERINE: But he's very abusive, has been very abusive.

THERAPIST: Well, because you think that there is still no way that you're going to encourage – how are you going to encourage Sophie to be with her father who you see as someone who is abusive and dangerous?

KATHERINE: He was. I didn't say he was dangerous, but he was abusive, so when I came to that first meeting I was telling you what happened in the past.

THERAPIST: Which makes me think, and the judge think, and the Dr and other professionals, that since you hold that image of him in your mind, you're going to transmit that to Sophie, whether you want to or not, or you are …

KATHERINE: I'm not.

THERAPIST: That's how she sees him. That's how she sees him. This thing about, "He's buying me things and it's called bribery", that's not a child's words.

KATHERINE: That's not my words!

THERAPIST: Well, I've heard you say it before…

KATHERINE: No, I haven't.

THERAPIST: I have heard you say it before.

KATHERINE: I would never say that to my daughter.

THERAPIST: Well, you may not say it to her directly, but your actions. She's a smart girl. She knows what you think about her father. How do you

expect Sophie to love her father, want to be with her father, spend time with him when she knows that her mother thinks her dad is abusive?
[Later on]

THERAPIST: I have been doing this job for 25 years, Katherine, I wasn't born yesterday. I've seen this kind of message through mothers and children before. This is exactly as [the psychiatrist] said, "it's as if mum is writing the letter".

KATHERINE: I haven't written the letter. I've been nowhere near that letter. I haven't.

THERAPIST: I know, but this is your influence, Katherine.

KATHERINE: I'm sorry, but what is wrong with a little girl wanting to be with her mum and saying that she wants to live with her mum? What is wrong with that?

THERAPIST: The thing that is wrong with it is that a few months ago this little girl who said "I hate my father. I don't ever want to see him again. I don't want to be in a room with him. I don't want him in my life", this is wrong, Katherine, this is wrong, and if we are going back to that stage then that is abusive to that child because a child who hates her father has been emotionally abused and alienated. I'm sorry. That's the way it is. Any child who says, "I hate my father", and cannot think of one good thing to say about them.

KATHERINE: I've never, ever, ever, ever said to her-

THERAPIST: So it comes out of you?

KATHERINE: I have never ever said to my daughter: "I hate your father".

THERAPIST: He's abusive. He's controlling, he abused me.

KATHERINE: Excuse me?

THERAPIST: I'm sure she heard that. She told me, "My father was very controlling."

KATHERINE: Yes, because he's controlling her.

THERAPIST: No. I'm sorry. She's using the same words as you are.

KATHERINE: No, I'm sorry

THERAPIST: Exactly the same words as you are.

KATHERINE: I'm sorry. I would never, ever say to my daughter, "Your father is controlling", I haven't done it. I wouldn't do it. I don't do that. I wouldn't do that.

THERAPIST: We are not getting anywhere. What I want to say is we're going to have contact today with [your ex-husband] and we're going to go through some of the cases and just think about how we move on in the future. There are a few points that he wants to bring up. You can bring up a few points, but as far as shared care is concerned, we're not going there at all.

KATHERINE: Please I can't have a meeting with [ex-husband] now. I want an advocate because it's wrong [Katherine is crying heavily at this point]

THERAPIST: Yes, you can have an advocate. I'm also going to write to the social worker and just tell him that I'm going to write a child-friendly

judgment and that we're going to go through the child-friendly judgment with Sophie so she understands the situation, and it would be really
important that we both support it. I think that [your ex-husband] has
worked hard to collaborate with you.

[The meeting continues but the therapist agrees to Katherine's request
not to have a joint meeting with her ex-husband.]

Summary of session by the therapist

The therapist concluded: I then shared my concerns with Katherine about
Sophie writing the letter and the way that [her ex-husband] says things
are going back to the way they were slightly. Katherine was shocked to
hear this and said that she had no knowledge of the letter, but that Sophie is [age deleted] and her voice needs to be heard. I again explained,
as I have in the past, that the reason that Sophie's voice cannot be heard
completely is because we believe that it is not completely her voice, but
that she is being influenced by her mother. Katherine started to cry hysterically and throughout the session, saying that she had never influenced
Sophie, and that Sophie is just making her mind up about her father
because of his past actions etc I expressed my concern that this sounded
very much like the discourse Katherine used to have before and that I
felt that she had moved on since before the summer. I then explained
that I was thinking of talking to Sophie about the judgment so that she
understands the situation.

Following on from session nine, two further joint sessions took place two
months later, with both clinicians, Katherine's ex-husband, and Katherine.

The psychiatrist also met with Sophie alone and read through a child-
friendly version of the judgment. Sophie was told that it was unlikely that
anything she said or did would have the judgment overruled and changed
and that there would be costs involved that she would not be able to afford.
Sophie was told that her mother had negatively influenced her. "We also told
her that the care arrangements are not going to change and that if we remain
concerned about her negatively influenced by her mother against her father,
we will ask for the contact to be supervised again".

This account by Katherine reveals how North American parental alienation intervention theories and practices are being used in England and Wales,
although this may not be apparent because of the different terminology and
language used. While the ostensible goal of the 'therapy' was to try to establish shared care of Sophie by Katherine and her ex-husband, the underlying aim was to 'treat' parental alienation. The extracts from the recordings
highlight how the power of parental alienation discourse reinterpreted and
placed the focus on Katherine's protective behavior, rather than on the abuse
perpetrated by Sophie's father. It is apparent how Katherine was silenced by

the therapists' lack of understanding of coercive control, with the abuse constructed as historical by the focus on forward thinking.

References

Center for Judicial Excellence. *CJE Staff.* California, n.d., https://centerforjudicial-excellence.org/about-us/cje-staff/

Center for Judicial Excellence. *CA Commission on Judicial Performance Audit & Reform.* 2016, https://centerforjudicialexcellence.org/cje-projects-initiatives/ca-commission-on-judicial-performance-audit-reform/#:~:text=On%20August%2010%2C%20 2016%2C%20the, and%20yes%2C%20even%20California%20judges

Hagerty, Barbara Bradley. "Can Children Be Persuaded to Love a Parent They Hate?" *The Atlantic,* 2020, December, https://www.theatlantic.com/magazine/archive/2020/12/when-a-child-is-a-weapon/616931/#:~:text=Critics%20 like%20Geffner%20also%20point, 2009%20based%20on%20two%20complaints

Re H (Children). EWHC 237, 2019.

Re S (Parental Alienation: Cult) EWCA Civ 568, 2020.

Re T (Parental Alienation) EWHC 3854 (Fam), 2019.

Part 2

When a child avoids a parent

Identifying and treating problems

Chapter 5

Evaluations for the courts in child custody cases

An attorney's perspective

Nancy S. Erickson

Child custody evaluations are built on an extremely fragile foundation, and the ways in which the evaluations are used often violate rules of evidence. Custody evaluations can mislead judges, resulting in the removal of children from the custody of the more appropriate parent.

Regarding opinions by child custody evaluators, some of the most highly respected experts in psychological evaluations for the courts have asserted:

> [T]here is probably no forensic question on which overreaching by mental health professionals has been so common and so egregious. Besides lacking scientific validity, such opinions have often been based on clinical data that are, on their face, irrelevant to the legal questions in dispute.
>
> (Melton et al. 2007, 484)

Since the mid-1980s, a belief system we now call "parental alienation" – which lacks a scientific foundation – has been brought into the practice of custody evaluations by mental health professionals who accept that belief system and apply it in their work. Judges in custody courts are trained in the law, not in the sciences. Judges often genuinely believe that mental health professionals can be helpful in assisting in determining the best interests of children. The result has been a frightening number of custody cases that are not decided in the best interests of children because a judge has been persuaded by a custody evaluator steeped in the parental alienation belief system that one parent (usually the mother) has "alienated" the child from the other parent (usually the father). Judges have been persuaded that mothers' attempts to protect themselves and/or the children from an abusive parent are evidence of alienation.

To understand how parental alienation fits into the child custody evaluation process, we will discuss what child custody evaluations are, their history, who conducts such evaluations, what training (or lack thereof) custody evaluators have, how they are appointed, how they generally conduct their evaluations, the reports that they provide to the courts, and how the reports are used. With that background, we approach the question of how

DOI: 10.4324/9781003095927-7

evaluators who enter the child custody evaluation field believing in parental alienation or who have become proponents of parental alienation are able to turn custody cases away from the better parent and toward awarding custody to an abusive, neglectful, or simply angry and vengeful parent. This result is especially concerning in cases in which domestic abuse is an issue.

Child custody evaluations

What is a custody evaluation and when would a court want one?

In court cases involving custody and/or visitation, judicial officers usually hope that the parents will come to a settlement of the case. Settlements are encouraged to save valuable court time. Courts also assume that the parents will know better than a judge what arrangements for the child will be in the child's best interests. When settlement does not appear forthcoming, a court may order the parties to submit to a custody evaluation. Then, if no settlement occurs, the court will have what it believes (or at least hopes) will be an expert opinion on what is in the best interests of the child.

In the United States, each state has its own laws and rules regarding substantive family law and procedures that courts and litigants must follow. All states decide custody and visitation cases based on a determination what is in the best interests of the child. The job of a custody evaluator is to collect as much information as possible relevant to the best interests of the child and then analyze it, organize it, and present the information to the court in a written report. The court may ask the custody evaluator for recommendations as to which custody and visitation arrangements would be best, but some courts do not ask for recommendations.

When the parties are informed of the contents of the custody evaluation report, if one party is less favored by the evaluator than the other, the less favored parent may decide to settle rather than going to trial (Baerger et al. 2002, 35). Settlement may appear to be the better option, because the less favored parent will otherwise start out faced by a de facto presumption that the more favored parent should prevail.

If no settlement is reached, the matter must go to trial. The custody evaluator is usually called as a witness. The custody evaluation report is often admitted into evidence even if the evaluator does not testify, and its contents then become known to the judge. Custody evaluations are more often than not followed by judges in their rulings (Davis et al. 2011; Kunin, Ebbesen, and Konecni 1992, 572; Waller and Daniel 2004, 24). Therefore, one of the only ways for the less favored parent to counter what is in the report is to get an expert witness to do a "peer review" of the custody evaluation report (Tippins 2015). However, that is an expensive and difficult prospect, and many parents cannot find a peer reviewer or afford to pay for one.

Custody evaluations are within the practice of forensic psychology

Historically, the jobs of most mental health professionals – whether psychologists, psychiatrists, social workers, or others in the mental health professions – had little involvement with the legal system, and such is the case even today. Most mental health professionals spend the majority of their time treating patients, not working within or with the legal system. Their role as a care provider is different from the role of a forensic evaluator as an expert to assist the court (Greenberg and Shuman 1997, 50). An example of the difference between expert testimony and fact testimony is addressed in the immediately following paragraph.

Occasionally a mental health professional who is a care provider comes into contact with the legal system, but that contact usually is one of a fact-finding nature concerning the patient. For example, a psychiatrist might be served with a subpoena from an attorney representing one of the psychiatrist's patients, seeking the patient's records because the patient has been accused of homicide. The attorney is considering an insanity defense. The psychiatrist might even be subpoenaed to testify in the case. The psychiatrist's testimony would be limited primarily to facts: how long the psychiatrist has been treating the patient; what medications were prescribed for the patient; when the psychiatrist last treated the patient before the alleged homicide, etc. The psychiatrist might be asked one or two questions as a treating expert – e.g., to offer a clinical diagnosis. However, the treating psychiatrist would not be allowed to give an opinion concerning whether the patient was insane at the time of the murder. That question is a psycho-legal one requiring the opinion of a forensic expert. Most psychiatrists are not experts on the legal definition of insanity in a particular jurisdiction or how to determine whether someone was legally insane at a particular time. Those are issues for forensic experts.

Opinions of experts are governed by the rules of evidence. Each state has its own rules of evidence. During much of the 20th century, the rule in most jurisdictions concerning admissibility of expert opinions followed the opinion set forth in *Frye v. United States*, which holds that to be admissible into evidence, an expert opinion must be based on scientific principles that are "sufficiently established to have gained general acceptance in the particular field in which it belongs" (Frye 1923). Some states still follow Frye, but most have adopted the rule set forth in *Daubert v. Merrell Dow Pharmaceuticals* (Daubert 1993), which held that Rule 702 of the Federal Rules superseded Frye's "general acceptance" test. Rule 702 states:

> If scientific, technical, or other specialized knowledge will assist the trier of fact to understand the evidence or to determine a fact in issue, a witness qualified as an expert by knowledge, skill, experience, training, or education, may testify thereto in the form of an opinion or otherwise.....
> (Rule 702 Federal Rules of Evidence)

Rule 702 tells us three things. First, it tells us how someone becomes qualified as an expert in federal courts – by "knowledge, skill, experience, training, or education."

Rule 702 also tells us that an expert witness may testify only if "scientific, technical, or other specialized knowledge will assist the trier of fact [the judge or jury] to understand the evidence or to determine a fact in issue." The test is helpfulness. If the judge or jury does not need the help of an expert to understand the evidence or to determine a fact in issue, then the expert's testimony will not be permitted. Finally, Rule 702 tells us that the expert's opinion must be based on the specialized knowledge of the expert witness, not on personal beliefs or preferences. Personal beliefs and preferences are not based on the expert's knowledge, skill, experience, training, or education in the expert's field of expertise. These rules are important to keep in mind in assessing when expert testimony is permitted and who is qualified to act as an expert.

This chapter concentrates on custody evaluators from the field of psychology rather than from the other mental health professions and the weight that their opinions should be given in custody determinations.

History and scope of forensic psychology

Providing custody evaluations to courts in child custody cases is a subspecialty within the specialty of forensic psychology, along with many other subspecialties, such as civil commitment, deprivation of parental rights, divorce, employment litigation, guardianship, personal injury, testamentary capacity, workers' compensation, juvenile delinquency, criminal competencies, insanity, diminished capacity, criminal sentencing, and others (Varela and Conroy 2012, 410).

Custody evaluators are sometimes called "forensic evaluators," or "forensics" for short, but "forensic" is a broad term meaning "pertaining to the courts of law and judicial procedure" (Reber and Reber 2001, 282). Custody evaluators are not the only forensic evaluators involved in family law cases. Forensic psychology is one field, but there are many others, including forensic psychiatry, forensic social work, forensic science, and forensic accounting. For example, forensic accountants are sometimes used in divorce cases involving complex finances, to determine their incomes and assets for purposes of child support, maintenance, and division of marital property.

While forensic psychology was recognized in Europe by the early 20th century, (Shaw, Ohman, and van Koppen 2013, 643) forensic psychology was recognized in the United States only within the last 45 years. The Psychology and Law Division of the American Psychological Association dates only to 1980, and forensic psychology was recognized as a specialty within the field of psychology only in 2001 (Varela and Conroy 2012, 411).

History of court-appointed custody evaluators

In most areas of the law, each side is permitted to choose the experts they wish to use in its case. The practice of appointing one custody evaluator to evaluate a family and make a report to the court giving findings – and often recommendations – is a relatively recent practice. Earlier, the practice was for each parent to hire her or his own "expert" to testify at the custody trial (see, for example, Kirkland and Kirkland 2001, 172). A few states still allow this (e.g., N.J. Rule 5:3-3), but many others discouraged the practice. This "battle of the experts" was not viewed as helpful, because each parent would try to hire someone who would support that parent's position that he or she is best suited to get custody. Consequently, many states began to favor the use of a so-called "neutral" custody evaluator chosen by the court or agreed to by the parties. The term "neutral" is misleading, of course, because no individual is "neutral" in the sense of having no biases (Zapf and Dror 2017, 228).

Education and training to conduct custody evaluations

Some psychologists who work as expert witnesses in court are well educated and trained in forensic psychology. There are now more than 30 graduate programs in the United States where doctoral study in forensic psychology is provided (AP-LS 2020, 6–7). These programs usually provide students with some practice in forensic interviewing and report writing under the supervision of knowledgeable and experienced educators and practitioners. After graduation, those students who want to continue their work in forensics can apply for postgraduate programs.

In addition, the American Board of Forensic Psychology, a respected organization, offers board certification in Forensic Psychology (American Board of Forensic Psychology abfp.com/about). Unfortunately, there are also other programs that call themselves "forensic psychology" programs but do not grant valid degrees or certificates; instead, they grant certificates which may have some value or may be worthless scams, sometimes improperly used to impress courts. For example, a psychologist once managed to get his cat Zoe credentialed under the name Zoe D. Katze in three major hypnotherapy associations as having met their "strict training requirements" (Eichel 2011).

Most psychologists who do custody evaluations are not formally educated or trained in forensics at all. They are care providers who simply decide to add forensic work to their practice. They often do that by attending conferences or continuing education programs and/or by consulting with a psychologist who already is doing forensic work. Each jurisdiction determines what training is sufficient to qualify a mental health professional as a custody evaluator for courts. In a few states, such as California, the legislature has enacted detailed guidelines on the required training for custody evaluators, including specific training on domestic abuse, and the procedures they must follow (CA. Rules of Court, Rules 5.220, 5.225, 5.230). In most other states, there are few if any guidelines and no special training is required. Evaluators should obtain a basic understanding of how the court system works, their role in it, and how to deal with the attorneys who represent the parties and any attorney or guardian ad litem who may be appointed to represent the children. Further, they should know the custody laws of the state in which they are working and how the courts have interpreted those laws (although many custody evaluators do not believe that is part of their job). Custody evaluators who want to do a professional job need to add those other layers of research and information gathering to the challenges of keeping up with new research in their main field of psychology as well as with the law.

They also need to understand before they take on the role of custody evaluator that their work will put them in the middle of two often antagonistic parties, which can be uncomfortable and even dangerous. It is not unheard of for a custody evaluator to be offered bribes or to be threatened by a litigant or someone on the litigant's behalf if the custody evaluation report is not favorable to that parent. Offers of bribes could also tempt them to accept the bribes, and that could lead them to make recommendations that would not necessarily be in the best interests of the children of the families they are appointed to serve.

There are incentives for going into this subspecialty. Conducting custody evaluations for the courts can be lucrative, so those who decide to do this work could be drawn to it purely for financial objectives. There are other things that might make this an attractive area of work. For example, individuals who prefer not to have set schedules or for other reasons do not want to practice therapy with individuals, couples, or groups might decide to take on custody evaluation work. Therapists squeezed by "managed care" might want to escape from the need to hire billing assistants and wait months for their payments from insurance companies. Other mental health practitioners could simply believe that it would be an easier job, since in most states no special training is required, and the work can be done in a small office – even an office in the practitioner's home.

Additionally, the work of the custody evaluator is not supervised or controlled by anyone, and the consumers – judges, attorneys, and laypersons – normally know little about the concepts, theories, and practices followed by custody evaluators. Thus, serious challenges to their reports can seldom be mounted except by experts who know how to critique custody evaluations. The fees to hire those experts are generally beyond the reach of most parents. One type of such expert is the peer reviewer, discussed above (Tippins 2015). The peer reviewer reviews the custody evaluation with an eye toward its failings and then may be called as an expert witness to rebut the custody evaluation. The other type of expert who can critique the custody evaluation is the trial consultant, who works behind the scenes to aid the hiring attorney but does not testify (Wittmann 2008).

Finally, custody evaluators who are appointed by the courts are shielded from malpractice suits in most states by the doctrine of "quasi-judicial immunity." Judges are fully immune from lawsuits and criminal charges unless they take bribes (e.g., People v. Garson 2006), or otherwise engage in criminal activity regarding a case. When custody evaluators are appointed by the courts, they take on similar immunity (Kirkland et al. 2006). Therefore, professionals will usually refuse to take on any job as a neutral custody evaluator without being appointed by a court.

Although custody evaluators are usually shielded from malpractice suits, complaints can be filed against them to their licensing boards, and in theory, the evaluators could lose their licenses because of such complaints. That rarely happens (Kirkland and Kirkland 2001). Some licensing boards are more diligent than others in terms of investigating alleged wrongdoing or serious neglect on behalf of custody evaluators. For example, New York's Office of Professional Discipline has been criticized for failing to investigate complaints against custody evaluators. OPD claims that because the parents do not receive copies of their custody evaluation reports and OPD has no power to compel the courts to provide OPD with the custody evaluation reports, the Office's hands are tied. Legislation needs to be passed to solve this problem (Tippins 2016).

The custody evaluation process

Over the years, custody evaluators have used various methods of collecting information that they believe is relevant to the best interests of the child. Typical pieces of the process are:

1   Interviews of the parents and, depending on the age of the child(ren), interviews of the child(ren);
2   Interviews of "collaterals" (other individuals, such as family members, doctors, and teachers);
3   Collecting and reading court documents;
4   Collecting and reading documents from other sources, such as medical records and the child's school records;
5   Observations of interactions between each parent and the child(ren); and
6   Possibly psychological assessment instruments, such as so-called "tests" (Otto, Edens, and Barcus 2000).

Only custody evaluators who are trained in how to administer and analyze the results of various so-called "tests" would normally use them in their custody evaluations. In their graduate programs, psychologists may be given such training. The MMPI probably is the test most often used by child custody evaluators (Ackerman and Pritzl 2011). Of course, just because custody evaluators use certain tests, does not mean that those tests produce reliable and valid data that are relevant to the best interests of children (Martindale et al. 2012). Psychiatrists are usually not trained in testing, so they would not generally administer tests. However, they would normally use all or at least most of the other methods listed above and could make use of psychological testing as appropriate (Krause and Thomas 2011).

Each of these methods for collecting information is rife with legal problems. For example, standard psychological assessment instruments such as the MMPI were not created for the purpose of custody evaluations. They were developed to assist mental health professionals to formulate hypotheses regarding the patient's psychological functioning, in order to treat the patient. An individual should not be diagnosed with a particular psychological disorder based only on psychological tests. Such instruments can be helpful, along with other data, in making diagnoses and creating treatment plans for patients. Whether they are helpful or misleading when used as part of custody evaluations is unclear (Brodzinsky 1993; Erickson 2005; Melton et al. 2018, 5552–5553). Possibly tests such as the MMPI can be useful "to generate hypotheses about individual functioning that are subject to confirmation or disconfirmation of data from independent data sources" (Gould 2005, 55–56). There are some psychological assessment instruments that have been developed specifically for use in custody evaluations, but their reliability and validity have not been adequately demonstrated (LaFortune and Carpenter 1998, 222; Martindale 2005).

Regarding interviews and documents, hearsay is one of the most obvious problems. Whatever was reported to the custody evaluator by anyone else and whatever the evaluator read that was written by anyone else is hearsay once the evaluator sets it forth in a report. If there is a trial, the custody evaluator then testifies, but many of the evaluator's conclusions may be based on statements made by others who do not testify at the trial and therefore cannot be cross-examined (Scheinberg 2005; Tippins and DeLuca 2018).

Another problem with interviews is that there is sometimes an assumption that an interview by a psychologist or other mental health professional will lead to truths that cannot be determined by others. Indeed, interviews by custody evaluators are often called "clinical interviews," and the training and experience of the evaluator is supposed to bring something special to their interviewing that can lead to a "clinical opinion" or "clinical judgment" expressed by the evaluator. However, the opinion of the evaluator may not be an expert opinion. "It [may be] a personal opinion, albeit one being expressed by an expert" (Martindale 2001, 503).

The task of a custody evaluator is to assist the court in deciding what custody and visitation arrangements are in the best interests of the child. But the best interests of the child standard is vague and subject to the individual value judgments and biases of the custody evaluator, just as it is subject to the individual value judgments and biases of the judges, attorneys, and others involved in the cases.

In some states, such as New York, legislative guidance for custody evaluators and all the other actors in custody cases as to what constitutes the best interests of a child was, and still is, virtually non-existent. The only specific factor mentioned in the New York custody statutes – aside from child maltreatment – is domestic abuse, which is supposed to be a "weighty" factor (N.Y. D.R.L. Section 240; Memo in Support, 1996 N.Y. Laws, Ch. 85, 1). Consequently, attorneys and judges look for guidance to the case law that has developed over the years (e.g., Eschbach 1982; Friederwitzer 1982).

In many other states, the legislatures enacted statutes listing factors for the courts to consider when making best interests decisions. A commonly used list of factors is found in the statutes of those states that have adopted provisions from the Uniform Marriage and Divorce Act (Melton et al. 2018, 535). For example, Michigan adopted most of the custody factors set forth in that uniform act and added others, ending up with the following factors:

a   The love, affection, and other emotional ties existing between the parties involved and the child.
b   The capacity and disposition of the parties involved to give the child love, affection, and guidance, and to continue the education and raising of the child in his or her religion or creed, if any.
c   The capacity and disposition of the parties involved to provide the child with food, clothing, medical care, or other remedial care recognized and permitted under the laws of this state in place of medical care and other material needs.
d   The length of time the child has lived in a stable, satisfactory environment and the desirability of maintaining continuity.
e   The permanence, as a family unit, of the existing or proposed custodial home or homes.
f   The moral fitness of the parties involved.
g   The mental and physical health of the parties involved.
h   The home, school, and community record of the child.
i   The reasonable preference of the child if the court considers the child to be of sufficient age to express preference.
j   The willingness and ability of each of the parties to facilitate and encourage a close and continuing parent/child relationship between the child and the other parent or the child and the parents.
k   Domestic abuse, regardless of whether the abuse was directed against or witnessed by the child.
l   Any other factor considered by the court to be relevant to a particular child custody dispute (Mich. Comp. L. Section 722.23).

Although lists of factors give more guidance to judges and custody evaluators than the simple phrase "best interest of the child," the amount of discretion left to the judge or evaluator is still immense. Decisions may be made based on which parent is more liked and believed by the custody evaluator and the judge. Consequently, the biases of the evaluator and the judge can and usually do play a large part in the outcome of the case. We do not know whether custody evaluations lead to decisions that are in the best interests of children, because there are few if any follow-up reviews to determine the outcomes (Kelly and Ramsey 2009).

Parental alienation and custody evaluations

In the mid-1980s, a psychiatrist named Richard Gardner began writing about something he called Parental Alienation Syndrome (PAS). Other chapters in this book discuss Gardner and chronicle the changes in the nomenclature from parental alienation syndrome to parental alienation and then to alienation and other terms and the concepts Gardner invented. Originally, Gardner described these beliefs as most often involving mothers' false allegations of child sexual abuse (incest) against fathers. Gardner and his followers claim alienation was recognized by other professionals before he named and wrote about it. Some mental health professionals and others noted the not uncommon phenomenon of parents badmouthing each other, but Gardner tried to elevate that behavior to a mental disorder, calling it a syndrome – Parental Alienation Syndrome.

Gradually, Gardner's ideas spread and became accepted by some custody evaluators. From the custody evaluators, who started using parental alienation belief systems in their reports, the terminology spread to judges, who often simply copied into their decisions what they read in the custody evaluation reports.

How did parental alienation ideas come to the attention of so many custody evaluators and then develop so much traction? This probably happened for at least four reasons. First, children often, for good reasons, prefer one parent over the other. This is quite normal and is not caused by the preferred parent intentionally trying to make the child dislike the other parent (Kelly and Johnston 2001). Another probable reason why the parental alienation belief system caught on is that alienation can happen. Parents often do badmouth each other in front of the children, even in an ongoing marriage or relationship, and probably more if they are breaking up or have broken up. Usually this is not done with the intention of destroying the relationship between the other parent and the child – it is usually just out of anger and frustration. It is wrong and not good for children, but it happens and usually fades away after the litigation is over (Bruch 2001, 533). Whether this is viewed as rising to the level of "alienation" depends upon the weight the evaluator or judge gives to the evidence, including the impact on the children. Nonetheless, a parent's deliberate attempts to undermine the other parent's relationship with the child(ren) can and does happen. Another reason parental alienation caught on is sex bias. Gardner at first was quite clear that he thought PAS most often involved mothers, not fathers. Our society, including our legal system, remains biased against women, so it is not surprising that many people still believe the myths that are encapsulated in parental alienation, such as that the myth that many women lie about abuse to get a leg up in a divorce case (Dallam and Silberg 2006).

Finally, and perhaps most importantly, the American Psychological Association initially appeared to approve Gardner's notion of "parental alienation," but only in a circuitous manner. In 1994, the first version of the APA "Guidelines for Child Custody Evaluations in Divorce Proceedings" was promulgated (APA Guidelines 1994). At the end of the Guidelines, two lists of publications appear. The first list is called "References." It includes four publications by the APA and nine by others. The second list of writings is called "Other Resources." It includes three subcategories: State Guidelines, Forensic Guidelines, and "Pertinent Literature." In "Pertinent Literature," one author stands out, because three of his books are listed: Richard Gardner. Those three books – all self-published – are Family Evaluation in Custody Mediation, Arbitration, and Litigation (Gardner 1989), True and False Accusations of Child Abuse (Gardner 1992a), and The Parental Alienation Syndrome: A Guide for Mental Health and Legal Professionals (Gardner 1992b).

In its 1994 Guidelines, the APA did not officially endorse the concept of Parental Alienation Syndrome, but neither did it explain the status of the publications listed under "Pertinent Literature." An impression was given that psychologists who wished to conduct custody evaluations should read some, if not all, of the publications listed there.

The APA's listing of these three books by Gardner undoubtedly led many psychologists to think that his theories were sound. But listing the books as references was not equivalent to support of a new psychological "theory."

The theories of PAS flowed from custody evaluators to judges and attorneys – especially attorneys who were hired by abusive parents to obtain custody of their children. It seemed to attorneys representing domestic abuse survivors that the number of mothers who lost custody of their children after having been "found guilty" of parental alienation by custody evaluators and judges was increasing. They lost custody because Gardner's recommended "cure" for parental alienation was to remove the child from the so-called alienator parent (with whom the child wanted to remain) for at least several months, with no contact at all, and to place the child with the so-called "target" parent, whom the child was trying to avoid. Not surprisingly, this "cure" can have devastating impacts on children (Dallam and Silberg 2016).

Custody evaluations in cases involving domestic abuse or child abuse

Custody evaluators may pose a danger to children when domestic abuse or child abuse is alleged in a case. Custody evaluators often are not sufficiently trained in domestic abuse and child abuse, and they may share the same biases against women as are prevalent in the world at large (Erickson and O'Sullivan 2011; Haselschwerdt, Hardesty, and Hans 2011; Logan et al. 2002).

As a result of what may be a lack of understanding of the dynamics of abusive behavior, some child custody evaluators have recommended custody to abusive fathers on the theory that the protective mothers were trying to alienate the children from the fathers. When that happens, the protective parent may face three opponents in the judicial arena: the abusive parent, the child's representative, or an attorney for the child (who often is also lacking in domestic abuse training), and the custody evaluator. Fortunately, some judges know enough about domestic abuse to recognize the red flags and reject the recommendations of a parental alienation "expert" (Vinciguerra 2000). Justice Dollinger, in Monroe County, New York, in a scathing opinion in a case where the father alleged the mother had alienated the children from him, rejected the father's "experts" (J.F. v. D.F. 2018; Tippins 2019).

However, many judges accept parental alienation allegations and the custody evaluator's "findings" of parental alienation and grant custody to the abusive father (Meier et al. 2019); Silberg, Dallam, and Samson 2013). The extensive study by Meier et al. indicates that the mere presence of a custody evaluator in a case makes it almost 2 ½ times more likely that a mother will lose custody. If the mother alleges physical child abuse, then the presence of a custody evaluator makes it almost 3 times more likely, and if she alleges both physical and sexual child abuse, then the presence of a custody evaluator makes it 6 ½ times more likely that she will lose custody to the alleged abuser (Meier et al. 2019, 25).

For all the reasons stated above, the appointment of a child custody evaluator should generally be avoided in cases where abuse and alienation claims are raised. Attorneys should be prepared with arguments against such appointments (Erickson 2013) as it is often impossible to determine in advance whether an individual custody evaluator is a parental alienation proponent or whether that individual is even competent, unbiased, thorough, and professional.

The future of child custody evaluations and parental alienation

The tide may be starting to change direction, so that parental alienation allegations may not be as persuasive as they were when parental alienation was introduced into the legal arena in the 1980s before child custody evaluators and courts were required to consider domestic abuse. Now it is well established that allegations of domestic abuse must be considered in all custody cases. In 1990, Congress passed a resolution declaring that "credible evidence of physical abuse of a spouse should create a statutory presumption that it is detrimental to the child to be placed in the custody of the abusive spouse"

(U.S. Congress 1990). The National Council of Juvenile and Family Court Judges also recommended such a presumption (NCJFCJ 1994). Now the laws of all states require that judges must consider domestic abuse, and half of our states plus the District of Columbia have custody statutes that embody a presumption against custody to a parent found to have perpetrated domestic abuse (Saunders 2016). Therefore, domestic abuse would have to be considered by custody evaluators, and a decision by the judge that domestic abuse had occurred would have to be accepted by the custody evaluator. For that reason and other reasons, it would be best for the judge to hold a hearing first on the domestic abuse allegations and order a custody evaluation only after deciding on that issue (Meier 2021). Of course, even if a judge determines that not enough evidence of domestic abuse has been presented to the court, the evaluator might discover additional evidence of domestic abuse.

The American Psychiatric Association has rejected the pressures by parental alienation advocates to accept parental alienation into the *DSM*-5 (American Psychiatric Association 2020; Crary 2012). The National Council of Juvenile and Family Court Judges has warned of its dangers (Dalton, Drozd, and Wong 2006). Research shows the damage being done to children if courts accept parental alienation allegations (Meier et al. 2019; Silberg and Dallam 2019). Research also demonstrates the unwarranted power that allegations of parental alienation have in custody cases even when domestic abuse is also alleged (Meier et al. 2019). Judges are beginning to reject testimony by parental alienation "experts" (J.F. v. D.F 2018; Tippins 2019). Support is building for laws requiring that safety be the most important consideration in a custody case (U.S. Congress 2016). The myth that respected people are never violent criminals or otherwise abusive individuals has been broken down by the Catholic Church and Boy Scouts pedophile scandals, the "Me Too" Movement, and the revelations about famous men who have perpetrated domestic abuse (e.g., football player Ray Rice) and sexual assault (e.g., Bill Cosby).

These are positive developments. But it remains concerning that individuals and groups propounding parental alienation have spread their belief system not only to English-speaking nations but also to many other countries (Sol Bravo 2020; EAP 2017).

Conclusion

The practice of conducting child custody evaluations for the courts has never been a scientific endeavor and never can be because the concept of the best interests of the child is very vague. Custody evaluation reports can be rife with hearsay and tilted by the explicit and implicit biases of the evaluators. When parental alienation was introduced into the custody evaluation mix, the result was an explosion of cases in which custody evaluators recommended that custody go to abusive parents. Some judges accepted the abusers' claims of parental alienation simply because the evaluators credited them.

Currently, no reputable legal or mental health organization has accepted the parental alienation claims of its proponents. Those claims have been rejected by the American Psychiatric Association (APA 2020; Crary 2012), a Task Force of the American Psychological Association (APA 1996), the National Council of Juvenile and Family Court Judges (Dalton, Drozd and Wong 2006), and many others. Consequently, parental alienation proponents have renamed and reworked parental alienation claims to make them appear more acceptable to custody evaluators and judges. It remains to be seen whether these tactics will be successful.

Acknowledgment

The author wishes to acknowledge the inspiration and assistance of Betty Good and Chris O'Sullivan, PhD, in the preparation of this chapter.

References

Ackerman, Marc J., and Tracy Brey Pritzl. "Child Custody Evaluation Practices: A 20-year Follow-up." *Family Court Review* 49, 2011: 618–628. doi: 10.1111/j.1744-1617.2011.01397.x.

American Board of Forensic Psychology, abfp.com/about.

American Psychiatric Association. *Diagnostic and Statistical Manual of Mental Disorders, Fifth Edition*, 2020. doi: 10.1176/appi.books.9780890425596.

American Psychological Association. *Violence and the Family: Report of the American Psychological Association Presidential Task Force on Violence and the Family*. Washington, DC: American Psychological Association, 1996.

American Psychological Association, Practice Directorate. "Guidelines for Child Custody Evaluations in Divorce Proceedings." *American Psychologist* 49, 1994: 677–680. doi: 10.1037/0003-066X.49.7.677.

American Psychology-Law Society. *Guide to Graduate Programs in Forensic and Legal Psychology 2019–2020: A Resource for Prospective Students, Fifth Edition*, 2020. https://www.apls-students.org/uploads/4/6/5/6/46564967/guide_to_graduate_programs_in_forensic_and_legal_psychology_2020___1_.pdf.

Baerger, Dana Royce, Robert Galatzer-Levy, Jonathan W. Gould, and Sandra G. Nye. "A Methodology for Reviewing the Reliability and Relevance of Child Custody Evaluations." *Journal of the American Academy of Matrimonial Lawyers* 18, 2002: 35–73. https://cdn.ymaws.com/aaml.org/resource/collection/35664435-7DFC-48A0-B8A0-DC4FB0009474/a_methodology_for_reviewing-18-1.pdf.

Brodzinsky, David M. "On the Use and Misuse of Professional Testing in Child Custody Evaluations." *Professional Psychology: Research and Practice* 24, 1993: 213–219. doi: 10.1037/0735-7028.24.2.213.

Bruch, Carol S. "Parental Alienation Syndrome and Parental Alienation – Getting It Wrong in Child Custody Cases." *Family Law Quarterly* 35, 2001: 527–552. doi: 10.2139/SSRN.298110.

California Rules of Court, Rules 5.220, 5.225, and 5.230.

Crary, David. "Parental Alienation Not a Mental Disorder, American Psychiatric Association Says." *Huffington Post*, 2012. http://www.huffingtonpost.com/2012/09/21/parental-alienation-is-no_n_1904310.html.

Dallam, Stephanie, and Joyanna Silberg. "Myths That Place Children at Risk during Custody Disputes." *Sexual Assault Report* 9(3), 2006: 33–34, 42–47. http://www.leadershipcouncil.org/docs/Dallam&Silberg.pdf.

Dallam, Stephanie, and Joyanna Silberg. "Recommended Treatments for 'Parental Alienation Syndrome' (PAS) May Cause Children Foreseeable and Lasting Psychological Harm." *Journal of Child Custody* 13, 2016: 134–143. doi: 10.1080/15379418.2016.1219974.

Dalton, Clare, Leslie Drozd, and Frances Wong. *Navigating Custody and Visitation Evaluations in Cases with Domestic Violence: A Judge's Guide.* Reno, NV: National Council of Juvenile & Family Court Judges, 2006. Available at www.ncjfcj.org/images/stories/dept/fvd/pdf/navigating_cust.pdf.

Daubert v. Merrell-Dow Pharmaceuticals, 509 U.S. 579 (1993).

Davis, Michael, Chris O'Sullivan, Kim Susser, and Marjory Fields. "Custody Evaluations When There Are Allegations of Domestic Violence: Practices, Beliefs, and Recommendations of Professional Evaluators." US Department of Justice, Office of Justice Programs, 2011. http://www.ncjrs.gov/pdffiles1/nij/grants/234465.pdf.

Eichel, Steve. "Credentialing: It May Not be the Cat's Meow." 2011. http://www.dreichel.com/Articles/Dr_Zoe.htm.

Erickson, Nancy. "Use of the MMPI-2 in Custody Evaluations Involving Battered Women." *Family Law Quarterly* 39, 2005: 87–108. https://www.jstor.org/stable/i25758278.

Erickson, Nancy. "Fighting False Allegations of Parental Alienation Raised as Defenses to Valid Claims of Abuse." *Family & Intimate Partner Violence Quarterly* 6, 2013: 35–78.

Erickson, Nancy, and Chris O'Sullivan. "Doing Our Best for New York's Children: Custody Evaluations When Domestic Violence is Alleged." *NYS Psychologist* 23, 2011: 9–12. https://cdn.ymaws.com/www.nyspa.org/resource/dynamic/blogs/20180425_154600_26574.pdf.

Eschbach v. Eschbach, 56 N.Y.2d 167 (1982).

European Association for Psychotherapy. *A Statement from the European Association for Psychotherapy (EAP) on the Concepts of 'Parental Alienation Syndrome' (PAS) and 'Parental Alienation' (PA),* 2017. https://www.europsyche.org/quality-standards/eap-guidelines/parent-alienation-syndrome-pas-parental-alienation-pa/.

Federal Rules of Evidence, Rule 702.

Friederwitzer v. Friederwitzer, 55 N.Y.2d 89 (1982).

Frye v. United States, 293 F. 1013 (D.C. Cir. 1923).

Gardner, Richard. *Family Evaluation in Custody Mediation, Arbitration, and Litigation.* Cresskill, NJ: Creative Therapeutics, 1989.

Gardner, Richard. *True and False Allegations of Child Sex Abuse.* Cresskill, NJ: Creative Therapeutics, 1992a.

Gardner, Richard. *The Parental Alienation Syndrome: A Guide for Mental Health and Legal Professionals.* Cresskill, NJ: Creative Therapeutics, 1992b.

Gould, Jonathan. "Use of Psychological Tests in Child Custody Assessment." In *Psychological Testing in Child Custody Evaluations,* edited by James Flens and Leslie Drozd, 49–69. New York, NY: Haworth Press, 2005.

Greenberg, Stuart A., and Daniel W. Shuman. "Irreconcilable Conflict between Therapeutic and Forensic Roles." *Professional Psychology: Research & Practice* 28, 1997: 50–57. doi: 10.1037/0735-7028.28.1.50.

Haselschwerdt, Megan, Jennifer Hardesty, and Jason Hans. "Custody Evaluators' Beliefs About Domestic Violence Allegations During Divorce: Feminist and Family Violence Perspectives." *Journal of Interpersonal Violence* 26, 2011: 1694–1719. doi: 10.1177/0886260510370599.

J.F. v. D.F., 61 Misc.3d 1226 (Sup. Ct. Monroe Co. 2018).

Kelly, Joan B., and Janet R. Johnston. "The Alienated Child: A Reformulation of Parental Alienation Syndrome." *Family Court Review* 39, 2001: 249–266. doi: 10.1111/j.174-1617.2001.tb00609.x.

Kelly, Robert F., and Sarah H. Ramsey. "Child Custody Evaluations: The Need for Systems-level Outcome Assessments." *Family Court Review* 47, 2009: 286–303. doi: 10.1111/j.1744-1617.2009.01255.x.

Kirkland, Karl, and Kristen Kirkland. "Frequency of Child Custody Evaluation Complaints and Related Disciplinary Action: A Survey of the Association of State and Provincial Psychology Boards." *Professional Psychology: Research and Practice* 32, 2001: 171–174. doi: 10.1037/0735-7028.32.2.171.

Kirkland, Karl, Kale Kirkland, Glen King, and Guy Renfro. "Quasi-judicial Immunity for Forensic Mental Health Professionals in Court-appointed Roles." *Journal of Child Custody* 3, 2006: 1–22. doi: 10.1300/J190v03n01_01.

Kraus, Louis J., and Christopher R. Thomas. "Practice Parameters for Child and Adolescent Forensic Evaluations." *Journal of the American Academy of Child and Adolescent Psychiatry* 50, 2011: 1299–1312. doi: 10.1016/j.jaac.2011.09.020.

Kunin, Carla, Ebbe Ebbesen, and Vladimir Konecni. "An Archival Study of Decision-makinginChildCustodyDisputes."*JournalofClinicalPsychology*48,1992:564–573. doi: 10.1002/1097-4679(199207)48:4<564::aid-jclp2270480420>3.0.co;2-a.

LaFortune, Kathryn, and Bruce Carpenter. "Custody Evaluations: A Survey of Mental Health Professionals." *Behavioral Sciences & the Law* 16, 1998: 207–224. doi: 10.1002/(SICI)1099-0798(199821)16:2<207::AID-BSL303>3.0.CO;2-P.

Legislative Memorandum in Support of Chapter 85, 1996 N.Y. Laws.

Logan, T.K., Robert Walker, Carol E. Jordan, and Leah. Horvath. "Child Custody Evaluations and Domestic Violence: Case Comparisons." *Violence and Victims* 17, 2002: 719–742. doi: 10.1891/vivi.17.6.719.33718.

Martindale, David. "Cross-examining Mental Health Experts in Child Custody Litigation." *Journal of Psychiatry & Law* 29, 2001: 483–511. doi: 10.1177/009318530102900404.

Martindale, David. "Psychological Assessment: Evaluating the Evaluations." *The Matrimonial Strategist* 22, 2005: 3–5.

Martindale, David, Timothy Tippins, Yossef Ben-Poreth, Jeffrey Wittmann, and William Austin. 2012. "Assessment Instrument Selection Should Be Guided by Validity Analysis, Not Professional Plebiscite: Response to a Flawed Survey." *Family Court Review* 50, 2012: 502–507. doi: 10.1111/j.1744-1617.2012.01466.x.

Meier, Joan S. "Denial of Family Violence in Court: An Empirical Analysis and Path Forward for Family Law." *GW Law Faculty Publications & Other Works* 2021: 1536. https://scholarship.law.gwu.edu/faculty_publications/1536.

Meier, Joan S., Sean Dickson, Chris O'Sullivan, Leora Rosen, and Jeffrey Hayes. "Child Custody Outcomes in Cases Involving Parental Alienation and Abuse Allegations." *GW Law Faculty Publications & Other Works*, 2019. doi: 10.2139/ssrn.3448062.

Melton, Gary, John Petrila, Norman Poythress, and Christopher Slobogin. *Psychological Evaluations for The Courts: A Handbook for Mental Health Professionals and Lawyers, Second Edition*. New York: Guilford. 2007.

Melton, Gary, John Petrila, Norman Poythress, Christopher Slobogin, Randy Otto, Douglas Mossman, and Lois Condie. *Psychological Evaluations for The Courts: A Handbook for Mental Health Professionals and Lawyers, Fourth Edition*. New York: Guilford, 2018.

Mich. Comp. L., Section 722.23.

National Council of Juvenile and Family Court Judges. *Family Violence: A Model State Code*, 1994. https://www.ncjfcj.org/wp-content/uploads/2012/03/modecode_fin_printable.pdf

New Jersey Rules Governing the Courts of the State, Rule 5:3-3.

New York Domestic Relations Law Section 240.

Otto, Randy, John Edens, and Elizabeth Barcus. "The Use of Psychological Testing in Child Custody Evaluations." *Family & Conciliation Courts Review* 38, 2000: 312–340. doi: 10.1111/j.174-1617.2000.tb00578.x.

People v. Garson, 6 N.Y. 3d 604 (Court of Appeals, 2006).

Reber, Arthur, and Emily Reber. *The Penguin Dictionary of Psychology, Third Edition*. London: Penguin Books, 2001.

Saunders, Daniel G. "State Laws Related to Family Judges' and Custody Evaluators' Recommendations in Cases of Intimate Partner Violence: Final Summary Overview." 2016. https://www.researchgate.net/publication/320426479_State_Laws_Related_to_Family_Judges%27_and_Custody_Evaluators%27_Recommendations_in_Cases_of_Intimate_Partner_Violence_Final_Summary_Overview.

Scheinberg, Elliott. "The Expert's Recommendation in Custody Cases." *New York Law Journal* 2005. https://www.law.com/newyorklawjournal/almID/900005431854/the-experts-recommendation-in-custody-cases/.

Shaw, Julia, Lisa Ohman, and Peter van Koppen. "Psychology and Law: The Past, Present, and Future of the Discipline." *Psychology, Crime & Law* 19, 2013: 643–647. doi: 10.1080/1068316X.2013.793979.

Silberg, Joyanna, and Stephanie Dallam. "Abusers Gaining Custody in Family Courts: A Case Series of Overturned Decisions." *Journal of Child Custody* 16, 2019: 140–169. doi: 10.1080/15379418.2019.1613204.

Silberg, Joyanna, Stephanie Dallam, and Elizabeth Samson. "Crisis in Family Court: Lessons from Turned Around Cases." *Final Report submitted to the Office of Violence against Women, Department of Justice*, 2013. https://irp-cdn.multiscreensite.com/0dab915e/files/uploaded/crisis-fam-court-lessons-turned-around-cases.pdf.

Sol Bravo, Maria. "PAS Application Despite of Its Rejection Three Axes That Serve as the Basis for Its Permanence." 2020. doi: 10.2139/ssrn.3546223.

Tippins, Timothy. July 2, 2015. "Peer-Review Experts in Custody Litigation." *New York Law Journal* 2015. https://www.law.com/newyorklawjournal/almID/1202731104057/.

Tippins, Timothy. "Custody Evaluators: Where Is the Oversight?" *New York Law Journal* 2016. https://www.law.com/newyorklawjournal/almID/1202751195988/custody-evaluators-wheres-the-oversight/.

Tippins, Timothy. "A Passel of Poppycock: Expert Witness Roles and Limitations." *New York Law Journal* 2019. https://www.law.com/newyorklawjournal/

2019/03/15/a-passel-of-poppycock-expert-witness-roles-and-limitations/
?slreturn=20210301174801.

Tippins, Timothy, and Lauren DeLuca. "The Custody Evaluator Meets Hearsay:
A Star-crossed Romance." *Journal of the American Academy of Matrimonial Law-
yers* 30, 2018: 521–558. https://cdn.ymaws.com/aaml.org/resource/collection/
B64341B0-6413-4F0B-AF32-DA6037C2AEAD/MAT211_4.pdf.

U.S. Congress. House. *Expressing the Sense of Congress that, for Purposes of Determining
Child Custody, Evidence of Spousal Abuse Should Create a Statutory Presumption that
It Is Detrimental to the Child to Be Placed in the Custody of an Abusive Parent.* H.Con.
Res.172 – 101st Congress (1989–1990).

U.S. Congress. House. *Expressing the sense of Congress that Child Safety Is the First
Priority of Custody and Visitation Adjudications, and that State Courts Should Improve
Adjudications of Custody Where Family Violence Is Alleged.* H.Con.Res.150 – 114th
Congress (2016).

Varela, Jorge and Mary Alice Conroy. 2012. "Professional Competencies in Forensic
Psychology." *Professional Psychology: Research and Practice* 43, 2012: 410–421. https://
doi.org/10.1037/a0026776. doi: 10.1080/01926180801960658.

Vinciguerra v. Vinciguerra, 294 A.D.2d 565 (2d Dept. 2000).

Waller, Erika, and Annaseril E. Daniel. "Purpose and Utility of Child Custody Evaluations: From the Perspective of Judges." *Journal of Psychiatry & Law* 32, 2004:
5–27. doi: 10.1177/009318530403200102.

Wittmann, Jeffrey. "Expert Witness vs. Trial Consultant." *New York Family Law
Monthly* 9, 2008: 1–2, 6–7.

Zapf, Patricia, and Itiel Dror. "Understanding and Mitigating Bias in Forensic Evaluation: Lessons from Forensic Science." *International Journal of Forensic Mental Health*
16, 2017: 227–238. doi: 10.1080/14999013.2017.1317302.

Chapter 6

Distinguishing parental alienation from child abuse and adverse parenting

Madelyn Simring Milchman

Ever since Richard Gardner proposed the Parental Alienation Syndrome to explain a child's rejection of a parent in divorce cases when child sexual abuse is alleged, the same eight factors have been used to identify alienated children (Gardner 1986). These factors have been assumed to refer to behaviors that can be observed directly, as if they were objective facts. If alienation were an objective fact, it would be identifiable from the evidence available to the senses. In other words, identifying its presence would be a matter of *perception*. However, alienation cannot be perceived. It is not a thing in nature. It is a concept. There are no behavioral observations that specifically and uniquely indicate alienation (Saini, Johnston, Fidler, and Bala 2012, 2016) though examples *interpreted* as revealing alienation abound in the alienation literature (Milchman, Geffner, and Meier 2020a, b). Rather than being perceived, alienation is *inferred* when behaviors interpreted as caused by alienation are observed.

The inferential nature of alienation is generally not recognized or acknowledged by proponents of alienation. This is a significant omission because implying that something is directly perceived rather than inferred makes it appear to be objective and therefore beyond dispute. It obfuscates the higher-order cognitive processes that are involved in making inferences. Those higher-order processes are subjective and are therefore open to dispute. For example, while there would be no dispute about whether an observed object is a shoe or a bridge or a tree or the like, there would be ample room for dispute in interpreting whether a disproven child sexual abuse allegation was made with malicious intent or was an innocent error. That interpretation, along with other comparable ones related to each of the eight alienation factors, is the basis for inferences about whether alienation is or is not present. Failure to acknowledge the inferential nature of alienation creates an appearance of objectivity that is misleading.

Nevertheless, despite omitting explicit discussions about the inferential nature of alienation, authors who contribute to theories about alienation agree that alienation should not be identified as the cause of parent rejection without assessing and eliminating other possible causes (e.g., Bernet and Freeman 2013; Drozd, Olesen, and Saini 2013). Unfortunately, this theoretical

DOI: 10.4324/9781003095927-8

complexity is not generally carried over into practice where evaluators tend to be overly ready to identify alienation (Warshak 2020). There are many reasons for this gap between theory and practice.

One is that in practice, the standard for ruling out abuse is overly simplistic and so the validity of ruling in alienation is inflated. Another is that the specific evidence needed to assess each plausible alternative cause of parent rejection, including different types of abuse, is often not obtained and the absence of evidence is equated with evidence of absence. Attorneys and judges often are not aware of these problems (Meier 2019, Milchman 2017, Silberg and Dallam 2019). To date, one pioneering protocol, the "Decision Trees" protocol (Drozd et al. 2013), has been published that guides evaluators to assess multiple factors related to a wide range of custody issues, including abuse and alienation. The focus in the Decision Trees protocol is methodological, addressing sources of evidence (e.g., police records, witnesses, interviews, psychological tests) that evaluators should obtain to assess the relevant psycholegal issues. The Decision Trees protocol moves practice from simplistic analyses to appreciating the complexity associated with child custody and parenting time evaluations, which is its purpose (Drozd et al. 2013).

Nevertheless, from the narrower perspective of guiding evaluators to assess child abuse allegations in custody evaluations, the Decision Trees protocol (Drozd et al. 2013) has limitations. It does not divide child abuse into subtypes and therefore does not counteract failure to assess each type's specific evidentiary needs. It contains only one mention of child sexual abuse assessment (and two citations) and that only warns evaluators to use a standard interview protocol. It omits psychological maltreatment entirely. The methodological focus of the Decision Trees protocol means that it tells evaluators where to look, but with few exceptions, discussed below, it does not tell them what to look *for*. The purpose of this chapter is to expand beyond those limitations. It addresses the specific evidence needed to assess two types of child abuse (sexual abuse, psychological maltreatment), other parenting practices recognized as causing harm well beyond that caused by normal or sub-par parenting (adverse parenting), and parental alienation.

The chapter begins with a critique of the commonly accepted standard for decision-making about whether parents have abused their child. This critique provides the basis for recommending that evaluators with the proper education and training should assess the different types of child abuse allegations themselves in some cases. The chapter then proposes a protocol to guide them in this task, the "Multidimensional Assessment of Causes of Parent Rejection" (MAP) (Milchman, in press). The MAP presents the specific evidence evaluators should obtain in order to provide courts with well-founded opinions about the causes of parent rejection in an instant case. These causes should then be addressed in the parenting plans that evaluators recommend. The MAP and the Decision Trees protocols (Drozd et al. 2013) complement each other. The MAP focuses on the kinds of evidence to obtain – the what to look for – from the various sources of evidence – the where to look – identified in the Decision Trees.

The Commonly Accepted Standard for Assessing
Child Abuse in Custody Cases is Inadequate

The commonly accepted standard is official decisions

Parental alienation authors generally agree that validated child abuse cases cannot be alienation cases, meaning that alienation cannot be considered the primary cause of parent rejection when abuse or other kinds of harmful parenting are identified. Nevertheless, alienation writings often bypass the problem of accurately identifying child abuse in custody cases by deferring to child protective services' findings or judicial opinions. The rationale is that these are the institutions officially charged with the responsibility of deciding the credibility of child abuse allegations whereas mental health professionals have no special expertise in deciding credibility (Melton, Petrila, Poythress, and Slobogin 2007; Myers 1992). However, the reliability of deferring to child protective agency findings and judicial opinions is problematic as there is considerable evidence that these governmental decisions should not be *assumed* to be accurate. Some judges, recognizing the weaknesses in child protective service investigations in custody cases, choose not to rely on them. Instead, they rely on experts and *Guardians Ad Litem*, without, however, being aware of problems in those sources of evidence (Silberg and Dallam 2019).

Child protective services' unsubstantiated decisions do not reliably indicate no abuse

Canada has conducted National Incidence Studies (CIS) for more than 20 years (Saini, Black, Fallon, and Marshall 2013). They reveal the fallacy of relying exclusively or heavily on unsubstantiation by child protective service agencies to conclude that no abuse occurred. In CIS-98 (Trocme and Bala 2005), caseworkers substantiated 7% fewer child custody cases (40%) than child protection cases (47%). However, they also decided that 14% of the unsubstantiated child custody cases had residual abuse suspicions. While this is fewer than in child protection cases (19%), it still is a warning that failing to substantiate a case leaves many children in custody cases with credible suspicions of abuse. In CIS-2003 (Saini et al. 2013), caseworkers again substantiated 4% fewer child custody cases (45%) than child protection cases (49%), but now decided that there were 7% *more* unsubstantiated custody cases that had residual abuse suspicions (19%) compared with child protection cases (12%). Increased professional awareness about child abuse in custody disputing families could have contributed to caseworkers' awareness of residual abuse suspicions even when cases could not be substantiated (Trocme, Fallon, MacLaurin, et al. 2010).

The risk that child protective service agencies could fail to substantiate true abuse cases appears to have several causes. Saini, Black, Godbout, and Deljava (2019) report discussions with caseworkers who cited a lack of training in investigating abuse in custody cases; the burden of overwhelming child protection caseloads to which custody cases only add; and pressure from parents and attorneys to take sides. My colleagues and I have had several cases that reveal other institutional pressures. In one, a child protective service administrator testified that the agency had downgraded a finding of substantiated sexual abuse administratively because the perpetrator threatened to appeal the finding legally, had the resources to do it, and pressured the agency. That administrator identified specific firms that specialize in aggressively appealing agency decisions and admitted that the agency takes special care with their cases. His admission is consistent with another case in which one of those firms threatened to appeal substantiated physical abuse and the threat alone was sufficient to downgrade the finding administratively. In another case, a caseworker admitted that there is an unwritten agency policy not to investigate abuse allegations in family matters, but to defer the responsibility to the family court judge who has ultimate oversight of the matter anyway.

Judicial opinions that allegations are false may not reliably indicate no abuse

Relying on judicial opinions is similarly problematic. There is evidence that some judges depend heavily on the opinions of experts and *Guardians Ad Litem*, which may be tainted by ideological biases in favor of alienation as well as by a lack of specialized knowledge about trauma and child abuse (Milchman, Geffner, and Meier 2020a, Saunders et al. 2012, Silberg and Dallam 2019). Milchman (2017) found that judges' opinions that abuse allegations were false were often based on the absence of evidence rather than on the presence of evidence that affirmatively disproved abuse. Meier (2019) found that judges' opinions discrediting abuse were much higher when alienation was used as a rebuttal than they were when abuse claims were raised without alienation rebuttals. Neither of these studies had affirmative evidence proving that the abuse allegations were valid and the alienation ones were not. However, Silberg and Dallam (2019) found 27 U.S. cases in which courts credited alienation claims over abuse claims and granted custody to the allegedly abusive parents, but then subsequent court proceedings had to overturn those decisions because the children were reabused by the parents who had been accused of abuse and to whom custody had been transferred.

Young children's disclosure process can make abuse validation difficult

The difficulty of identifying child abuse in custody cases is not limited to questionable decisions when child abuse is disclosed. For child sexual abuse, the reliability of official decisions is also undermined by the complexity of the disclosure process, especially when the children are young and the alleged abusers are parents, which are the kinds of cases that beleaguer family courts.

Pipe, Lamb, Orbach, and Cederborg (2007) have tracked the child sexual abuse disclosure process in detail. Their results suggest that one fairly common sexual abuse disclosure process disfavors identifying true abuse. They found that official interviews of young children were often triggered by prior disclosures to immediate family members (40% of 4–6 year olds; 27% of 6–8 year olds) (88, T. 5.4). For older children (9–13 year old), official interviews were more often triggered by disclosures to peers and neighbors (14%) than to immediate family (12%) (88, T. 5.4), but the difference was not dramatic. Most of the disclosures to immediate family members for children of all ages were followed consistently with disclosures in official interviews (Pipe et al. 2007, 88, T. 5.3). Virtually all but the youngest children who initially disclosed to immediate family members also disclosed in their official interviews (93–99% of 6–13 year olds) (88, T. 5.3). Even the young children (4–6 year olds) typically followed their initial disclosure to immediate family members with disclosures in their official interviews (77%) (88, T. 5.3). However, a 77% rate of consistent disclosures in both interviews still leaves 23% of 4–6 year olds who disclosed to immediate family members who did *not* repeat their allegations during their official interviews.

The problem of young children's inconsistency in disclosing to immediate family members but not to official interviewers cannot be trivialized, especially in custody cases. Some of the inconsistency could be related to young children's general reluctance to disclose abuse (Hershkowitz et al. 2014). This problem is especially pronounced when the abuse is sexual abuse by a parent. Hershkowitz et al. (2014) found that the vast majority of children aged 3–6 years did not disclose sexual abuse by a parent (over 80%) (1209, T. 3). Pipe et al. (2007, 85) found that young children were much less likely to disclose abuse in their official interviews when the abuser was a biological father than when it was anyone else (59% for 4–6 year olds compared with 29% for other suspects; 53% of 6–8 year olds compared with 8% for other suspects). Their findings are consistent with the repeated finding that nearly 2/3 of sexual abuse victims do not disclose until they become adults (London, Bruck, Ceci, and Shuman 2007).

Inconsistent disclosures could be interpreted as cause to doubt the truth of the allegations that young children make to immediate family members but do not repeat beyond the family. Since mothers are usually the primary custodians (Nielsen 2014), they would be most likely to be the immediate family members in whom the children initially confide. Even if the children disclosed to other family members, the mothers would have to be informed in order for the allegations to be brought to family courts. When family court judges are confronted with mothers claiming that their children alleged sexual abuse by the fathers to them, and the children do not repeat the allegations to official interviewers precisely *because* the allegations are against their fathers, the stage is set for judges to perceive the mothers as overly zealous and blame them for pursuing baseless claims (Pipe et al. 2007). They might not appreciate that protective mothers would be expected to make every effort to have the allegations investigated officially when they believe their children. The perception that the mothers are overzealous can prime judicial skepticism about the truth of the allegations (Meier 2019), especially if judges are not aware that a common childhood disclosure pattern could be responsible for the children's inconsistency.

The difficulties in obtaining disclosures from young children in official interviews is a reason that properly trained evaluators with advanced expertise in child trauma should carefully scrutinize the basis for prior decisions invalidating sexual abuse, whether they were made by child protective services, experts, or *Guardians Ad Litem*. A trauma-informed perspective is essential to discriminate between post-traumatic responses such as avoidance, numbing, and dissociation and non-traumatic anxiety, fear, and phobic responses. Evaluators whose expertise is primarily in the areas of child custody and alienation are likely to fail to make such distinctions or to appreciate their importance (e.g., Fidler, Ward, and Deutsch 2017). This failure can be dangerously misleading to family courts (Silberg and Dallam 2019) because it normalizes children's responses to abusive parents, which diminishes their significance.

While evaluators should not routinely assess child sexual abuse in all custody evaluations in which allegations are made, evaluators with the proper expertise should assess sexual abuse allegations when the official decisions do not appear to be well-founded in the evidence considered or in other evidence that should have been considered but was not. The purpose of such assessment is not to pre-empt child protective services' investigative authority but to provide judges with more adequate evidence on which to base their decisions. If evaluators lack the proper expertise, they should refer to other evaluators with the requisite expertise for supplementary evaluations. Of course, evaluators assessing child sexual abuse allegations must also comply with all applicable reporting requirements as well as other legal and ethical requirements in their jurisdictions and professions. This chapter now turns to the proposed MAP protocol to guide evaluators, attorneys, and judges in the evidence that should be considered in custody cases with allegations of child abuse and/or parental alienation (Figure 6.1).

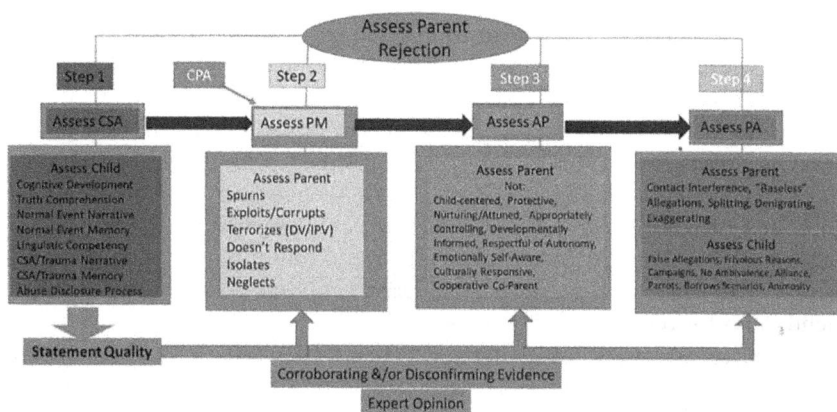

Figure 6.1 Multidimensional assessment of causes of parent rejection in child custody cases.

CSA = Child Sexual Abuse; CPA= Child Physical Abuse, PM = Psychological Maltreatment; AP = Adverse Parenting; PA = Parental Alienation

Overview

The MAP is a schema for organizing generally accepted psychological knowledge about two types of child abuse (sexual abuse, psychological maltreatment), adverse parenting, and alienation. It does not provide novel scientific knowledge about any of these parenting problems and therefore its use by evaluators should not be challenged on that basis. The MAP contextualizes the evidence it identifies as necessary to assess each type of parenting problem by advising evaluators to collect corroborating and/or disconfirming evidence for each and to rely on the totality of the evidence in formulating their expert opinions and parenting plan recommendations.

The value of using the MAP is twofold. One, like the Decision Trees protocol (Drozd et al. 2013), it guides evaluators to be comprehensive in their data collection. Two, it makes the evidence needed to provide well-founded expert opinions and recommendations more transparent. Increasing transparency could help evaluators be more self-critical in conducting their evaluations and formulating their opinions; help attorneys with direct and cross-examination of the evaluators; and help judges weigh expert testimony in making their decisions. The MAP, like the Decision Trees protocol (Drozd et al. 2013), provides a rational framework for collecting and analyzing evidence. It is intended to minimize the likelihood that evaluators would quickly and superficially interpret behaviors that appear to fit the alienation factors without assessing the complexity of all plausible causes that could contribute to parent rejection (Warshak 2020).

Sequential organization of assessment in the MAP

The MAP organizes the causes to be assessed sequentially as Steps 1 through 4, with the first three steps representing abuse and adverse parenting and the fourth representing alienation. The sequence in the MAP is a matter of logic. The first three steps represent assessment of justified reasons for parent rejection. Since alienation is *defined* as unjustified parent rejection (Bernet and Freeman, 2013, Fidler and Ward 2017), alienation cannot be identified without first ruling out justified causes of parent rejection. The sequential organization in the MAP prioritizes the several causes of justified parent rejection over alienation in developing parenting plans, particularly recommendations for reunification therapy.

Sequential assessment is a major difference between the MAP and the Decision Trees whose authors say that they "do not propose giving specific weights to various factors … because there is no evidence that there is predictive value in organizing the data in any specifically weighted way" (Drozd et al. 2013, 26). They seem to be arguing that in order to justify assessment priorities scientifically, there needs to be empirical evidence that parenting plans based on those priorities result in better outcomes for children. This argument is unrealistic. It is doubtful that such empirical research could ever be done because the complexity of variables within the child as well as within the family and outside it, all of which change over time, pose insurmountable obstacles to identifying the effects of various parenting plans on children. The scientific basis for the assessment priorities in the MAP does not depend on their relative predictive values, which are unknowable, but on logic.

Cases with co-occurring abuse and alienation (hybrid cases) illustrate the disagreements caused by failing to agree on the logic of prioritizing abuse over other causes of parent rejection. Though there is widespread consensus that children's safety from abuse is paramount (Fidler, Ward, and Deutsch 2017), and no responsible expert would knowingly put children's safety at risk, disagreement about the need to prioritize abuse over alienation still exists and can be seen in conflicts about reunification therapy. Some alienation authors assert that protective parents can intensify their children's resistance to abusive parents and therefore recommend reunification therapy to treat the protective parents' behavior "whether it is justified or needlessly protective" (Fidler, Ward, and Deutsch 2017, 255). They also argue that past abuse, "regardless of its nature or severity," does not preclude reunification therapy (Fidler, Ward, and Deutsch 2017, 255). While they advise carefully assessing such variables as the severity of the abuse; the children's level of trauma and willingness to have contact with their abusive parents; and the parents' ability to benefit from therapy (Fidler and Ward 2017), all of which are sensitive, conceptualizing protective parenting as a treatment problem (Drozd and Olesen 2004, Fidler and Ward 2017; Fidler, Ward, and Deutsch 2017, Johnston and Sullivan 2020, Worenklein 2013) puts the primary emphasis on re-establishing connections with abusive parents rather than on healing from trauma.

Some alienation authors making this argument also take the position that "children should not be retraumatized by being pushed too vigorously to reunify" (Fidler, Ward, and Deutsch 2017, 255). While, again, that position is sensitive, it also avoids the problem of whether to prioritize the children's contact resistance or the parents' contact demands. What specifically does "too vigorously" mean? If the children's contact resistance is not attributed primarily to the nature and severity of the abuse, then what should guide courts' decisions about whether to honor that resistance or whether to honor parents' demands? The problem is not solved by citing children's unwillingness to have contact with their abusive parents as the criterion. If the children's unwillingness is considered disproportionate and attributed to the alienating influence of protective parents, the criterion becomes meaningless.

In making these arguments, alienation theorists are at odds with trauma theorists whose recognition of the complex damage to children's developing personalities caused by parent-inflicted trauma (Briere and Spinazzola 2009, Ford and Cloitre 2009, Ford and Courtois 2009, Ford, Albert, and Hawke 2009, James 1989) implies a possibly prolonged and unpredictable recovery period. Trauma experts are more likely to emphasize children's need to master the trauma than they are to emphasize their need to re-establish contact with their abusive parents. Unlike alienation theorists, they are unlikely to blame protective parents for the children's resistance or see protective parenting as a treatment issue. Whereas alienation experts are more likely to emphasize children's physical safety in reunification therapy due to the physical presence of the therapists, trauma experts are more likely to emphasize the emotional danger to children of premature exposure to abusive parents in reunification therapy sessions even though therapists are in the room.

Judges face a profound dilemma when they are faced with disputing experts in which one side offers them a way to protect parents' constitutional rights without risking the children's safety and the other side insists that this might be impossible. It is tempting to believe that science could resolve the conflict between parents' rights and children's needs if only predictive validity studies could be done. While alienation theorists argue that alienation causes harm to children (Bernet 2010) and critics assert the lack of well-designed scientific studies that assess such harm (Saini et al. 2012, 2016), and while harm from all types of abuse is well-established, the issue for experts making parenting plan recommendations is not harm *per se*, but whether there is any expert knowledge that could justify deciding which harms are more important. There is not. Decisions about whether it would be better to move quickly toward reunification at the risk of re-traumatization, or better to delay reunification indefinitely at the risk of losing the relationship with the rejected parent, are not scientific decisions. They are moral decisions.

They are based on choices about what is more or less important. It is a myth to hold out science as a moral arbiter, as comforting as that myth might be.

Experts may be able to contribute knowledge that could help judges make such choices. Depending on their discipline-specific education and training, they might have the expertise to advise the court as to which causes of parent rejection they deem to be at play. They might have the expertise to recommend the types of therapeutic interventions needed for the children, the abusers, and the families. They might have the expertise to advise courts as to the therapeutic benchmarks that would indicate the children's, the abusers', and the families' readiness for reunification therapy. However, decisions about whether to count on therapy to repair abusive parent-child relationships and whether a family's resources should be expended in this way are decisions that are based on values and law, not science. Such decisions are beyond the expertise of mental health professionals (Melton, et al. 2007, Myers 1992).

The MAP does not guide expert opinions about whether judges should give harm caused by child sexual abuse, psychological maltreatment, or adverse parenting greater or lesser weight than harm caused by parental alienation. It does not guide expert opinions about whether judges should give parents' constitutional rights or children's psychological needs greater or lesser weight. These are decisions about which science cannot speak. They are the sole prerogative of the family court.

Assessing child sexual abuse with the MAP: Step 1

History of child sexual abuse assessment

Child sexual abuse assessment is based in part on assessing the quality of children's statements alleging sexual abuse. Child sexual abuse assessment is the first step in the MAP because knowledge about the factors that affect the quality of children's sexual abuse statements is the largest body of scientifically validated knowledge related to assessing the reliability of children's testimony. Official forensic interviewing protocols rely on techniques that are based on that undisputed body of knowledge (American Prosecutors Research Institute 2003; Hershkowitz, Lamb, and Katz 2014; Lamb, Orbach, Hershkowitz, Esplin, and Horowitz 2007; Lyon 2005).

Research findings that inform child sexual abuse assessment

Scientifically validated research on the factors that influence the quality of children's sexual abuse statements comes from studies of children's memory, language, suggestibility, truthfulness, statement characteristics, trauma, abuse disclosure, sexual knowledge, and sexual behavior. This research shows that, while there are no characteristics of child sexual abuse allegations that are *invariably* associated with known sexual abuse (Brilleslijper-Kater, Friedrich; and Corwin 2004; Corwin 1995; Everson and Faller 2012; Friedrich 2005), there are characteristics of children's sexual abuse statements, which, in the context of the totality of case-specific evidence, are more likely to be associated with actual sexual abuse (Ackerman, Kane; Gould, and Dale 2015; Brown, Scheflin; and Hammond 1998 McNally 2005).

In brief review, high-quality statements tend to be informative, containing who/what/where/when/why details. Those statements tend to have details that identify specific events. The statements tend to have language reflecting a child's point of view and exhibit precocious sexual knowledge that cannot be explained by exposure to non-abusive sexually informative experiences (e.g., inadvertently witnessing a sex act; media exposure). While high-quality statements tend to be organized logically, this can be deceptive. Deficits in logical organization could reflect factors unrelated to the veracity of the child's sexual abuse statements such as lower intelligence, limited language development, and less familiarity with adult-child discussions of children's experiences.

Generalizing children's sexual abuse statement characteristics to other types of child abuse

There is nothing about most of the characteristics of children's sexual abuse statements that would conceptually be expected to be specific to sexual abuse statements. Some logical exceptions would be the presence of sexually precocious knowledge and the use of child language to describe sexual experiences that the child doesn't understand and lacks the language to describe. These factors would be specific to sexual abuse. However, the other factors which characterize reliable child sexual statements would be likely to apply to statements about other kinds of parent-perpetrated abuse and/or adverse parenting. The MAP therefore proposes that the factors which contribute to the general quality of children's sexual abuse statements could be generalized to their statements about psychological maltreatment, adverse parenting, and parental alienation.

Assessing psychological maltreatment with the MAP: Step 2

Research findings that inform psychological maltreatment assessment

The psychological maltreatment assessment factors in the MAP are taken from the *APSAC Practice Guidelines* (2019) which define maltreatment in terms of factors related to the maltreating parent. While assessment methods may involve parents and children (Wheeler 2018), defining psychological maltreatment in terms of parent factors rather than child factors increases the legal system's ability to protect children because it does not make verification dependent on symptoms that children might or might not manifest at the point of assessment (Hart, Brassard, Binggeli, and Davidson 2002).

The psychological maltreatment factors are taken from a broad body of scientifically validated research related to children's psychological needs and the parenting practices that meet or thwart them. These research areas include human needs theory, which is central, as well as attachment theory, psychosocial stage theory, interpersonal acceptance-rejection theory, learned helplessness theory, and others (Brassard, Hart, Baker, and Chiel 2019; Hart, Brassard, Bingelli, and Davidson 2002; Hart, Brassard, Davidson et al. 2011). Parenting practices that are deficient in these areas thwart children's needs for a sense of safety, love, belonging, trust, security, acceptance, self-esteem, and agency. These harms affect the foundation of children's developing personalities, which is why the damage caused by psychological maltreatment is severe.

Deciding when to assess psychological maltreatment

Psychological maltreatment is the psychological context in which abused children live. It might exist on its own but also might accompany other types of abuse. Child physical abuse would always be associated with psychological maltreatment. While this relationship is included in the MAP, the factors associated with assessing child physical abuse are not included because they are medical not psychological factors.

Child custody evaluators should assess psychological maltreatment whenever it or any other type of child abuse or adverse parenting is alleged. However, they should not limit themselves to parents' allegations of psychological maltreatment. Parents may not be aware that many of the behaviors defining psychological maltreatment are relevant to the issues they are litigating. Further, children raised in an atmosphere of psychological maltreatment may not understand that they should tell evaluators about these experiences. Being treated in psychologically maltreating ways might feel normal to them, minimizing their disclosures. Also, they might blame themselves and therefore not realize that they should tell someone about their parent's actions. Evaluators should assess this form of child abuse whenever they obtain evidence that suggests to them that psychological maltreatment may be involved.

Assess adverse parenting with the MAP: Step 3

Research findings that inform assessment of adverse parenting

To provide a comprehensive and thorough guide to assessing adverse parenting, the MAP coordinates two relevant but independent research areas that have hitherto been siloed: divorce research (Ackerman et al. 2015; Kuehnle and Drozd 2012) and 60 years of research on parenting competency reviewed in the Social Policy Report of the Society for Research on Child Development/SRCD (Teti, Cole, Cabrera, Goodman, and McLoyd 2017).

Assessment of adverse parenting is the area where the Decision Trees protocol (Drozd et al. 2013) broadens its methodological focus on sources of evidence to include substantive psychological factors that should be assessed in the various sources of evidence. It labels adverse parenting "parenting problems," and identifies parenting that is alienating, mis-attuned, too lax or too rigid, self-centered, intrusive, and enmeshed. The SRCD Policy Report (Teti et al. 2017) uses the label "competent parenting," identifying parenting that is protective, nurturing, appropriately controlling, developmentally informed, mindful, culturally aware, and capable at coparenting. Failures in these areas identify incompetent parenting.

The SRCD Policy Report (Teti et al. 2017) focuses on parents whose risk of incompetent parenting is largely associated with poverty. Many have been involved in child protection proceedings, not child custody proceedings. Custody litigating parents tend to be more affluent, better educated, have higher social status and less history with child protection agencies than parents involved in child protection proceedings (Saini, Black, Godbout, and Deljava 2019). Nevertheless, the parenting competency variables that have been empirically validated for parents involved in child protection proceedings are consistent with general theories of child development and largely overlap with parenting problems identified in divorce research, suggesting that several factors relating to parenting quality apply across social-economic lines (Pruett, Cowan, Cowan, Pradhan, Robins, and Pruett 2016).

The label "adverse parenting" is intended to encompass the parenting failures identified in both the divorce and parent competency research. The label also relates the concept of severe deficiencies in the quality of parent-child relationships to the concept of adverse childhood experiences (ACEs; Felitti et al. 1998). ACEs have been defined in terms of child abuse, domestic violence, substance abuse, serious mental illness or suicidality, and incarceration and have been shown to have serious and long-term medical consequences. ACEs have not been defined to include parenting quality. The use of the same term in the MAP is not intended to imply that the medical outcomes of the ACEs are likely to occur in response to adverse parenting, though this is an empirical question worth exploring, but to call attention to the severity of the parenting deficits identified in the divorce and parent competency literatures.

Adverse parenting practices identified by both divorce and parenting competency research

Protective parenting

All authors in the divorce and parenting competency literatures agree that children's safety is essential. Many different parenting behaviors other than abuse can threaten children's safety (e.g., letting children ride bikes without a helmet; not monitoring alcohol at teens' parties; failure to get children vaccinated). The MAP references threats to safety that do not come from abuse with the term "unprotective."

Developmentally responsive parenting

Authors contributing to both the divorce and parenting competency literatures are concerned about relationships between children's development and parenting. The divorce research recognizes the importance of children's developmental needs in relation to specific issues that are raised in custody litigation (e.g., overnights and relocation for young children, Ackerman et al. 2015; impact of children's stages on family alliances, Drozd et al. 2013). The parent competency literature focuses on parents' ignorance of children's developmental abilities. Ignorance is more likely to be a central problem for poor parents than for custody litigants because poor parents are likely to be less educated about child development (e.g., inappropriate achievement expectations for different aged children; Teti et al. 2017). The MAP uses the label "developmentally uninformed" to refer to general and specific deficits in parents' developmental knowledge.

Culturally responsive parenting

Both the parenting competency (Teti et al. 2017) and the divorce (Bhatia and Saini 2016) literatures address cultural issues, largely focusing on immigrant parents whose adjustment to U.S. cultural norms might cause parenting problems. Such problems could be caused by parents' lack of information about U.S. cultural norms or by their moral, religious, or cultural opposition to those norms even if they know what they are. Lack of information (e.g., about the harmful effects of spanking) might be a greater problem for less educated immigrant parents involved in the child welfare system, which are the types of parents largely studied in parenting competency research. Opposition to cultural norms might be more of a problem for custody litigants, which are the types of parents largely studied in divorce research. While custody litigating parents often have higher levels of education and/or professional accomplishment that provide information about cultural norms, and they might comply with them in their work lives, they might nevertheless oppose them as parents (e.g., objecting to their daughters' attendance at "away" games for sports teams). The MAP uses the label "culturally unresponsive" to refer to lack of information about cultural norms and opposition to them.

Parenting quality

Divorce studies (Drozd et al. 2013 Pruett, Cowan, Cowan, Pradhan, Robins, and Pruett 2016) and parenting competency studies (Teti et al. 2013) both address the quality of children's relationships with their parents. The two research areas overlap nearly completely.

The concept of mis-attuned parenting in the divorce literature overlaps with the concept of parenting that is not nurturing in the parent competency literature. These two concepts refer to somewhat different aspects of parental sensitivity. Parents could be attuned to a child's needs but still fail to nurture them (e.g., depressed or overworked parents who feel guilty about neglecting their children but are unable to meet their needs for food, clothing, and supervision). The MAP refers to such problematic parenting with the hybrid term "not nurturing/attuned" to capture both aspects of parental insensitivity.

The concept of too lax or too rigid parenting in the divorce literature overlaps with the concept of parenting that is inappropriately controlling in the parent competency literature.

The MAP refers to both parenting problems with the broader term "not appropriately controlling" (Pruett et al. 2016). Parents who are neither too lax nor too rigid could nevertheless fail to control their children appropriately. They could use harsh disciplinary methods that are neither too lax nor too rigid by their cultural standards (e.g., spanking for behavior that deserves punishment). Similarly, they could fail to supervise appropriately for reasons that are also unrelated to being too lax or too rigid (e.g., inconsistent supervision due to pain or illness).

The concept of alienating parenting in the divorce literature overlaps with the concept of incompetent coparenting in the parenting competency literature. The MAP uses the term "uncooperative coparenting" (Pruett et al. 2016) to refer to both alienating and incompetent coparenting. That term captures most of the problems classified as incompetent coparenting, many classified as alienating, and some that are neither (e.g., lack of cooperation caused by differences in religious values).

Adverse parenting practices identified by divorce research only

Problematic parenting practices in the divorce literature that are not identified in the parenting competency literature consist of parenting practices that are self-centered, intrusive, and enmeshed (Drozd et al. 2013). Self-centered parenting is referenced in the MAP with the term "not child centered," which is synonymous. The terms "intrusive" and "enmeshed" are replaced by "not respecting the child's autonomy," which is a broader concept that could subsume both of these problematic parenting practices as sub-types. The MAP relabeled these terms to put them into the negative for consistency with the other adverse parenting terms.

Adverse parenting practices identified by parenting competence research only

Problematic parenting practices identified in the parenting competency literature that are not identified in the divorce literature are practices that are not mindful. "Mindfulness" refers to parents' awareness and regulation of their own emotions in response to their awareness of the children's emotions. In the MAP, this kind of parent-child emotional exchange would be included in the assessment of "nurturing/attuned" parenting. However, mindful parenting also includes parents' emotional self-awareness in the moment (Teti et al. 2017). Since this factor is not necessarily part of nurturing/attuned parenting, it is included in the MAP.

Need for longitudinal assessment of adverse parenting

Evaluators assessing adverse parenting should collect data about the quality of the parent-child relationship before, during, and, when relevant, after the divorce proceedings. They should not merely accept rejected parents' assertions that their prior relationship with the children was positive (e.g., Baker 2020). They should not assume that evidence of adverse parenting or good parenting during custody litigation reflects the parent's general parenting competency. It could reflect the impact of situational factors such as the divorce crisis, which could intensify parenting deficits, or attempts at positive impression management, which could conceal those deficits to gain a litigation advantage.

Assessing parental alienation with the MAP: Step 4

Alienation factors are proposed but not scientifically validated

Unlike child sexual abuse, psychological maltreatment, and adverse parenting factors, alienation factors are only "proposed" factors, because, despite vociferous claims to the contrary (Bernet 2010), they have not been empirically validated by any well-designed scientific study (Saini et al. 2012, 2016). There is no scientific evidence that the proposed factors can validly identify alienated children and distinguish them from abused children. The evidence cited to support them is largely anecdotal (Saini et al. 2016). Efforts to identify different degrees of alienation (Darnall 2013, Warshak 2013, Worenklien 2013) might be perceived as making its identification more precise. However, such efforts just extend the basic scientific error of relying on anecdotal evidence to define a concept. Anecdotes are intrinsically case-specific. They are examples. However, science requires general rules, known as "operational definitions," to define a concept, not examples. Operational definitions consist of objectively observable behaviors that are found across examples. When anecdotes define a concept, subjective judgment must be used to decide whether a new example is similar enough to the defining example to be considered an instance of the concept.

Subjective judgment is not the only problem with anecdotal evidence. Even if the similarity among examples is clear, the lack of scientific validation for the proposed alienation factors means that the behaviors in the examples might or might not indicate the alienation concept. While the examples might be like each other, alienation might not be identified by any of them. This is especially problematic because the interpretation of the proposed alienation factors is ambiguous and could just as logically be interpreted as abuse factors, which is why recognizing the inferential nature of alienation identifications is so important (Milchman 2019).

Factors proposed to identify alienating parents do not differentiate them from protective parents

In the MAP, parents' proposed alienating behaviors (e.g., Clawar and Rivlin 2013) are grouped into three overarching factors: Baseless Allegations, Contact Interference, and Negative Statements ("Bad Mouthing"). Negative statements include splitting, denigrating, and exaggerating. All these factors could just as logically be related to protective parenting in response to abuse allegations as they could to alienation. The reliability of the interpretation depends on the relationship between the parents' behavior and other case-specific facts. Reliability cannot be determined based on the behavior in isolation, which is why experts reject checklists to identify alienation (Warshak 2020).

Baseless allegations

Parents' refusal to accept official decisions that the abuse allegations are false does not prove them to be baseless. The refusal must be interpreted in relation to the quality of the evidence upon which the official decisions were based. Parents who live with their children, who are the children's confidants, and who communicated the children's allegations to legal authorities might be neglectful if the decisions were based on evidence that left residual suspicions and they did not continue to make every effort to protect their children. Failure to act on residual suspicions might be more indicative of wishful thinking than of cooperative parenting.

Contact interference

Parents' interference with contact cannot be interpreted as unjustified on the face of it. It must be assessed in relation to the type of interference in which the parents engage. Behaviors that obstruct contact with an alleged abuser but are arguably help-seeking – e.g., calling child protective services repeatedly, telling school staff not to permit after school pick-ups, filing motions – must be differentiated from behaviors that obstruct contact but cannot reasonably be interpreted as help-seeking – e.g., repeatedly scheduling preferred activities when visitation is scheduled, insisting on the rejected parent's incompetence at routine tasks, making repeated contact with the children during supervised visitation. While obstructing contact in ways that are not relevant to protection could indicate alienation, failure to obstruct contact by seeking help from appropriate sources could indicate neglectful parenting.

Bad mouthing

Parents' negative statements about the other parents cannot be assumed to be unwarranted or harmful to the children. The negative statements must be assessed in relation to their content and the persons to whom they are made. Negative statements that are limited to the abuse allegations and are made to appropriate persons (e.g., caseworkers, lawyers) would be protective parenting and likely to be perceived as such by the children, making them feel safer. Making such statements privately to confidants to get emotional support might be necessary. None of this would indicate denigration, exaggeration, devaluation, or splitting. However, if the negative statements were general indiscriminate character assassinations, not limited to abuse allegations, then there would be better grounds to suspect alienation.

Decision-makers who devalue or dismiss parental concern when abuse has not been affirmatively disproven put protective parents in an impossible position. Fear of being perceived as alienating forces protective parents to choose between temporarily failing to protect their children by permitting visitation, or permanently failing to protect them by risking loss of custody (Meier 2019). To avoid such error, decision makers must understand that the lack of scientific validity for the proposed parent alienation factors requires extreme caution in interpreting questionable abuse allegations, contact interference, and negative statements about alleged abusers as evidence of alienation.

Factors proposed to identify alienated children do not differentiate them from abused children

The MAP itemizes the eight factors proposed to identify alienated children (Gardner 1986, Lorandos 2013). Two are necessary; the other six are supportive (Lorandos 2013). The interpretation of all of them is ambiguous. Each one could just as logically be interpreted as abuse-related rather than as alienation-related. The risk of misinterpretation increases when the children's behavior is understood in terms of factors related to normal child development, child psychology, and family dynamics rather than from a trauma-informed perspective. In the context of alienation vs. abuse cases, the normal psychological framework explains children's disturbed behaviors as irrational responses to external manipulation and blames the allegedly alienating parent. In contrast, the trauma-informed perspective explains children's disturbed behaviors as rational adaptations to their perception of threat and blames perceived or actual abuse as the source of the threat. The reliability of the interpretation increases when children's perception of threat is not assumed to be irrational.

False allegations

Alienation thinking relies heavily on suggestibility research to give plausibility to their argument that children, especially young ones, can be led by their favored parents to make false sexual abuse allegations (Barden 2013, Campbell 2013, Lorandos 2013). However, the research they cite to support this argument largely consists of experimental studies in which the suggestions are markedly different from abuse suggestions. They range from neutral to mildly upsetting but are never traumatic. This research has been strongly criticized on the grounds that getting children to accept false information about trivial details that are inconsequential for their lives has little bearing on getting them to accept suggestions that they have been sexually assaulted by a loved parent (Eisen, Quas, and Goodman 2002, Eisen, Goodman, Quin, Davis, and Crayton 2007, Malloy and Quas 2009).

   Pipe et al.'s (2007) research on the sexual abuse disclosure process provides some empirical data that can be brought to bear on the suggestibility argument. They investigated the proportion of children who made sexual abuse disclosures to immediate family or other people and then did or did not follow up with disclosures to official investigators. If disclosure to immediate family is interpreted as a proxy for exposure to abuse suggestions, and age is interpreted as a proxy for suggestibility, then these findings are relevant to the question of whether children's suggestibility for experimental events is similar to their suggestibility for abuse events. Of course, caution is needed in interpreting data that is proxy and not a direct measure of the phenomenon of interest. Nevertheless, Pipe et al.'s (2007) findings are intriguing as a first step toward investigating suggestibility for real-world sexual abuse.

It would be logical to interpret a higher rate of disclosure in official interviews following disclosures to immediate family as indicating that children might have accepted suggestions made by immediate family. Some of Pipe et al.'s (2007) findings could support this interpretation. She and her colleagues found that young children (4–8 years old) who first disclosed to an immediate family member were more likely to follow through by making an allegation in their official interview (68%) than they were if they disclosed either to a family member who was not immediate family (20–40%) or to other people who were not family members (17–58%) (89, T. 5.5). However, other findings in this study cast doubt on this interpretation.

If suggestibility by immediate family were responsible for children's allegations to official interviewers, then the youngest children – who have consistently been found to be more suggestible than older ones in experimental studies – should have made more allegations in their follow-up interviews than did the older children. However, Pipe et al. (2007) did not find age differences in the rate of allegations made in follow-up interviews. In all age groups (4–5 years, 6–8 years, 9–13 years), the same proportion of children who first disclosed to immediate family members also disclosed to official interviewers (68%) (89, T. 5.5). The finding that younger and purportedly more suggestible children did not make any more abuse disclosures in follow-up interviews than did older and purportedly less suggestible children raises doubt that suggestions made by immediate family members were responsible for the children's subsequent abuse disclosures.

The fact that approximately 2/3 of the children disclosed to immediate family and to official interviewers means that 1/3 did not, a proportion that is large enough to raise the possibility that forces outside the family might inhibit many children from making sexual abuse disclosures. Children who did not disclose in follow-up interviews or did not do so with sufficient information to meet legal standards (Lindblad 2007, Lyon 2007), might have been worried that the interviewers would not be receptive, a phenomenon observed even in experimental research where the questions were about neutral events and the answers inconsequential for the children (Brubacher, Timms, Powell, and Bearman 2019).

Evaluators who have a receptive demeanor could encourage the children to make more complete disclosures and they should not suppress children's attempts to communicate freely if they indicate a willingness to do. The children might speak more freely to receptive evaluators as a last-ditch attempt to get help in a world where they are being ignored or dismissed or misperceived. Evaluators should question the children using approved techniques (APSAC 2003, Hershkowitz et al. 2014, Lyon 2005) to elicit as much information as possible. If children's statements to evaluators differ from those, they made to family members or previous interviewers, then evaluators should question the children to discover the reasons for the differences. Evaluators should look for differences in the amount of information communicated and for differences in the details communicated. Children's more complete statements should be assessed to see whether they have at least some of the characteristics of the statements itemized in Step 1 of the MAP.

If the children's statements to the evaluator merely repeat statements made previously, evaluators should explore the reason the children are making those same statements to *them*. They should consider whether the children are merely reciting a "script" or whether they have different expectations of the evaluators than of previous interviewers. They should also assess the consistency in the statements, looking not for differences in details, which would be expected for memories recalled at different times and to different people, but for actual contradictions. If their statements contain information not previously reported, evaluators should probe them fully, document them completely, and comply with their states' requirements for mandated reporters. While empirical data is very limited, experimental studies of suggestibility do not appear to provide a reliable basis for arguing that full descriptions of actual abusive events could be suggested. The very limited evidence that exists, which is relevant for suggestibility of actual sexual abuse, appears to suggest the opposite.

Frivolous reasons

Alienation thinking characterizes children's reasons for contact refusal as frivolous when the reasons appear trivial or illogical to an adult and the resistance appears to be disproportionate to the stated reasons. In some cases, children might give seemingly frivolous reasons because they do not have good reasons. In other cases, the seemingly frivolous reasons might be defensive disclosures to elicit help without risking the consequences of direct and full disclosures against allegedly abusive biological parents (Pipe et al. 2007).

Evaluators should assess seemingly frivolous reasons by relating them to the factual record and to the children's interview behavior when questioning them about their contact refusal. They should investigate the factual record to see if there is any evidence that would affirmatively disconfirm abuse. They should attempt to detect defensiveness by looking for such interview behaviors as refusal to answer abuse-specific questions but not neutral ones; changes in affect, behavior, and demeanor in response to abuse-specific questions but not neutral ones; and statements that indicate denial, minimization, or rationalization. When there is no disproof of abuse and the child appears defensive, evaluators should probe the defensive behavior with non-leading questions that communicate receptivity to further communication. Evaluators should not equate the absence of evidence with the absence of abuse and they should not dismiss residual suspicions of abuse when abuse was not substantiated or proven.

Campaigning

Alienation thinking asserts that children who repeatedly allege abuse to multiple people are conducting campaigns of vilification against their innocent parents. In some cases, this might be true. However, in others, children's repeated abuse allegations might represent desperate attempts to find someone who will believe them. They could be reaching out for help to people they reasonably expect would be able to protect them (e.g., family members, friends and their parents, neighbors, teachers, school staff, therapists). They might be particularly determined to find support if they are aware that they, or their protective parents, are not believed. Evaluators should identify the people the children are telling, find out what they are saying, when they said it, and what they expected or wanted to happen. Evaluators should differentiate between indiscriminate "bad mouthing" and reasonable help-seeking.

Lacking ambivalence

While some alienation proponents recognize the pathology of children's bonds to abusive parents (Baker and Schneiderman 2015), alienation thinking asserts that all children, even abused ones, feel ambivalence and long for their abusive parents (Bernet and Baker 2013). This assertion is based largely on children in child protection cases. Alienation thinking gives little if any recognition to the possibility that the differences between the custody context and the child welfare context might explain why children in custody cases fail to express ambivalence toward their abusers whereas children in foster care do express ambivalence.

In foster care cases, where children may either remain in the care of their abusers or be removed from both parents by the state, the love they proclaim for their abusers may be rationalizations made to convince themselves that they are safe. It might be intended to convince authorities that they can return home. It might express their wish that the abuse will not happen again. In contrast, in custody cases, children who remain in the care of loving protective parents and are only removed from abusive parents might not have to convince themselves that they love and need their abusers. Thus, they might genuinely not feel ambivalent, at least not close in time to when the separation from the abusers first occurs. They might be too angry to be ambivalent. They might only feel relief. The differences between foster care and custody cases are too great to permit ready generalizations from the one to the other. Children in foster care want to go home. Children in custody cases are home. They don't want to leave. The difference in contexts makes the children's reactions incomparable.

Evaluators in custody cases should not accept abusers' claims that their prior relationships with their children were good and that the children's lack of ambivalence is a clear indication of alienation. They should seek external information about the quality of the children's prior relationships with the alleged abusers in areas that did not involve the alleged abuse. They should probe children's thinking to see whether it is generally realistic, whether it generally recognizes good and bad feelings, and whether it relates bad feelings to rational causes. Evaluators should not assume that a lack of ambivalence indicates alienation.

Allying with preferred parents

Alienation thinking asserts that children's alliances with preferred parents indicate alienation, especially if the children also exaggerate or fabricate bad experiences with their rejected parents. While this might be true in some cases, in cases where abuse is alleged, the alliances might serve safety needs. Children might ally with a preferred parent and exaggerate or fabricate the failings of the rejected parent to enhance the credibility of protective parents, especially if they are aware that their abuse allegations are not believed. They might be trying to curry favor with the preferred parents to elicit their support if they fear that support is questionable, a dynamic sometimes observed when the preferred parents are victims of domestic violence whose fear of the abuser caused them to fail to protect the children in the past. They might ally with preferred parents and exaggerate or fabricate bad experiences with rejected parents to get revenge, to feel powerful, or for other abuse-related reasons unrelated to any influence by the preferred parents.

Evaluators should assess whether the children are aware of past and current threats to the preferred parents' custody and how that awareness is affecting their alliances. They should seek external corroboration to assess whether children are reporting some abusive events accurately even if they are also exaggerating or fabricating others. Evaluators should probe children's feelings about their preferred parents, paying special attention to whether the children perceive those parents as weak. They should probe whether children are normally independent but have allied with a preferred parent under the threat of contact with their abusers. Evaluators should probe whether the rejected parents' behavior has contributed to the children's alliances with the other parents. Finally, they should probe whether the children's alliances are developmentally normal but misperceived by the rejected parent.

Parroting

Alienation thinking claims that children's accusations against their rejected parents parrot their allied parents' complaints when the two complaints are similar. In some cases, this might be true, but in others, it is possible that the allied parents are reporting the children's statements and not the other way around. Simply put, the parents might be the "parrots," not the children.

Evaluators should assess the timeline that accompanies the children's statements, paying particular attention to evidence indicating whether the children made the statement before the parents did. When specific terms match and the children's vocabulary seems adult-like (e.g., vulva, scrotum), evaluators should assess whether those terms are part of the children's general vocabulary. When the evidence suggests that the children are parroting, evaluators should probe the reasons why. They should pay special attention to whether the children believe they must support their favored parents to protect themselves or whether the favored parents need the children to be extensions of themselves. If such pathological enmeshment is involved, evaluators should assess whether the preferred parents also need the children to reject the other parents, in which case alienation might be suspected (Fidler, Ward, and Deutsch 2017).

Borrowing scenarios

Alienation thinking claims that children's accusations against their rejected parents are borrowed scenarios when the two accusations are similar. In some cases, this might be true, but in others, the parents and children may have had similar experiences (e.g., of financial deprivations not experienced before the marital breakup). When children describe scenarios that are similar to those described by their preferred parents, evaluators should assess whether the children provide specific details of their own experiences. The similarities might be caused by the rejected parents' similar behaviors toward the children and the preferred parents and not by alienation.

Spreading animosity

Alienation thinking claims that children's antagonism toward their extended family indicates alienation. However, children might be legitimately angry at extended family for several reasons. The family may be siding with the abusers. They may be pressuring the children to deny the abuse. They may be accusing the children of lying. They might be invalidating the children by praising the alleged abuser. Evaluators should assess the reasons for the child's spread of animosity and not assume it is irrational and manipulated by the preferred parent.

Conclusion

The risk of discrediting children's true abuse allegations appears to be particularly high in cases where parental alienation allegations are asserted to rebut abuse allegations. These are precisely the kinds of cases that child protective services are least equipped to handle and the family court system most at risk of disbelieving. As a result, a protocol is needed that specifies and coordinates the particular evidence required to assess each type of child abuse specifically as well as parental alienation.

The MAP serves this purpose. It itemizes the specific evidence needed to assess sexual abuse, psychological maltreatment, adverse parenting, and parental alienation, coordinating them by putting them into a sequence so that abuse and adverse parenting are ruled out before alienation can be identified as the primary cause of parent rejection. The MAP guides evaluators to collect evidence related to abuse and alienation allegations that has not been collected by prior investigations or has been collected but not relied upon. Further, by focusing on evidence related to multiple possible causes of parent rejection, the MAP guides evaluators to collect evidence that *both confirms and disconfirms* each possible cause. The purpose is to enhance evaluators' ability to discriminate between abused or badly parented children, on the one hand, and alienated children, on the other. The goal is to inform the court as to whether there is evidence not previously considered or insufficiently considered that would warrant giving specific allegations serious concern or more serious concern.

The value of the MAP is not limited to guiding experts' evaluations and the testimony based on them. It also can be used to guide attorneys to identify the evidence evaluators should have collected and to cross examine them more precisely. Further, directly by itemizing specific evidence related to each possible cause, and indirectly in response to more effective cross-examination, the MAP also guides judges to be more aware of limitations in the foundations of opinions that are offered by experts and *Guardians Ad Litem*.

The MAP protocol should *not* be interpreted as advising evaluators to opine on the issue of whether the children's specific allegations (who/what/when/where/why) are or are not true. Those opinions are opinions about the credibility of the children, which are not allowed in the U.S. on the grounds that mental health professionals have no more expertise in detecting truthfulness than do lay people (Melton et al. 2007, Myers 1992). Rather, the MAP protocol supports expert opinions about whether specific evidence is more consistent with one of the four particular causes and less consistent with the other three causes. As a result, it could help reduce the risk of false negatives and false positives by providing courts with a stronger evidentiary foundation for each particular cause than they would otherwise have. The MAP's focus on descriptive testimony about psychological evidence and the interpretation of that evidence leaves decisions about whether the allegations are true or not to judges' discretion. Testimony that is carefully crafted to avoid credibility judgments, while presenting evidence that helps judges make those judgments, is likely to enhance judicial perceptions that the mental health testimony as a whole in an instant case is well-grounded and therefore reliable, enhancing experts' ability to protect children.

References

Ackerman, Mark J., Andrew Kane, Jonathan Gould, and Milfred Dale. *Psychological Experts in Divorce Actions, Sixth Edition*. New York: Wolters Kluwer, 2015.

American Prosecutors Research Institute. *Finding Words: Half a Nation by 2010: Interviewing Children and Preparing for Court*. National District Attorneys Association, 2003. http://www.daa.org/contactus.html also available as the *RATAC Child Forensic Interview* [Rapport, Anatomy, Touch, Abuse, Closure] from Cornerhouse Interagency Child Abuse Evaluation and Training Center: 1502 10th Ave. So. Minneapolis, MN 55404-4510.

American Professional Society on the Abuse of Children/APSAC. *APSAC Practice Guidelines (2019): The Investigation and Determination of Suspected Psychological Maltreatment of Children and Adolescents*. Columbus, OH: Author, 2019.

Baker, Amy J. L. "Reliability and Validity of the Four-factor Model of Parental Alienation". *Journal of Family Therapy* 42, 2020: 100–118.

Baker, Amy J. L., and Mel Schneiderman. *Bonded to the Abuser: How Victims Make Sense of Childhood Abuse*. New York: Rowman & Littlefield, 2015.

Barden, Richard C. "Protecting the Integrity of the Family Law System: Multidisciplinary Processes and Family Law Reform". In *Parental Alienation: The Handbook for Mental Health and Legal Professionals*, edited by Demosthenes Lorandos, William Bernet, and Richard Sauber (263–288). Springfield, IL: Charles C. Thomas, 2013.

Bernet, William. *Parental Alienation, DSM-5, and ICD-11*. Springfield, IL: Charles C. Thomas, 2010.

Bernet, William, and Bradley Freeman. "The Psychosocial Assessment of Contact Refusal". In *Parental Alienation: The Handbook for Mental Health and Legal Professionals*, edited by Demosthenes Lorandos, William Bernet, and Richard Sauber (47–73). Springfield, IL: Charles C. Thomas, 2013.

Bhatia, Gitu, and Michael Saini. "Cultural Dynamics of Divorce and Parenting". In *Parenting Evaluations, Second Edition: Applied Research for the Family Court*, edited by Leslie Drozd, Michael Saini, and Nancy Olesen (463–487). New York: Oxford University Press, 2016.

Brassard, Marla, Stuart Hart, Amy Baker, and Zoe Chiel. *The APSAC Psychological Maltreatment Monograph* [Digital Document]. Columbus, OH: APSAC, 2019. Available at APSAC.org, on the Home Page/Store to non-members.

Briere, John, and Joseph Spinazzola, J. (2009). "Assessment of the Sequelae of Complex Trauma: Evidence-based Measures". In *Treating Complex Traumatic Stress Disorders: An Evidence-based Guide*, edited by Christine Courtois and Julian Ford (104–123). New York: Guilford Press, 2009.

Brilleslijper-Kater, Sonja, William Friedrich, and David Corwin. "Sexual Knowledge and Emotional Reaction as Indicators of Sexual Abuse in Young Children: Theory and Research Challenges". *Child Abuse & Neglect* 28(10), 2004: 1007–1017.

Brown, Daniel, Alan Scheflin, and D. Corydon Hammond. *Memory, Trauma , and the Law*. New York: W.W. Norton, 1998.

Brubacher, Sonja P., Lydia Timms, Martine Powell, and Madeleine Bearman. "'She Wanted to Know the Full Story': Children's Perceptions of Open Versus Closed Questions". *Child Maltreatment* 24(2), 2019: 222–231.

Campbell, Terence W. "Sexual Abuse Allégations in the Context of Custody and Visitation Disputes". In *Parental Alienation: The Handbook for Mental Health and Legal Professionals*, edited by Demosthenes Lorandos, William Bernet, and Richard Sauber (163–189). Springfield, IL: Charles C. Thomas, 2013.

Clawar, Stanley, and Brynne Rivlin. *Children Held Hostage: Identifying Brainwashed Children, Presenting a Case, and Crafting Solutions, Second Edition.* Chicago, IL: American Bar Association, 2013.

Corwin, David. "Child Sexual Abuse Assessment and Professional Ethics: Commentary on Controversies, Limits and When to Just Say No". *Journal of Child Sexual Abuse* 4(4), 1995: 115–122.

Darnall, Douglas. "Mild Cases of Parental Alienation". In *Parental Alienation: The Handbook for Mental Health and Legal Professionals*, edited by Demosthenes Lorandos, William Bernet, and Richard Sauber (74–96). Springfield, IL: Charles C. Thomas, 2013.

Drozd, Leslie, Nancy Olesen, and Michael Saini. *Parenting Plan and Child Custody Evaluations: Using Decision Trees to Increase Evaluator Competence and Avoid Preventable Errors.* Sarasota, FL: Professional Resource Press, 2013.

Eisen, Mitchell, Gail Goodman, Jianjian Qin, Suzanne Davis, and John Crayton. "Maltreated Children's Memory: Accuracy, Suggestibility and Psychopathology". *Developmental Psychology* 43(6), 2007: 1275–1294. doi:10/1037/0012–1649.43.6.1275.

Eisen, Mitchell, Jodi Quas, and Gail Goodman. *Memory and Suggestibility in the Forensic Interview.* Mahwah, NJ: Lawrence Erlbaum, 2002.

Everson, Mark, and Kathleen Faller. "Base Rates, Multiple Indicators and Comprehensive Forensic Evaluations: Why Sexualized Behavior Still Counts in Assessments of Child Sexual Abuse Allegations". *Journal of Child Sexual Abuse* 21, 2012: 45–71.

Felitti, Vincent, Robert Anda, Dale Nordenberg, David Williamson, Alison Spitz, Valerie Edwards, et al. "Relationship of Childhood Abuse and Household Dysfunction to Many of the Leading Causes of Death in Adults: The Adverse Childhood Experiences (ACE) Study". *American Journal of Preventive Medicine* 14(4), 1998: 245–258.

Fidler, Barbara, and Peggie Ward. "Clinical Decision-making in Parent-child Contact Problem Cases: Tailoring the Intervention to the Family's Needs". In *Overcoming Parent-child Contact Problems: Family-based Interventions for Resistance, Rejection, and Alienation*, edited by Abigail Judge and Robin Deutsch (13–62). New York: Oxford University Press, 2017.

Fidler, Barbara, Peggie Ward, and Robin Deutsch. "Translating the *Overcoming Barriers* Approach to Outpatient Settings". In *Overcoming Parent–child Contact Problems,* edited by Abigail Judge and Robin Deutsch (13–62). New York: Oxford University Press, 2017.

Ford, Julian, David Albert, and Josephine Hawke. "Prevention and Treatment Interventions for Traumatized Children: Restoring Children's Capacities for Self-regulation". In *Treating Traumatized Children: Risk, Resilience and Recovery,* edited by Danny Brom, Ruth Pat-Horenczyk, and Julian Ford (195–209). New York: Routledge, 2009.

Ford, Julian, and Marylene Cloitre. "Best Practices in Psychotherapy for Children and Adolescents". In *Treating Complex Traumatic Stress Disorders: An Evidence-based Guide*, edited by Christine Courtois and Julian Ford (116–139). New York: Guilford Press, 2009.

Ford, Julian, and Christine Courtois. "Defining and Understanding Complex Trauma and Complex Traumatic Stress Disorders". In *Treating Complex Traumatic Stress Disorders: An Evidence-based Guide*, edited by Christine Courtois and Julian Ford (195–209). New York: Guilford Press, 2009.

Friedrich, William. "Correlates of Sexual Behavior in Young Children". In *Child Custody Litigation: Allegations of Child Sexual Abuse*, edited by Kathryn Kuehnle and Leslie Drozd (41–55). New York: Haworth Press, 2005.

Gardner, Richard. *Child Custody Litigation: A Guide for Parents and Mental Health Professionals*. Cresskill, NJ: Creative Therapeutics, 1986.

Hart, Stuart, Marla Brassard, Nelson Binggeli, and Howard Davidson. "Psychological Maltreatment". In *The APSAC Handbook on Child Maltreatment, Second Edition*, edited by John Myers, Lucy Berliner, John Briere, C. Terry Hendrix, Carole Jenny, and Theresa Reid (79–103). Thousand Oaks, CA: Sage Publications, 2002.

Hart, Stuart, Marla Brassard, Howard Davidson, Erin Rivelis, Vielka Diaz, and Nelson Binggeli. "Psychological Maltreatment". In *The APSAC Handbook on Child Maltreatment, Third Edition*, edited by John Myers (125–144) Thousand Oaks, CA: Sage Publications, 2011.

Hershkowitz, Irit, Michael Lamb, and Carmit Katz. "Allegation Rates in Forensic Child Abuse Investigations: Comparing the Revised and Standard NICHD Protocols". *Psychology, Public Policy, and Law* 20(3), 2014: 336–344.

James, Beverly. *Treating Traumatized Children: New Insights and Creative Interventions*. Lexington, MA: Lexington Books, 1989.

Johnston, Janet, and Matthew Sullivan. "Parental Alienation: In Search of Common Ground for a More Differentiated Theory". *Family Court Review* 58(2), 2020: 270–292.

Kuehnle, Kathryn, and Leslie Drozd. *Child Custody Litigation: Allegations of Child Sexual Abuse*. New York: Haworth Press, 2012.

Lamb, Michael, Yael Orbach, Irit Hershkowitz, Philip Esplin, and Dvora Horowitz. "A Structured Forensic Interview Protocol Improves the Quality and Informativeness of Investigative Interviews with Children: A Review of Research Using the NICHD [National Institute of Child Health and Development, U.S.] Investigative Interview Protocol". *Child Abuse & Neglect* 31, 2007: 1201–1231.

Lindblad, Frank. "Reflections on the Concept of Disclosure". In *Child Sexual Abuse: Disclosure, Delay, and Denial*, edited by Margaret-Ellen Pipe, Michael E. Lamb, Yel Orbach, and Ann-Christin Cederborg (291–301). New York: Routledge, Taylor & Francis Group, 2007.

London, Kamala, Maggie Bruck, Steven Ceci, and Daniel Shuman. "Disclosure of Child Sexual Abuse: A Review of the Contemporary Empirical Literature". In *Child Sexual Abuse: Disclosure, Delay, and Denial*, edited by Margaret-Ellen Pipe, Michael Lamb, Yael Orbach, and Ann-Christin Cederborg (11–39). New York: Routledge, 2007.

Lorandos, Demosthenes. "Legal Interventions in Cases of Parental Alienation". In *Parental Alienation: The Handbook for Mental Health and Legal Professionals*, edited by Demosthenes Lorandos, William Bernet, and Richard Sauber (232–262). Springfield, IL: Charles C. Thomas, 2013.

Lyon, Thomas D. *Ten Step Investigative Interview*. State of Michigan, Governor's Task Force on Child Abuse and Neglect and Department of Health and Human Services, 2005.

Lyon, Thomas D. "False Denials: Overcoming Methodological Biases in Abuse Disclosure Research". In *Child Sexual Abuse: Disclosure, Delay, and Denial*, edited by Margaret-Ellen Pipe, Michael Lamb, Yael Orbach, and Ann-Christin Cederborg (41–62). New York: Routledge, 2007.

Malloy, Lindsay C., and Jodi Quas, "Children's Suggestibility: Areas of Consensus and Controversy". In *The Evaluation of Child Sexual Abuse Allegations: A Comprehensive Guide to Assessment and Testimony*, edited by Kathryn. Kuehnle and Mary Connell (267–297). Hoboken, NJ: John Wiley & Sons, 2009.

McNally, Richard J. *Remembering Trauma*. Cambridge, MA: Belknap Press/Harvard University Press, 2005.

Meier, Joan S. "Child Custody Outcomes in Cases Involving Parental Alienation and Abuse Allegations". *GWU Law School Public Law Research Paper No. 2019–56; GWU Legal Studies Research Paper No. 2019–56*, 2019. https://ssrn.com/abstracte=3448062.

Melton, Gary B., John Petrila, Norman Poythress, and Christopher Slobogin. *Psychological Evaluations for the Courts: A Handbook for Mental Health Professionals and Lawyers, Third Edition*. New York: Guilford Press, 2007.

Milchman, Madelyn S. "Misogyny in NYS Custody Decisions with Parental Alienation Versus Child Sexual Abuse Allegations". *Journal of Child Custody* 14, 2017: 234–259.

Milchman, Madelyn S. "How Far Has Parental Alienation Research Progressed Towards Achieving Scientific Validity?" *Journal of Child Custody* 16(2), 2019: 115–139.

Milchman, Madelyn S. "Assessing Children's Contact Resistance or Refusal in Child Custody Evaluations: Differentiating Parental Alienation from Child Sexual Abuse, Psychological Maltreatment, and Bad Parenting". In *Handbook of Interpersonal Violence Across the Lifespan*, edited by Robert Geffner, Victor Vieth, Viola Vaughan-Eden, Alan Rosenbaum, L. Kevin Hamberger, and Jacquelyn White. A Publication of the National Partnership to End Interpersonal Violence across the Lifespan (NPEIV): Global Partners for Peace, in press.

Milchman, Madelyn S., Robert Geffner, and Joan Meier. "Rhetoric Replaces Evidence and Reasoning in Parental Alienation Literature and Advocacy: A Critique". *Family Court Review* 58(2), 2020a: 340–361.

Milchman, Madelyn S., Robert Geffner, and Joan Meier. "Putting Science and Reasoning Back into the 'Parental Alienation' Discussion: Reply to Bernet, Robb, Lorandos, and Garber". *Family Court Review* 58(2), 2020b: 375–385.

Myers, John E.B. *Legal Issues in Child Abuse and Neglect*. Newbury Park, CA: Sage, 1992.

Nielsen, Linda. "Shared Physical Custody: Summary of 40 Studies on Outcomes for Children". *Journal of Divorce & Remarriage* 55, 2014: 613–625.

Pipe, Margaret-Ellen, Yael Orbach, Michael Lamb, and Ann-Christin Cederborg. "Seeking Resolution in the Disclosure Wars: An Overview." In *Child Sexual Abuse: Disclosure, Delay, and Denial*, edited by Margaret-Ellen Pipe, Michael Lamb, Yael Orbach, and Ann-Christin Cederborg (1–10). New York: Routledge, 2007.

Pruett, Marsha K., Carolyn P. Cowan, Philip Cowan, Lisa Pradhan, Sarah Robins, and Kyle Pruett. "Supporting Father Involvement in the Context of Separation and Divorce". In *Parenting Evaluations: Applied Research for the Family Court, Second Edition*, edited by Leslie Drozd, Michael Saini, and Nancy Olesen (85–117). New York: Oxford University Press, 2016.

Saini, Michael, Tara Black, Barbara Fallon, and Alana Marshall. "Child Custody Disputes within the Context of Child Protection Investigations: Secondary Analysis of the Canadian Incident Study of Reported Child Abuse and Neglect". *Child Welfare* 92(1), 2013: 115–137.

Saini, Michael, Tara Black, Elisabeth Godbout, and Sevil Deljavan. "Feeling the Pressure to Take Sides: A Survey of Child Protection Workers' Experiences about Responding to Allegations of Child Maltreatment within the Context of Child Custody Disputes". *Children and Youth Services Review* 96, 2019: 127–133.

Saini, Michael, Janet Johnston, Barbara Fidler, and Nicholas Bala. "Empirical Studies of Alienation". In *Parenting Evaluations: Applied Research for the Family Court*, edited by Kathryn Kuehnle and Leslie Drozd (399–441). New York: Oxford University Press, 2012.

Saini, Michael, Janet Johnston, Barbara Fidler, and Nicholas Bala. "Empirical Studies of Alienation". In *Parenting Evaluations: Applied Research for the Family Court, Second Edition*, edited by Leslie Drozd, Michael Saini, and Nancy Olesen (374–430). New York: Oxford University Press, 2016.

Saunders, Daniel G., Kathleen Faller, and Richard Tolman. *Child Custody Evaluators' Beliefs about Domestic Abuse Allegations: Their Relationship to Evaluator Demographics, Background, Domestic Violence Knowledge and Custody-visitation Recommendations.* Washington, DC: U.S. Dept. of Justice, 2012.

Silberg, Joyanna, and Stephanie Dallam. "Abusers Gaining Custody in Family Courts: A Case Series of Overturned Decisions". *Journal of Child Custody* 16(2), 2019: 140–169.

Teti, Douglas M., Pamela Cole, Natasha Cabrera, Sherryl Goodman, and Vonnie McLoyd. *Social Policy Report. Supporting Parents: How Six Decades of Research Can Inform Policy and Best Practice.* Washington, DC: Society for Research in Child Development/SCRD, 2017.

Trocme, Nico, and Nicholas Bala. "False Allegations of Abuse and Neglect When Parents Separate." *Child Abuse & Neglect* 29(12), 2005: 1333-1345.

Trocme, Nico, Barbara Fallon, Bruce MacLaurin, Vandna Sinha, Tara Black, Elizabeth Fast, Caroline Felstiner, Sonia Helie, Daniel Turcotte, Pamela Weightman, Janet Douglas, and Jill Holroyd. *Canadian Incidence Study of Reported Child Abuse and Neglect – 2008: Major Findings.* Public Health Agency of Canada: Ottawa, 2010. http://www.phac-aspc.gc.ca/cm-vee/public-eng.php.

Warshak, Richard. "Severe Cases of Parental Alienation". In *Parental Alienation: The Handbook for Mental Health and Legal Professionals*, edited by Demosthenes Lorandos, William Bernet, and S. Richard Sauber (125–162). Springfield, IL: Charles C. Thomas, 2013.

Warshak, Richard. "Parental Alienation: Overview, Management, Intervention, and Practice Tips". *Journal of the American Academy of Matrimonial Lawyers* 28, 2015: 181–248.

Warshak, Richard (2020). "When Evaluators Get It Wrong: False Positive IDs and Parental Alienation". *Psychology, Public Policy, and Law* 26(1), 2020: 54–68.

Wheeler, Jennifer. "Psychological Assessment of the Child and the Family". In *the APSAC Handbook on Child Maltreatment, Fourth Edition*, edited by J. Bart Kilka and Jon Conte (163–181). Thousand Oaks, CA: Sage Publications, 2018.

Worenklein, Abe. "Moderate Cases of Parental Alienation". In *Parental Alienation: The Handbook for Mental Health and Legal Professionals*, edited by Demosthenes Lorandos, William Bernet, and S. Richard Sauber (97–124). Springfield, IL: Charles C. Thomas, 2013.

Chapter 7

Comparison of parental alienation treatments and evidence-based treatments for children and families

Sarah T. Trane, Kelly M. Champion, and Stephen D. A. Hupp

Parent-child relationship problems have been studied extensively within the developmental and psychological literature. Even for families with an intact marriage, it is common for children to become increasingly resistant to parental control as they develop, especially in adolescence and emerging adulthood. Most families manage these developmental shifts without intervention. However, sometimes resistance to parental control becomes more extreme and includes substantial rule-breaking, frequent defiance, and even aggressive behavior. These more extreme behaviors in youth are often preceded by coercive strategies used by parents as they attempt to maintain some level of control. Coercive parenting has been studied for over 40 years (see Dishion, Forgatch, Chamberlain, and Pelham 2016 for review), generating volumes of basic and applied research that informs clinical practice for families to help resolve these conflicts. Relatedly, many treatments for families have been developed to help youth and parents cope with the challenges associated with the youth's growing independence. In contrast, the treatments described below to specifically address parental alienation focus primarily on increasing contact between family members without including established evidence-based methods for youth well-being and without providing clinically meaningful outcome data.

When parents are separating from each other, the family dynamics indeed become more complicated. Developmentally appropriate behaviors associated with the youth's independence take on new meaning and begin occurring in two separate households. The youth is now on two separate but intertwined paths toward independence from each parent. Oftentimes, these two paths follow similar trajectories, but other times these trajectories differ considerably. That is, sometimes youth continue to be dependent on one parent but become independent from the other parent. In the more extreme situations, one of the parents can end up feeling left out in the cold.

In the context of separating/divorced families, parental alienation was defined in Chapter 1 as situations in which a preferred parent encourages their child's avoidant behaviors toward the nonpreferred parent, which in turn

DOI: 10.4324/9781003095927-9

causes the youth to reject the nonpreferred parent. That is, the youth may attempt to avoid spending time with the nonpreferred parent altogether.

As discussed in earlier chapters, there are many controversies surrounding parental alienation. This chapter will focus on treatments for parental alienation that are often court ordered. Specifically, the chapter will examine the level to which parental alienation treatments can be considered supported by research. We will also consider other treatments aimed at improving meaningful outcomes for both youth and parents in these complex circumstances. In addition to defining what it means for a treatment to be considered "evidence-based", we will also compare parental alienation treatments to other interventions with the strongest research support. In this chapter we will frequently use the term *youth* to refer to both children and adolescents.

Parental alienation treatments

For families with frequent court contact, court professionals often recommend treatments that aim to reunify youth with a rejected parent. *Reunification* is a term borrowed from the foster care system for youth who have spent time away from their primary caregiver and recognizes that the youth may have experienced some type of traumatic circumstance necessitating foster care. In the case of parental separation, however, the nonpreferred parent has usually not been absent but has been present in the youth's life to some degree. Proponents of parental alienation treatments describe how reunification family treatment may be predicated on one parent's apparent alienation of the other parent (Sullivan, Ward and Deutsch 2010). Other recent conceptualizations do not use the term *alienation* but label a youth's persistent efforts to avoid a nonpreferred parent as a *resist and refuse dynamic* (RRD; Walters and Friedlander 2016). Such treatments often choose to neutralize the many possible factors that might be related to a youth's rejection of a parent and move forward with reunification in the absence of substantiated claims of abuse or maltreatment. As described in earlier chapters, parental alienation is thought not to be present in cases where child maltreatment is documented; however, situations where allegations of maltreatment have been made but not substantiated are considered to be comparable to families without any abuse allegations.

Programs that are used for parental alienation include Overcoming Barriers Family Camp (Sullivan et al. 2010), Family Bridges[TM] (Warshak 2010), Family Reflections Reunification Program (Reay 2015), High Road (Childress 2015), Multi-Modal Family Intervention (Friedlander and Walters 2010), Restoring Family Connections (Baker, Fine and Baker 2020), Transitioning Families Therapeutic Reunification Model (Judge et al. 2016), Multi-Modal Family Intervention (MMFI; Friedlander and Walters 2010), Turning Points for Families (TPFF; Gottlieb n.d.), and Child-Centered Conjoint Therapy (CCCT; Greenberg 2019). Mercer (2019) provides a comprehensive overview of most of these programs, and they will also be described below. Each named treatment is provided at substantial cost to families as health insurance tends not to cover these programs.

Overcoming Barriers Family Camp

The Overcoming Barriers Family Camp (Sullivan, Ward, and Deutsch 2010) is a five-day camplike setting using psychoeducational interventions, along with milieu and family therapy methods. This program allows both preferred and nonpreferred parents to attend with their children, usually under court order. Youth engage in recreational activities with their nonpreferred parent and participate in family meetings in attempts to promote reunification. A mental health provider leads co-parent groups to address negative attitudes and behaviors within and between families. Parents provide feedback to each other in a large group setting for support as well as helping each other have realistic expectations with their children.

Saini (2019) used an online survey with 40 parents who had previously completed the program between two and ten years (with a mean of five years) earlier. Overall, 25.0% of the participants reported that the program "did meet their expectations" and 42.5% indicated the program "did not meet their expectations" (the other participants did not provide a response to the question). About half (48.1%) of the parents indicated their conflict with the other parent stayed the same after the program, and an equal number of parents reported that their conflict got better (25.9%) or got worse (25.9%). The article provided additional data on the participants' perceptions of their strained relationships. For most items, their perceptions stayed the same or got better. For example, on the item "My ability to emotionally regulate," none of the parents reported that this ability got worse after the program while 41.7% indicated this ability got "vastly better," 29.2% indicated it got "somewhat better," and 29.2% stayed "the same." On the other hand, on the item "My ability to problem solve with the other parent," 37.5% got "vastly worse," 12.5% got "somewhat worse," 33.3% stayed "the same," 12.5% got "somewhat better," and 4.2% got "vastly better."

Overall, all of these results (both positive and negative) should be interpreted extremely cautiously because the data collection design is severely limited. In particular, there is not a control group. Thus, there is no way to tell if the program led to any of the reported changes. As evidence of this problem, 63% of the parents reported that other therapists or programs were involved after they attended the Overcoming Barriers Family Camp. Thus, these other resources (and many other variables) could have influenced their relationships. Rigorous research about the effectiveness of this program could not be found.

Family Bridges™

In the Family Bridges™ program (Warshak 2010), youth are transported to a facility that is typically far from home, their cell phones are taken away, and they are allowed little to no communication with their preferred parent. The program uses psychoeducation, with an emphasis on teaching youth and parents about cognitive bias and influence, including discussion, for example, of the controversial Milgram study on obedience (Milgram 1963). Youth watch a prepared video about ways they may have been influenced, and they later engage in role plays as modeled on the video. Goals include helping the youth have a balanced point of view, which is a point of view consistent with the content taught within the program. Goals for parents include strengthening their parenting skills to be more nurturing while still setting limits. Mercer (2019) describes reports of prior attendees as teenagers who reported being highly coerced to participate under threat of negative outcome for their preferred parent (e.g., they were told that their parent would go to jail).

Little empirical research has examined this program. One recent survey of 83 youth reported that "between 75% and 95% of children overcame their alienation" (Warshak 2019, 645); however, the data collection methods had major methodological limitations, such as having no control group and having poorly defined outcomes. Thus, these reported results should be interpreted extremely cautiously. Rigorous research about the effectiveness of this program could not be found.

Family Reflections Reunification Program

The Family Reflections Reunification Program (FRRP; Reay 2015) uses a camplike setting in southern British Columbia, Canada. Youth initially attend without their parents and receive psychoeducation about families while preparing for recreational activities with their nonpreferred parent as a means to reconnect. A mental health professional works with the nonpreferred parent prior to their engaging with their child, although the specific topics are not described in detail. In general, the youth participate in psychoeducational groups to improve their "critical thinking skills" as a program goal. Both preferred and nonpreferred parents are encouraged to continue working with a mental health professional following participation in the formal program, preferably one trained in the FRRP model.

Outcome data described by Reay (2015) includes 12 families by using parents' and children's "own statements" at various intervals, up to 12 months after participation, reporting a 95% "success rate in re-establishing and maintaining a relationship between children and once-rejected parents" (Reay 2015, 197). The data collection methods had serious methodological problems including no control group and the specific outcome questions asked are not reported. Rigorous research about the effectiveness of this program could not be found, and it is unclear if this program is continuing to operate given the difficulty in finding information from general web search and the website previously created appears to be currently defunct.

High Road to Family Reunification

The High Road program (Childress 2015) is similar to Family Bridges, using "intensive psychoeducational intervention," requiring separation from a preferred parent for 60–90 days in addition to youth attending a 4-day program with their nonpreferred parent. High Road is based on work by a life coach without a mental health license. This program at times has recommended up to nine months separation of youth from their preferred parent. Youth who continue to report rejection of their nonpreferred parent require longer treatment, while youth who reduce their rejection have shorter treatment length. Thus, there is a clear coercive motivation for youth to deny rejecting their nonpreferred parent. Rigorous research about the effectiveness of this program could not be found.

Multi-Modal Family Intervention and Restoring family connections

Rather than being camplike, the Multi-Modal Family Intervention (MMFI; Friedlander and Walters 2010) and the Restoring Family Connections program (Baker, Fine and Baker 2020) both include intensive outpatient family and individual psychotherapy that address parent rejection using protocols for interventions that include all family members. MMFI also includes the court system, using the term "customized confidentiality" to describe the program's insistence on open communication between therapists and other involved professionals (e.g., judge, parenting coordinator, or counsel). These programs have similar goals of reunification along with emphasis on addressing the youth's coping skills with post-divorce conflict and reducing alignment with one parent over the other. Both parents are expected, and often court-ordered, to participate along with their children. The program by Baker (2020) describes therapeutic methods for adult children to reconnect with their parents. Rigorous research about the effectiveness of this program could not be found.

Transitioning Families Therapeutic Reunification Model

Originally developed for nonfamilial abductions, the Transitioning Families Therapeutic Reunification Model (TFTRM; Judge et al. 2016) has also been used for parental alienation. Isicoff (2015) describes the use of TFTRM as part of the Stable Paths program, which uses workshops in a private setting to help parents and youth reconnect. Activities include swimming with dolphins, horseback riding, and other recreational activities. Youth access to the preferred parent is limited and supervised. Rigorous research about the effectiveness of this program could not be found.

Turning Points for Families

Turning Points for Families (TPFF; Gottlieb n.d.) is another camplike program using a 4-day format for youth and nonpreferred parents often following a court order and no contact with the preferred parent. Preferred parents are asked to write a letter to their child at treatment onset encouraging them to engage with the treatment program. The program may choose to shorten or lengthen the no-contact period based on the content of this letter. If, during treatment, a youth recalls negative memories, such as abuse by the nonpreferred parent, this memory can be "corrected" by the nonpreferred parent saying that they did not do what was claimed. Gottlieb explained that this is necessary to prevent the child developing post-traumatic stress disorder out of the belief that he or she had been abused and even goes so far as to discuss false memory syndrome with youth and nonpreferred parents directly. Rigorous research about the effectiveness of this program could not be found.

Child-Centered Conjoint Therapy

Not specifically designed for parent alienation, child-centered conjoint therapy (CCCT; Greenberg 2019) is designed to assist clinicians and court evaluators with conceptualizing and treating youth and parents in situations with allegations of violence, past experiences with family violence, harsh parenting, abandonment, parental disengagement, and alienation. CCCT addresses issues of false allegations of threats or harm, and assumes that youth cannot reliably identify, describe, or express emotions and ideas independent of a parent if parents are in conflict (Greenberg 2019). There is almost no attention to the past two decades of research on child memory and child forensic interviewing nor evidence-based child protection. The authors report using the clinical literature to support evidence-informed interventions but do not provide any direct empirical data on this type of intervention. Rigorous research about the effectiveness of this program could not be found.

Family therapy as reunification therapy

It should be noted that in addition to the above therapies, many family courts and well-intended therapists may be offering something referred to as "reunification therapy", another family therapy option that is without empirical evidence for these cases. See Kleinman (2017) for a more detailed review of the ethical and clinical challenges such recommendations present. This chapter does not allow space to review the multitude of permutations of this type of "therapy" being offered. Indeed, a recent survey of 14 experienced clinicians known to offer this type of treatment revealed "substantial variance among practitioners' underlying theoretical frameworks which inform clinical practice and service delivery models" (Polak 2020), demonstrating the somewhat arbitrary nature of interventions being offered. As one example, Smith (2016) provides a detailed case report of family therapy, which is helpful toward delineating useful steps for intervention and perhaps as a pilot for future intervention research which remains lacking. There are no randomized nor quasi-experimental reports on the safety or effectiveness of this type of intervention for families in situations of youth refusal of parent contact.

Summary of parental alienation treatments

Overall, very little data on the safety and effectiveness of parental alienation treatments has been published. Overcoming Barriers Family Camp (Saini 2019), Family Bridges (Warshak 2019), and FFRP (Reay 2015) provide some published survey data from families who have attended their programs; however, even these attempts at providing evidence had serious methodological problems. Even less data appears to be available for the other programs. Anecdotal claims about a program do not constitute convincing research. In the next sections, we describe important elements to look for in treatments that are evidence-based. We will use this information to compare and contrast evidence-based treatments with the commonly used programs for parental alienation.

Classification frameworks for identifying evidence-based treatment

A rich literature exists within the fields of clinical child and developmental psychology that speaks to the important elements of family relationships and optimal youth development. The literature is so vast, however, that it can be challenging to identify which treatments have the strongest research support. Fortunately, multiple organizations have created frameworks to help identify treatments. This section will identify four valuable resources for identifying evidence-based treatments for youth and families. These include Blueprints for Healthy Development, California Evidence-Based Clearinghouse, and two clinically focused societies within the American Psychological Association (i.e., Society of Clinical Child and Adolescent Psychology, and the Society of Clinical Psychology). Before further describing these resources, we will briefly describe some gold standards that they rely on for identifying *evidence-based treatments* (EBTs) – interventions with modest to strong research support. The term evidence-based treatments is a somewhat recent label; earlier iterations included the terms *empirically validated treatments* (EVTs) and *empirically supported treatments* (ESTs). Although there have been minor tweaks across these iterations, the criteria used to define them have been relatively stable over time.

Gold standards for identifying evidence-based treatments

Research studies come in all shapes and sizes. When science-informed professional organizations label interventions as having modest to strong research support, specific criteria are used when choosing which research studies merit inclusion. For example, more weight is given to studies with higher levels of evidence regarding (a) specific descriptions of participants (e.g., age, gender, ethnic-racial identifiers), (b) specific descriptions of the treatment including its ethical safety, (c) reliable and valid measures (i.e., do they measure what they say they are measuring, and are they consistent over time), and (d) substantial improvements in outcomes. Beyond these basics, there are a few Gold Standards for selecting studies to help identify best treatments.

Gold standard #1: randomized controlled trials

For a treatment to be identified as having modest or strong research support, studies are prioritized when they employ *randomized controlled trial* (RCT) designs. These group design studies include at least one experimental group (i.e., receives the treatment) and at least one control group (i.e., does not receive the same treatment or any treatment at all). The *randomized* aspect of group selection in an RCT is particularly important. That is, each participant's assignment to one group or the other needs to be determined randomly in order for the study to have a true experimental design, thus minimizing threats to validity. A threat to validity would be something different about the groups other than the treatment(s). A group design study *without* random assignment is instead known as a *quasi-experimental design* (QED), and is much less convincing due to the various potential threats to validity. Even a group design study without random assignment, however, is more informative than a study without any control group for comparison. The control group (and especially the randomly assigned control group) helps researchers evaluate if variables other than the treatment itself are causing participants to change or do better. For example, many people start feeling better simply because time has passed. If this is the case, *any* treatment that was used could falsely look as if it helped even if the participants would have gotten better over time anyway without the treatment.

Studies that use other treatments (including placebo treatments) for the control group are more valued than studies in which the control group receives no treatment at all. That is, control groups function best when they control for common factors related to all treatments. For example, simply talking to someone about one's problems can make many people feel better. Also, just expecting a treatment to work can also help many people feel they are getting better. Thus, to some extent any treatment at all has the potential for people to start feeling better in the short-term but these improvements in perception tend to be fleeting. Thus, the science of psychotherapy seeks to discover benefits beyond the common factors of treatment that make people feel better in the short term.

Randomized controlled trials commonly use a waitlist approach for identifying their groups. That is to say, participants in the control group are often put on a waitlist to one day receive the same treatment as the experimental group. Thus, they will eventually get the same treatment, though it may be several months after the data is collected. The waitlist framework is not needed for a study to demonstrate experimental control; however, it helps mitigate ethical issues regarding withholding treatment for the half of the participants that are assigned to a control group. Another way of accomplishing this goal is to encourage the control group to seek services in their community, also called *treatment as usual*. This method too produces an acceptable comparison group from the active treatment group in a research study.

Gold standard #2: independent replication

If one RCT is good, then two RCTs are better. However, if the same team of researchers conducted both of the RCTs (or even ten RCTs), then the available pool of RCT studies is problematic for a few reasons. First, the initial team of researchers is probably the most invested in making sure they find significant differences between the experimental group and the control group. This is often because this initial team is the one that developed the treatment in the first place and may be subject to confirmation bias. In the worst-case scenario, they could fabricate their results or otherwise manipulate the data in unethical ways to promote a new treatment or program. Hopefully, this result does not occur often. More likely, personal biases might creep in, and they can fool themselves into believing there is a difference between groups by unintentionally making poor design and statistical choices. Or perhaps they are implementing the treatment in a unique way that is not well described for others to replicate. Regardless, lack of objectivity is a real threat to research integrity, validity, and reliability.

For all these reasons, it is valuable to have at least one other research team conduct an independent replication of an RCT, especially within the treatment literature for a vulnerable population including youth. Of course, this second team of researchers could also falsify data, make poor design choices, or implement the treatment in unique ways, but having two independent teams considerably minimizes these possibilities. Unfortunately, academia has tended to reward *innovators* more than *replicators*. For example, the initial

RCT is more likely to get published in a competitive journal than the replication. However, replications are becoming more appreciated and in fact constitute a gold standard for identifying treatments that work.

Gold standard #3: low potential for harm

Theoretically, just about any treatment has some potential for harm. Many pharmaceutical interventions, for example, often come with side effects even though they are effective. Psychological interventions can also have unintended effects, and some treatments have a much greater potential for harm than others. Lilienfeld (2007) described several ways that psychological treatments might cause harm. For example, psychological treatments have the potential to (a) make symptoms worse, (b) prompt new symptoms to develop, (c) cause an overreliance on therapy, (d) prompt premature therapy drop-out, (e) prevent future use of therapy, (f) cause physical harm (including death), (g) cause harm to family or friends, and (h) waste financial resources. Mercer (2017) has since expanded on Lilienfeld's work by further defining potentially harmful psychological treatments and identifying several that have been used with youth. When scientific and ethical organizations attempt to identify the best treatments, they prioritize treatments with a relatively low potential for harm. Similarly, research studies on treatments with youth are often required to receive approval from an institutional review board (IRB) documenting appropriate protection of human subjects. IRB approval is often required for a study to be published in a respected peer-reviewed journal.

Blueprints for Healthy Youth Development

Blueprints for Healthy Youth Development (hereafter called Blueprints) provides a registry of evidence-based treatments that was launched in 1996 by the Institute of Behavioral Science. Initially, the registry focused on programs that targeted violence prevention but has since broadened to include many other aspects of social-emotional health (the up-to-date registry can be found at www.blueprintsprograms.org).

Not every treatment included in the Blueprints register should be considered "evidence-based"; however, many of them can be considered as such. Particularly, some programs are certified as *Model Plus Programs*, the strongest level of support, if they meet multiple criteria related to (a) intervention specificity, (b) evaluation quality, (c) intervention impact, (d) dissemination readiness, (e) and independent replication. Of particular importance is that the treatment needs to be supported by at least two randomized controlled trials (RCTs) or at least one RCT and at least one quasi-experimental design (QED) study. Further, there must be independent replication and at least one long-term follow-up study of one year or longer. Overall, to be considered a Model Plus Program, a treatment only needs two very-well designed studies (by two different research teams) to be identified as having strong research support. That is to say, it should not be that challenging for an effective treatment to reach even this strongest level of research support. Still, very few programs are considered a Model Plus Program.

Some programs in the Blueprints registry are identified as *Model Programs* (notice this label does not include the word *Plus*), the second strongest level of support (i.e., modest support). To be a Model Program, a treatment must meet most of the same criteria as Model Plus Programs; however, the criteria of independent replication by another research team is not required for this level.

Lastly, a program is identified as a *Promising Program* based on the same criteria as for the Model Program level; however, the requirement for two RCTs (or one RCT and one QED) is not needed for this level. Thus, the bar to be identified as a Promising Program is very low, and the word "promising" is likely overstated in many situations. A more accurate term might be "Possibly Promising Programs." Promising programs should not be considered evidence-based at this time, although there is some glimmer of hope that they could reach the higher levels one day.

California Evidence-Based Clearinghouse for Child Welfare

The California Evidence-Based Clearinghouse for Child Welfare (CEBC; www.cebc4cw.org) maintains an active database of evidence-based practices for families and children involved in the child welfare system to promote effective program implementation. This registry ranks programs using a scientific rating scale using studies in published peer-reviewed journals, taking into account the study's safety and focus on child/family well-being. Although initially focused on state policy for California, the majority of programs reviewed in this database are available nationwide, are rated by national experts across the country, and can apply to youth who are involved in public or commercial intervention. Programs are rated along the following 5-point scale: 1 – *Well-Supported by Research Evidence*; 2 – *Supported by Research Evidence*; 3 – *Promising Research Evidence*; 4 – *Evidence Fails to Demonstrate Effect*; and 5 – *Concerning Practice*. Programs without sufficient research evidence are rated as NR – Not able to be Rated, as long as there are no data suggesting a program causes a risk of harm. Programs that are either not effective or shown to be at risk of causing harm are rated at the 4 or 5 level. The specific criteria are very similar to Blueprints with regard to randomized control trials and evidence of effectiveness and safety.

Clinically focused societies of the American Psychological Association

The American Psychological Association has two clinical psychology divisions that have been at the forefront of identifying EBTs for mental health since the mid-1990s. First, the Society of Clinical Psychology (Division 12) created a task force that developed criteria for EBTs for adults and children (at first the criteria were for the earlier iterations of EVTs and ESTs). This society also began to identify which treatments met the developed criteria (Chambless and Hollon 1998). Subsequently, the Society of Clinical Child and Adolescent Psychology (Division 53) used the same criteria to specifically identify EBTs for youth and families (Southam-Gerow and Prinstein 2014).

These societies use similar criteria and levels as Blueprints and CEBC but with different names. The highest level of empirical support is called *Well-Established Treatments*. This level is also labeled on their websites as "Strong Research Support" and "Works Well." Of particular note is that a treatment needs at least two well-designed RCTs by two different teams (i.e., independent replication) to meet the criteria for this level. The control group also needs to provide some type of placebo intervention or else compare the treatment to a previously identified well-established treatment. The next level of support comprises *Probably Efficacious Treatments*, also labeled as "Modest Research Support" or "Works." For this level, one well-designed RCT could be sufficient (e.g., as long as the control group includes a placebo) or two RCTs from independent teams (but without placebo controls) could be sufficient.

The Society of Clinical Child and Adolescent Psychology further identifies three additional levels that should not be considered "evidence-based" at this time. These include *Possibly Efficacious Treatments* (i.e., has only one RCT without placebo controls), *Experimental Treatments* (i.e., not yet tested in an RCT), and *Treatments of Questionable Efficacy* (i.e., research demonstrates the treatment does not work), although there is hope that some of these could one day be considered evidence-based if more studies are conducted. Additionally, the Society of Clinical Psychology uniquely identifies treatments with *Controversial Research Support* for treatments with mixed findings (e.g., they have an implausible primary component).

An updated list of identified treatments can be found on the web for both the Society of Clinical Psychology (https://div12.org/treatments) and the Society of Clinical Child and Adolescent Psychology (https://effectivechildtherapy. org/therapies). These are excellent resources for anyone interested in staying current on psychosocial EBTs for children, teens, and families.

Specific evidence-based treatments

Blueprints and CEBC note strong evidence for programs assisting families with children in divorce or with mild to moderate behavioral problems and parenting concerns. However, neither Blueprints, CEBC nor the APA societies have identified any effective treatments for parental alienation specifically, likely due to the lack of professional acceptance of this diagnosis or categorization at the level of *Diagnostic and Statistical Manual* or the *International*

Classification of Diseases. Thus, court professionals who want to refer families for treatment regarding parental alienation have difficult decisions to make. Should they refer families to expensive, time-consuming treatments that do not have rigorous research support but claim to specifically treat parental alienation? Or should they help connect families with treatments that are evidence-based for related and relevant issues but do not claim to address parental alienation specifically?

Before making this decision, it would be helpful for court professionals to know which interventions are considered evidence-based treatments by respected professional organizations. Indeed, there are published and research-supported treatments that may be helpful for families experiencing challenges related to separation. These challenges can include emotion regulation, internalizing issues, externalizing behaviors, exposure to violence/ trauma, and coercive parent–child relationships. In this chapter, we will highlight many (but not all) of the programs identified by Blueprints, CEBC, and the clinically focused societies of APA as showing strong to modest research support for these issues. The interested reader is invited to visit their websites (included above) for a complete list of programs.

Coping with divorce/separation

Only one program has been identified by Blueprints that specifically focuses on separating/divorced families. The New Beginnings program (Herman et al. 2015; Wolchik et al. 1993) was classified as a Model Program by Blueprints and earned a rating of Well-Supported by Research Evidence (1) by CEBC. New Beginnings involves about ten sessions (2 hours each) for parents and youth (ages 3–18 years old) in a group format. New Beginnings is based on well-established cognitive-behavioral and parent training approaches with robust evidence. For youth, it has been shown to decrease internalizing issues (e.g., anxiety, depression), decrease externalizing behaviors (e.g., oppositional defiance, aggression), and improve the mother-child relationship. Recently, the results from a 15-year follow-up of an RCT with 240 families demonstrate long-lasting benefits of the program (Wolchik et al. 2020) as well as cost-effectiveness of this preventive intervention (Herman et al. 2015). It is important to note that Blueprints certified the program for mothers but did not have enough data to do so for fathers, although the CEBC did not make such distinction. Unfortunately, fathers tend to systematically participate in parent-child research less often. An independent replication is needed before the program can be classified as Model Plus by Blueprints.

The APA societies have not identified any treatment programs specifically for separating or divorced families. Both societies tend to focus on behavioral or emotional disorders and/or psychological processes that impact parent-child relationship quality rather than a specific event like divorce or separation. Youth and parents can experience relationship conflict regardless of the structure of the family unit, whether married, intact, or separated families. The APA Societies do recognize treatment for youth who struggle with post-traumatic stress symptoms following traumatic events including abuse, emotional threats or conflict, interpersonal violence, or have traumatic grief, specifically Trauma Focused-Cognitive Behavioral Therapy (TF-CBT; Judith Cohen, Anthony Mannarino, and Esther Deblinger 2006). CEBC rates TF-CBT as 1 – Well Supported by Research Evidence and is an intervention that involves youth (aged 3–18) and caregivers together.

Internalizing issues

Blueprints has identified the Blues Program (Rohde et al. 2015) as a model program for depression; CEBC similarly rates this program as Supported by Research Evidence (2). The Blues Program is a cognitive-behavioral, school-based group intervention that targets adolescents of ages 15–18 years for six sessions (one hour each). The Society of Clinical Child and Adolescent Psychology has labeled Cognitive Behavioral Therapy (CBT) as a Well-Established Treatment for adolescents with depression (Weersing et al. 2017), youth with anxiety disorders (Higa-McMillan et al. 2016), and youth who have been exposed to trauma (Cohen, Mannarino and Deblinger 2006; Dorsey et al. 2017). Another variation of CBT, Alternative for Families CBT (AF-CBT), has been developed specifically for families with high conflict and/or allegations of child abuse with and without substantiation (Kolko et al. 2011). In CBT for older children and adolescents, it is common to use about 10–12 one-hour sessions. It is also common for parents to be involved in the treatment. Moreover, the Society of Clinical Psychology also classifies multiple variations of both Cognitive Therapy and Behavior Therapy as Well-Established for *adults* with depression, anxiety, and exposure to trauma.

Externalizing behaviors

Blueprints has identified several behavioral interventions as Model Plus for externalizing behaviors, and CEBC rates them strongly as well. These programs include Parent Management Training Oregon (PMTO; aged 3–18), Functional Family Therapy (FFT; aged 12–18), and Multisystemic Therapy (MST; aged 12–18). Similarly, the Society of Clinical Child and Adolescent Psychology labels multiple variations of Parent Behavior Therapy, such as PMTO, as a Well-Established Treatment for youth with externalizing behaviors such as defiance and aggression (Kaminski and Claussen 2017). PMTO involves about 25 sessions, FFT involves about 30 hours of intervention, and for MST, the intervention can begin as daily but then gradually taper to weekly session over the course of about four months. Readers are referred to Blueprints and CEBC for additional evidence-based treatment options, as there are several for younger children as well.

Parent-child relationship

All the programs listed in the above section on externalizing behaviors also directly target the parent-child relationship for both mothers and fathers. In particular, these programs focus on increasing positive attention from parents while decreasing conflict including coercive and harsh discipline. Additionally, based on 15 studies with several RCTs (e.g., Olds et al. 2004), Blueprints has identified the Nurse-Family Partnership, a home-visiting program, as being a Model program for improving reciprocal mother-child warmth among other variables. This program begins during pregnancy and continues to the child's second birthday; however, it does not target the ages most commonly associated with the idea of parental alienation.

Summary of evidence-based treatments

Blueprints, CEBC, and the clinically focused societies of APA have identified *many* relevant evidence-based treatments that all have low potential for harm. These treatments have been shown to improve functioning related to divorce/separation, internalizing issues, and externalizing behaviors. To date, there have been no evidence-based treatments identified for parental alienation specifically; however, there are strong evidence-based treatments for parent-child relationships more broadly as well as treatments for youth and adults who have experienced trauma or been exposed to high levels of conflict and violence.

Evidence-based treatments compared with parental alienation treatments

Evidence-based treatments are clearly defined and treat specific issues and relational processes. By definition, these treatments meet several gold standards including: (1) randomized controlled trials, (2) independent replication, and (3) low potential for harm. Studying whether a treatment is safe and effective pre-supposes approval by an institutional review board to ensure the treatment meets ethical and legal standards of care for vulnerable populations, namely the minors involved. Treatment goals of evidence-based treatments are clearly defined using reliable and valid measures and often include reports from parents, clinicians, and youth themselves. Goals are focused on meaningful and functional variables, such as improved mood, decreased externalizing behaviors, and improved daily functioning at home and school.

In contrast, the parental alienation treatments aim to create reunification, assuming the youth has no rational ground for resisting contact with their nonpreferred parent and that youth are dishonest or irrational in their refusal. However, none of these programs have been subject to rigorous treatment research with consistent outcome data on effectiveness and safety for the youth or family members involved. In fact, at face value, it appears that many of these programs may indeed have the potential to increase stress and potential harm for already vulnerable youth by abruptly removing them from their preferred caregiver for extended periods. Although some of the authors of parental alienation treatments have described parental alienation as "emotional abuse," there is no definition within the literature beyond theoretical descriptions to support this point of view. Indeed, the American Professional Society on the Abuse of Children has *not* included parental alienation within its definition of child maltreatment ("APSAC announces..." 2019). The substantial lack of quantifiable data raises serious concerns about program safety, utility, and feasibility. It seems problematic that the desired outcome of treatment focuses on the youth accepting time with a nonpreferred parent, rather than clearly defining characteristics of the relationship that are expected to develop and the promotion of the youth's well-being. Parent alienation treatments appear to engender some of the very issues they report wanting to reduce, such as extended time away from a parent. That is, a youth is forced to spend extended time with a nonpreferred parent, often against the youth's wishes and often without the ability to communicate with the preferred parent. In addition, the youth's point of view is often confronted, challenged, and negated in this coercive power dynamic established by court-ordered treatment.

Another purported primary treatment goal for most parental alienation treatments is an improved relationship between the youth and the nonpreferred parent, the quality of which is often ill-defined. If contact between a youth and a nonpreferred parent cannot be achieved with parent agreement, then a specific treatment plan is developed with a goal that both parents support a relationship between the nonpreferred parent and the youth (Sullivan et al. 2010; Walters and Friedlander 2016). The priority appears to be that the child and the nonpreferred parent spend time together, with minimal consideration placed on identifying or ameliorating the possible multitude of factors that led toward the initial and ongoing rejection.

To date, there are *no* rigorous studies that demonstrate the positive or negative impact of re-establishing a relationship with a nonpreferred parent after time spent in a parental alienation treatment program. Research in this area that has been published relies on retrospective accounts of a small number of adults rather than prospective reports from youth. Some publications have included measures from the parent's point of view or have discussed outcomes as increased time spent with the previously rejected parent but fail to include any behavioral or psychological outcome measures of these parents and their children that would be developmentally or clinically meaningful.

Another primary goal of these treatments is that the preferred parent expresses behavioral and emotional support of a relationship between the child and the nonpreferred rejected parent (Sullivan et al. 2010; Walters and Friedlander 2016). The fact that nonpreferred parents often have engaged in concerning behaviors (e.g., behavior that predicts poor parent-child relationships and poorer child social-emotional adjustment) is treated as one neutral factor. This neutral stance often rests on an assumption that only a positive finding of ongoing abuse by a parent from child protection authorities has merit in terms of identifying any need for child protection. Rarely are parents required to provide any evidence that they have adopted attitudes and behaviors consistent with safe, secure, and nurturing parenting. Improving the likelihood of child safety from exposure to family violence, hostile parenting, physical or sexual abuse, or child neglect seems to be put on equal footing with a demand that the other parent demonstrate attitudes and beliefs supportive of co-parenting. Walters and Friedlander (2016) discuss how in fact a nonpreferred parent will "counter-reject" their child during the reunification treatment, creating even more distress for this vulnerable youth yet specific data are again lacking on the frequency of such events during any parental alienation treatment as well as the clinical or developmental sequelae.

We were unable to find any published peer-reviewed outcome data on youth functioning in various meaningful domains of their life after parent alienation treatment. Does reunification with a parent lead to improved academic functioning? Improved social skills and peer relationships? Improved parent-child interaction quality? None of these questions have been adequately addressed within the publications linked to parental alienation, as there have been no RCTs comparing this treatment modality to even a wait-list control sample, let alone a different intervention. Without these data, there remains little evidence upon which these treatments can be described as evidence-based for youth. The small number of existing publications describe parents' satisfaction about their relationship with their child, but descriptions of the treated sample are not researched and often neglect to include meaningful descriptions of improvements among the youth involved. As Mercer (2019) describes, any outcome data from these programs cannot assume only treatment effects given numerous potential confounding effects, including the youth's experience of loss of contact from their preferred caregiver, peers and other social contacts, unfamiliar environments, as well as possible covert or overt influence from staff to move forward with the treatment model. Moreover, the retail costs of such programs are reported to be as high as $20,000, an expense that can be ordered by the court to be paid by the preferred parent who is often denied any contact with their child for up to 90 days or longer.

Alternatively, evidence-based treatments have considerable research support, and many evidence-based treatments for families have been identified. Different variations of Parent Behavior Therapy (e.g., PMTO) and Cognitive-Behavioral Therapy (e.g., TF-CBT) include parent components and do not involve separating a child from a preferred parent. In addition, they encourage the child to use well-researched skills for improving emotion regulation and challenging maladaptive thinking patterns. Treatment goals include the improvement of parent-child relationship skills and helping parents create and maintain nurturing environments. Lastly, the evidence-based treatments are considerably less expensive than most programs that target parental alienation and are a covered benefit among most health insurances including state-sponsored health insurance, reducing disparities among families who would indeed benefit from psychological intervention to address parent-child relationship issues.

Conclusion

Psychology and other social sciences have delineated the importance of research methods for describing treatments as evidence-based (e.g., Bedics 2020). Parental alienation treatments lack the evidence required to be considered evidence-based by agreed-upon professional standards. In addition to the review provided in this chapter, a 2017 review also concluded that no rigorous research could be identified for parental alienation treatments (Templer et al. 2017). Moreover, their safety remains in question, let alone their effectiveness at reaching purported treatment goals. If treatment goals are the reduction of coercion among parents and children, psychology research has a lot to say about best methods and procedures for improvements in this regard. Indeed, methods almost universally suggest the need for parents to demonstrate improvements in their own emotion regulation skills, communication skills, and ability to create a safe and supportive environment for their children before their children can be expected to demonstrate such skills. It behooves the Court, attorneys, and other professionals involved with these most challenging cases to understand that there remains a distinct lack of evidence to assure that the existing parental alienation programs are psychologically safe or effective for families. While it is possible that these programs emerged with the best of intentions to assist distressed and desperate parents, they do not rise to the ethical imperative to create EBTs that warrant court-ordered participation.

References

"APSAC Announces Revisions to Its Definitions of Psychological Maltreatment and Adds a Cautionary Note." 2019. Accessed April 15, 2021 at https://www.apsac.org/single-post/2019/08/16/apsac-announces-revisions-to-its-definitions-of-psychological-maltreatment-and-adds-a-cau.

Baker, Amy, Paul Fine, and Alianna L Baker. *Restoring Family Connections.* Lanham, MD: Rowman and Littlefield, 2020.

Bedics, Jamie D. "Recommendations and Future Directions for the Scientific Study of Dialectical Behavior Therapy: Emphasizing Replication and Reproducibility." In *The Handbook of Dialectical Behavior Therapy*, edited by Jamie D. Bedics, 361–379. Cambridge, MA: Academic Press, 2020. doi: 10.1016/B978-0-12-816384-9.00016-6.

Chambless, Dianne L., and Steven. D. Hollon. "Defining Empirically Supported Therapies." *Journal of Consulting and Clinical Psychology* 66, 1998: 7–18.

Childress, Craig. *An Attachment-Based Model of Parental Alienation: Foundations*. Claremont, CA: Oaksong Press, 2015.

Cohen, Judith A., Anthony P. Mannarino, and Esther Deblinger. *Treating Trauma and Traumatic Grief in Children and Adolescents*. New York: Guilford Press, 2006.

Dishion, Thomas, Marion Forgatch, Patricia Chamberlain, and William E. Pelham. "The Oregon Model of Behavior Family Therapy: From Intervention Design to Promoting Large-scale System Change." *Behavior Therapy* 46, 2016: 812–837. doi: 10.1016/j.beth.2016.02.002.

Dorsey, Shannon, Katie A. McLaughlin, Suzanne E. Kerns, Julie P. Harrison, Hilary K. Lambert, Ernestine C. Briggs, Julia Revillion Cox, and Lisa Amaya-Jackson. "Evidence Base Update for Psychosocial Treatments for Children and Adolescents Exposed to Traumatic Events." *Journal of Clinical Child & Adolescent Psychology* 46, 2016: 303–330. doi: 10.1080/15374416.2016.1220309.

Gottlieb, Linda. "Children Are Harmed When Professionals Reject Science." Accessed January 15, 2021. https://turningpoints4families.weebly.com/uploads/2/2/5/4/22545256/children_are_harmed_when_professionals_reject_science.pdf.

Gottlieb, Linda. "Family Access Fighting for Children's Rights." Accessed March 24, 2021. https://www.familyaccessfightingforchildrensrights.com/linda-gottlieb.html.

Graham-Berman, Sandra A., and Suzanne Perkins. "Effects of Early Exposure and Lifetime Exposure to Intimate Partner Violence (IPV) on Child Adjustment." *Violence and Victims* 25, 2010: 427–439. doi: 10.1891/0886-6708.25.4.427.

Greenburg, Lyn, Barbara J Fidler, and Michael A Saini. *Evidence-Informed Interventions for Court-Involved Families: Promoting Healthy Coping and Development*. New York: Oxford University Press, 2019.

Herman, Patricia, Nicole E. Mahrer, Sharlene A. Wolchik, Michele M. Porter, Sarah Jones, and Irwin N. Sandler. "Cost-benefit of a Preventive Intervention for Divorced Families: Reduction in Mental Health and Justice System Service Use Costs 15 Years Later." *Prevention Science* 16, 2015: 5586–5608.

Higa-McMillan, Charmaine K., Sarah E. Francis, Leslie Rith-Najarian, and Bruce F. Chorpita. "Evidence Base Update: 50 Years of Research on Treatment for Child and Adolescent Anxiety." *Journal of Clinical Child & Adolescent Psychology* 45, 2016: 91–113.

Judge, Abigail Rebecca Bailey, JoAnn Behrman-Lippert, Elizabeth Bailey, Cynthia Psaila, and Jane Dickel. "The Transitioning Families Therapeutic Reunification Model in nonfamilial abductions." *Family Court Review* 54, 2016: 232–249.

Kaminski, Jennifer W., and Angelika H Claussen. "Evidence Base Update for Psychosocial Treatments for Disruptive Behaviors in Children." *Journal of Clinical Child & Adolescent Psychology* 46, 2017: 477–499.

Kleinman, Toby. "Family Court Ordered 'Reunification therapy': Junk Science in the Guise of Helping Parent/Child Relationships?" *Journal of Child Custody* 14, 2017: 295–300. doi: 10.1080/15379418.2017.1413699.

Kolko, David J., AMR Iselin, and Kevin J Gully. "Evaluation of the Sustainability and Clinical Outcome of Alternatives for Families: A Cognitive-Behavioral Therapy (AF-CBT) in a Child Protection Center." *Child Abuse & Neglect* 35, 2011: 105–116.

Lilienfeld, Scott O. "Psychological Treatments That Cause Harm." *Perspectives on Psychological Science* 2, 2007: 53–70.

Mercer, Jean. "Evidence of Potentially Harmful Psychological Treatments for Children and Adolescents." *Child and Adolescent Social Work Journal* 34, 2017: 107–125.

Mercer, Jean. "Are Intensive Parental Alienation Treatments Effective and Safe for Children and Adolescents?" *Journal of Child Custody* 16, 2019: 67–113. doi: 10.1080/15379418.2018.1557578.

Milgram, Steven. "Behavioral Study of Obedience." *The Journal of Abnormal and Social Psychology* 67, 1963: 371–378.

Olds, David L., Harriet Kitzman, Robert Cole, JoAnn Robinson, Kimberly Sidora, Dennis W Luckey, Charles Henderson, Carole Hanks, Jessica Bondy, and John Holmberg. "Effects of Nurse Home Visiting on Maternal Life Course and Child Development: Age 6 Follow-up Results of a Randomized Trial." *Pediatrics* 114, 2004: 1550–1559. doi: 10.1542/peds.2004-0962.

Polak, Shely. "Mental Health Professionals' Practice of Reintegration Therapy for Parent–child Contact Problems Post-separation: A Phenomenological Study." *Journal of Divorce & Remarriage* 61, 2020: 225–248. doi: 10.1080/10502556.2019.1699370.

Reay, Kathleen. "Family Reflections: A Promising Therapeutic Program Designed to Treat Severely Alienated Children and Their Family System." *American Journal of Family Therapy* 43, 2015: 197–207.

Rohde, Paul, Eric Stice, Heather Shaw, and Jeff M. Gau. "Effectiveness Trial of an Indicated Cognitive-behavioral Group Adolescent Depression Prevention Program Versus Bibliotherapy and Brochure Control at 1- and 2-year Follow-up." *Journal of Consulting and Clinical Psychology* 83, 2015: 736–747. doi: 10.1037/ccp0000022.

Saini, Michael. "Strengthening Coparenting Relationships to Improve Strained Parent–child Relationships: A Follow-up Study of Parents' Experiences of Attending the Overcoming Barriers Program." *Family Court Review* 57, 2019: 217–230.

Smith, Linda S. "Family-based Therapy for Parent-child Reunification." *Journal of Clinical Psychology* 72, 2016: 498–512. doi: 10.1002/jclp.22259.

Southam-Gerow, M. A., and Mitch Prinstein. "Evidence Base Updates: The Evolution of the Evaluation of Psychological Treatments for Children and Adolescents." *Journal of Clinical Child & Adolescent Psychology* 43, 2014: 1–6.

Sullivan, Michael, Peggie Ward, and Robin Deutsch. "Overcoming Barriers Family Camp: A Program for High-conflict Divorced Families When a Child Is Resisting Contact with a Parent." *Family Court Review* 48, 2010: 116–135.

Templer, Kate, Mandy Matthewson, Janet Haines, and Georgina Cox. "Recommendations for Best Practice in Response to Parental Alienation: Findings from a Systematic Review." *Journal of Family Therapy* 39, 2017: 103–122.

Walters, Marjorie G., and Steven Friedlander. "When a Child Rejects a Parent: Working with the Intractable Resist/Refuse Dynamic." *Family Court Review* 54, 2016: 424–445.

Warshak, Richard. "Family Bridges: Using Insights From Social Science to Reconnect Parents and Alienated Children." *Family Court Review* 48, 2010: 48–80.

Warshak, Richard. "Reclaiming Parent-child Relationships: Outcomes of Family Bridges with Alienated Children." *Journal of Divorce and Remarriage* 60, 2019: 645–667.

Weersing, V. Robin, Megan Jeffreys, Minh-Chau T. Do, Karen T. Schwartz, and Carl Bolano "Evidence Base Update of Psychosocial Treatments for Child and Adolescent Depression." *Journal of Clinical Child & Adolescent Psychology* 46, 2017: 11–43. doi: 10.1080/15374416.2016.1220310.

Wolchik, Sharlene A., Stephen G. West, Susan Westover, Irwin N. Sandler, Art Martin, Julie Lustig, Jen-Yun Tein, and Jennifer Fisher. "The Children of Divorce Parenting Intervention: Outcome Evaluation of an Empirically Based Program." *American Journal of Community Psychology* 21, 1993: 293–331. doi: 10.1007/BF00941505.

Wolchik, Sharlene A., Irwin N. Sandler, Nicole E. Mahrer, Roger E. Millsap, Emily Winslow, Clorinda Velez, Michele M. Porter, Linda J. Luecken, and Amanda Reed. "Fifteen-year Follow-up of a Randomized Trial of Preventive Intervention for Divorced Families: Effects on Mental Health and Substance Use Outcomes in Young Adulthood." *Journal of Consulting and Clinical Psychology* 81, 2013: 660–673. doi: 10.1037/a0033235.

Wolchik, Sharlene. A., Jenn-Yun Tein, Emily Winslow, Jessy Minney, Irwin Sandler, and Ann S. Masten. "Developmental Cascade Effects of a Parenting-focused Program for Divorced Families on Competence in Emerging Adulthood." *Development and Psychopathology* 33, 2021: 201–215.

Chapter 8

Gender credibility and culture
The impact on women accused of alienation

Margaret Drew

Background

Accusations of mothers alienating children from fathers is consistent with our cultural history of blaming women for the actions or inactions of men. When abusive fathers create unhealthy environments for their partner and their children, the result may be a child's unwillingness to be with the father. Rather than restricting the abusive parent's access to the child to a safe setting, the father is often awarded custody of the children and at a minimum, unsupervised parenting time. Safety of the child is not necessarily the primary factor when child access decisions are made. From a legal perspective, alienation claims require little to no proof. As alienation advocates argue, a child's unwillingness to be with a parent creates a presumption that the (typically) mother's actions cause the child's choice. This presumption of maternal interference is a result of a cultural refusal to respect women, to hear their voices, and to credit their decisions. This chapter focuses on the many ways in which women are discredited throughout our culture and the consequences for women during family court hearings, particularly those where alienation claims are alleged. Many U.S. statutory schemes assert that the child's preference can be a consideration (Alaska 2021). The child's choice is generally ignored, however, when a child chooses to live with the non-abusive parent and chooses not to see the other parent.

A telling bumper sticker is "Eve Was Framed." The slogan embraces the perfect combination of the consequences of being a woman in existing legal systems along with ancient religious and cultural support of women shaming. In the context of parenting, a better slogan might be "Eve Was Blamed".

Gender bias against women is embedded in most cultures and has strong historical roots. The bias is both conscious and unconscious. Patriarchal notions of the role of women in bearing responsibility for the well-being of all family members, whether those family members reside together or not, is astounding (Johnson 1988, 232). Not only do women bear greater (and unrealistic) responsibilities as partners and mothers (Johnson 1988, 77), but they are also double burdened by lack of credibility in legal and other forums.

DOI: 10.4324/9781003095927-10

Before exploring the diminished position women have in the family legal systems, it is informative to examine the long-standing global culture of not listening to, believing, and otherwise disregarding women. While much of the history discussed is drawn from U.S. culture, the same phenomenon is found wherever culture and institutions are male dominated and designed.

The U.S. "founding fathers," like founders of other countries, refused to eliminate racial atrocities and gender disparities as part of developing government and legal structures. In making that choice, men continued a culture where women failed to achieve any credible status, even in the newly formed "democracy". Women lacked status, except as property subject to social and financial governance by men. Enslaved women were in greater peril as legally and socially they had no recourse and frequently their children were taken from them and sold. White women had no legal claim to their children because the husband was the children's legal custodian (Grossberg 1983, 238). Even nominal recognition of women as individuals with agency was delayed by an additional 200 years from the founding. During the interim, many women achieved the right to vote, despite harsh physical and verbal opposition by men. The process of women achieving the right to vote was difficult and took generations. Switzerland granted the right of women to vote in federal elections only in 1971 (The Federal Assembly—The Swiss Parliament n.d.). In the United States, the "right" to vote was meaningless for Blacks until the latter half of the 20th century when the voting rights act was passed (Voting Rights Act of 1965). The 19th Amendment to the U.S. Constitution provides that the right to vote could not be denied on the basis of sex (U.S. Constitution, amend. 19). Race was not addressed. Women's voting rights brought the potential to shift the political power imbalance between men and other genders, but not all women were permitted to vote. Consequently, as Black women's voting power was not implemented until the mid-1960s, women's right to vote did not have an immediate effect. Voting power alone was insufficient to render cultural change so long as women had limited social capital. The recognition and permission for women to be decision makers is developing slowly, except in one arena. Women have incorrectly been assumed to be the primary decision maker regarding children and the primary influence on them. This misconception has further lowered women's status as parents as well as their credibility. As women were culturally assigned responsibility for family safety and wellness, this assigned role undercut their power and credibility generally and specifically within court systems (Schafran 1997, 40). Women are held responsible for the safety of children, even when other family members create harm or risk of harm (Morris 2009, 421). Misogyny is embedded in this blame, which itself is based upon impossible expectations of women as caregivers.

In addition to blaming women for the actions of others, women face additional barriers to autonomy and credibility. The first is the belief that women lie generally, and the second, more pointedly, that women particularly lie about abuse. including sexual abuse (Weiser 2017, 46).

The first line of defense when disputes between genders arise is that the less powerful gender is not credible (DeCosse 1992, 287). Women and other non-male people of color face double and triple dismissiveness. The cultural unwillingness to believe women flourishes despite extensive studies concluding that an overwhelming majority of women are truthful in their assertions and are rightfully concerned when making allegations of abuse, including sexual abuse of them and their children. One study indicates that 98% of women's allegations of sexual abuse of children are credible reports (Everson & Boat 1989, 231). Studies of reports by women of sexual assault find that roughly 95% of reports are credible (Drew 2017, 215).

Before moving to an analysis of women's discounted experiences in the family court, an exploration of women's experiences in other cultural and institutional settings is necessary to understand the pervasiveness of women's subservience and the ensuing discrediting. When one examines the dismissive attitude of women in cultural institutions, and the routine discrediting of women in courts, the punitive results they experience are not surprising.

Religions and institutional misogyny

As one author wrote "Women abuse is by no means a modern-day phenomenon. There is plenty of documentation from the ancient world onwards to show that women have always suffered abuse from intimate male partners" (Mooney 2021, VI).

Women's testimony not being credited similarly has ancient roots. Oppressors deny the truth of what the oppressed say. Because the oppressed carry little power and are easily dismissed, the tactic has been effective for millennia and continues to be useful in contemporary times. While the symbolism of untrustworthy women has varied over millennia, the result is the same. Women are designated as inferior, but at the same time, cunning; they are evil, although occasionally honored in a patronizing way. Women are the source of men's failings and most certainly the source of men's own malicious behavior (Taylor 2021, 33).

Examples of men's fears of female anatomy and sexuality are well documented. In ancient mythology, women were depicted as half human and half animal. And the animals were not typically friendly ones. Snakes, serpents, and goats were the symbols of female malevolence. Often grotesque animals were shown at the edges of women's genitals further demeaning the female sex. Women's beauty was considered the trap laid for men who would then be emasculated or caused to engage in vile affairs or "sins", which they would not have done but for the cunning woman. Much is wrapped into the symbolism. Men's fear of losing control to another, along with any guilt from engaging in mutual passion are merely two of the possible bases for the distorted views of women (Taylor 2021, 66–67). But at the heart of these wrongful depictions is men's unwillingness to take responsibility for their own actions or to meet women as separate, autonomous people. As we will see, these themes run through our contemporary culture and play out in our institutions.

From early mythology, women were assigned by men to be sinister and untrustworthy creatures. Even the beautiful mermaid disguised her dangerousness where she would snatch men from boats or the shore and drown them in the sea (Sax 2000, 44). From ancient mythologies to contemporary religious systems, women largely are subservient to men. Respecting sincerely held religious beliefs, no matter the reasons for those beliefs, differing roles for men and women subtlety support secondary roles for women. Beyond role limitation, however, is a belief system that women are evil, wily, and responsible for men's failings.

The writings of Paul, Timothy, and other early writers are a staple of most Christian sects. These early authors relied upon the Adam and Eve story to "justify excluding women from participating in church administration" (Moore 2015, 24). "Adam was not deceived, but the woman was deceived and became a transgressor. It was Eve and not Adam who was responsible for human sin (Moore 2015, 24)." Eve, after all, partook from the tree of knowledge. Women's illiteracy and lack of formal education remains a tool for those who wish to control women (Kocieniewski and Gately 2006) (Winsor & Morgan 2021). Men's fear of female biology was another source for much discrimination against women in ancient religious organizations and traditions. Menstruating women are sometimes still considered unclean (Robertson 2007).

Early Christians' decision to polarize the sexes created enormous barriers to women achieving religious or personal autonomy which exists to this day. Some faiths prohibit women from participating as priests, and by extension, those positions further up in the hierarchy. While other Christian sects and Jewish congregations permit women to be preachers, pastors, or rabbis, their numbers are limited (Sandstrom 2016), and many women who achieve that status are discriminated against in those roles (Gritz & Barkhorn 2012).

Both some Jewish and some Christian sects responded to female functions, such as menstruation and childbirth, by associating them with impurity.

> The unfortunate link to impurity comes from the Book of Leviticus (12:1–8) where women were pronounced as unclean for a week after the birth of a son (two weeks after the birth of a daughter) and then had to wait for another one to two months before they could be purified.

The Catholic Church ended the practice of "churching" post-birthing women after Vatican II because of the impression that the ceremony was for purification, rather than a blessing for the mother (Kasten 2015).

The early white European travelers to the "new" world brought disdain of women from the "old world". As one author wrote in discussing Puritans and witchcraft,

> Powerful women and/or women who transgressed the boundaries of the gender binary were seen as evil. Female bodies, as the weaker sex and descendants of Eve, were more vulnerable to 'the Devil's influence. Having little autonomy and agency, women were easy targets for blame.

The story of Eve, the original sinner, was projected onto women living in the Puritan society. Women were "worthy of honor" for being wives but deemed witches if they disrupted their traditional functionality in society (Rosen 2017, 23). As one author notes, 21st century women who break through cultural boundaries are compared to witches, "Contemporary witch-hunts exist in spaces where women hold positions of power or possess similar characteristics to that of the women who were deemed witches centuries ago (Rosen 2017, 22)." "Having little autonomy and agency, women were easy targets for blame (Rosen 2017, 24)." Words used to describe the plight of women in Puritan times are equally relevant in this era. In 1998, the Southern Baptist Convention amended its essential teachings to make clear that women must "graciously" submit to their husbands (Niebuhr 1998).

Women's health and their medical and psychiatric providers

Medical systems and their actors historically have discounted women patients' complaints and observations. Several stereotypes of women come into play when women enter the medical world as patients. As one author notes, the position of women's credibility was countered by "historical Western social and scientific conceptions of women as excessively emotional beings with questionable decision-making ability" (Madeira 2012, 342). In addition, the stereotype that women are "hysterical" and otherwise inaccurate reporters is an invisible companion to the female client entering medical offices. A recent demonstration of this concerns Serena Williams' complaints of blood clots following the birth of her daughter.

The day following her delivery, Ms. Williams complained of difficulty breathing, which she attributed to a possible pulmonary aneurism. Medical personnel refused to credit her complaint, despite that Ms. Williams earlier had been sidelined from tennis due to blood clots in her lung. A nurse suggested that pain medication had confused Ms. Williams. A doctor insisted that instead of the CT-scan and heparin drip Ms. Williams requested, an ultrasound of her leg was in order. The result of the ultrasound showed nothing irregular, and a CT-scan was ordered. After the scan revealed several lung clots, Ms. Williams was placed on a heparin drip.

Ms. Williams, both wealthy and famous, had insufficient power and credibility with her medical team to cause an urgent response to her complaints. Women during and following childbirth often are ignored when voicing or demonstrating concerns about complications. Ms. Williams was further disadvantaged as a Black woman. Post-delivery concerns are minimized for many mothers. With a high maternal death rate, the United States leads developed countries in the rate of maternal deaths and has a higher death rate than many developing countries (Douthart et al. 2021). So much so that a campaign begun in 2012 called Stop. Look. Listen! is aimed at increasing medical personnel's awareness of maternal complications (Rutgers n.d.). But maternity is not the only circumstance under which women's medical complaints are minimized. Women with temporary or chronic pain are affectively treated at a slower rate than men. "Women in pain are much more likely than men to receive prescriptions for sedatives, rather than pain medication, for their ailments" (Kiesel 2017). "Women are half as likely as men to receive pain killers after surgery because doctors often do not take their complaints seriously" (UPI 1989). These articles reference a study completed by Karen Calderone which documented the slowness with which women were treated for pain compared with men. Ms. Calderone found

> The results revealed that male patients were administered pain medication significantly more frequently than female patients, and that female patients were administered sedative medication significantly more frequently than male patients. Also, patients 61 years or younger received pain medication significantly more frequently than those patients 62 years and over.
>
> (Calderone 1990)

Two frightening conclusions from this study include that women's pain complaints are attributed to exaggeration of their status and that older women are even less likely to receive appropriate pain relief (Calderone 1990). When one adds age discrimination and with a presumption of impaired mental incapacity, the bleakness of women's medical care over their lifespan is exacerbated.

While the exact roots of this dismissive attitude toward women can be argued, no doubt the attitude of women as property enhanced the medical profession's disregard of women's complaints and demands. When women were "owned" by their husbands, women's choice was irrelevant to most decisions. Whether the source of this ownership and obedience to the husband was religious, cultural, or law-based or all of that, women's lack of autonomy and control over their bodies was institutionalized (Orford 1994, 86). Instances of women's lack of control over their bodies are numerous.

There has been a long history of subjecting marginalized women to forced and coerced sterilization. In recent years, the practice has been documented in countries in North and South America, Europe, Asia, and Africa. It has targeted women who are ethnic and racial minorities, women with disabilities, women living with HIV, and poor women.

(Patel 2017)

Recently, immigrant women held in a detention center were sterilized without their consent by a prison doctor (Manian 2020). More than 40 women detained at a Georgia Immigration and Customs Enforcement (ICE) detention center complained of abuses by the gynecologist engaged by the private prison (Bekiempis 2020).

Petitioners were victims of non-consensual, medically unindicated, and/or invasive gynecological procedures, including unnecessary surgical procedures under general anesthesia, performed by and/or at the direction of [gynecologist Dr Mahendra Amin], the petition said. 'In many instances, the medically unindicated gynecological procedures Respondent Amin performed on Petitioners amounted to sexual assault' (Guardian 2020).

Sterilization of the immigrant women was the most common form of unauthorized surgery. And those detainees who objected or complained were penalized, sometimes with deportation and other times with solitary confinement. Sterilizing women, particularly indigenous, immigrant women and women of color, and all poor women has a long history in the United States. Both men and women were sterilized during the Eugenics era, (roughly 1920–1945); however, those violated were disproportionately women. One study of Latinx that looked at sterilization incidents during the Eugenics era, found that Latina women were sterilized at a much higher rate than Latino men (Novak et al. 2018). Poor women, indigenous women, women of color, those receiving public assistance and those incarcerated were the primary targets (Stern 2005). When the intersections of race and ethnicity are combined with gender, the use of forced or coerced sterilization rises (Manjeshwar 2020). Women with HIV have routinely been sterilized (Bi & Klusty 2015, 952).

Historical treatment of women's claims of gender violence

Women's claims of sexual assault exemplify the active employment of the stereotype that women are not credible. US women's early experiences with the credibility barrier may well have been in various court systems because as parents, women historically had no rights of child custody. Children were considered the property of the father (Woodhouse 1992, 1037). Women's assessed lack of credibility in sexual and domestic assault matters carried over into civil matters particularly in divorce and custody disputes even after women gained rights in both arenas (Grossberg 1983). Even though culturally women are assigned as primary caregivers of the children, this is no advantage in court, where abusive parents ignore the history of the child with the mother and demand equal if not sole custody of them. Men's judgments that mothers lie are credited, particularly when allegations of abuse are involved, and even more so with allegations of sexual abuse. And why not? Those stereotypes are in our consciousness. No one did more harm to women's credibility on issues of child sexual abuse than Sigmund Freud. At one point in his early practice, Freud met with women who were suffering from what he described as hysteria. Woman after woman told of child sexual abuse by family members, most often their fathers. Freud connected child sexual abuse to behavior of adult victims (Azzopardi et al. 2017, 255). Freud's male peers ranged from not supporting his research to outright hostility, "They lashed out at him with the strength of indignation which only the guilty can muster (Cogley 2003)." Freud altered his interpretations to declare that women were fantasizing. Thus, the theories of Oedipal Complex and the promotion of Hysteria accelerated. After this theoretical change, the popular notion that women are not credible reporters of abuse flourished. The switch in focus changed from fathers and other family members sexually abusing daughters to the victims' reporting deficiencies. By the latter half of the 20th century, Freud's retraction and its source was being uncovered, but the damage to those (primarily women) reporting child sexual abuse had been done (Schusdek 1966). While many other advocates and authors, most notably social worker Florence Rush, exposed Freud's duplicity (the cover-up theory), the cultural practice of discounting reports of sexual abuse continues. Cultural acceptance of Freud's creation led to men (the dominant group) denying abuse of all sorts. Without the power of this stereotype of women as fantasizers or liars, parental alienation claims in cases involving abuse and the low rate of sexual abuse convictions, could not flourish. Given the discreditation of women in U.S. and other histories, as well as the mythology and misinterpretation of women's bodies and personas, it should come as no surprise that when women enter the legal systems, the negative stereotypes with which women are burdened accompany them into the courtroom.

Women in U.S. legal systems

Criminal court

Given the embedded cultural bias against women, no one will be surprised to know that the bias presents barriers for women within the legal system. Bias against women in court did not originate there. Rather, the bias is an implementation of the biases and stereotypes that court actors brought into the legal arena. In addition to a cultural view of women as property, women encounter another related societal expectation—behavioral expectations. Women are expected to meet gender norms of male expectations. One of these expectations is that women are responsible for any perceived flaws in a family and while they are required to meet behavioral stereotypes expected of all women e.g. to act "like ladies" (Fox 1977). For example, women accused of committing criminal acts are more harshly treated in the criminal justice system. Often egregious acts that are disturbing when committed by men, demonize women. Women are given harsher sentences for the same crimes committed by their male counterparts. One study found that when men and women act together in the commission of a crime, women receive longer sentences (Grabe et al. 2006). Another found that for various reasons, women receive harsher sentences than men for spousal homicide. Of applicable factors, the Defendant's inability "to fit with notions of appropriate femininity may be the most significant" (Newby 2011).

In addition, women prosecuting domestic and sexual assault cases face two intense barriers. The first is that the expected victim demeanor is to be "scared, helpless, meek, and blameless" (Goodmark 2008, 83). Second, criminal court uses a standard of "beyond a reasonable doubt" in deciding guilt or not-guilty. In the United States, this is the highest standard of proof used in legal cases. Because of its high standard of proof, evidence of a not-guilty finding is not admissible in civil cases. Conversely, evidence of a guilty finding is admissible in civil cases. Family Court and other civil judges hearing domestic abuse cases often know—from either defense counsel or by examining court dockets—when a party to a protection order hearing or custody dispute has been acquitted of related criminal charges. This evidence of an acquittal is not properly brought before the court in these civil hearings because a not-guilty is not proof that the defendant is innocent of the allegations. A not-guilty means the judge or jury determined that the state did not prove its case. Civil court judges and lawyers representing the alleged abuser often interpret a non-guilty as evidence that the crime did not happen and concurrently reach the unfounded conclusion that the victim (typically the mother) has lied (Kohn 2003, 743).

Family court

When a mother who suggests that their partner is dangerous to herself or the children arrives at the courthouse, all the above-described stereotypes, myths, and misinterpretations of her actions preceded her. Court players, including judges, clerks, and other actors, have lived for decades in a world that presumptively discredits women. Women of color bring even less power into the legal arena (Epstein & Goodman 2019). Often there is a presumption that addictive substances and sex work are part of Black women's lives (Arthurs 2014; Ternet 2016). At minimum, parents of color may face a higher standard of scrutiny of their parenting abilities, resulting in overrepresentation of their children in state custody (U.S. Department of Health and Human Services 2016).

Should an abused mother show anger or other distress or be unable to formulate her arguments in a logical manner, her testimony is often dismissed as not credible (Goodmark 2007). Women who deviate from the expected norms are not believed, nor is their behavior assessed as a trauma or fear lens (Long n.d.).

> The symptoms of their trauma—the reliable indicators that abuse has in fact occurred—are perversely wielded against their own credibility in court. Because PTSD symptoms can make abused women appear hysterical, angry, paranoid, or flat and numb, they contribute to credibility discounts that may be imposed by police, prosecutors, and judges.
>
> (Epstein & Goodman 2019, 399)

When counsel for the alleged abusive father raises that the mother is not credible, and worse is vengeful, the allegations may feel familiar and even comfortable to court actors. "For all these women, credibility discounts both harm they experience and create yet another obstacle to healing and justice" (Epstein & Goodman 2019, 403).

Many family court judges, and some statutory schemes (Alaska 2021) begin with the assumption that parents have an equal right to custody of the children. There are flaws in this approach. First, this view protects the rights of the parents, which may be contrary to the "best interests of the child" standard so many courts purport to use. Second, this presumption minimizes the child's wishes and the child's caregiving history placing the burden of persuasion on the caregiving parent that co-parenting is not in the child's best interest. The history of stability in the child's life is a factor to be considered but that consideration can be at odds with a presumption of 50-50 custody (Alaska 2021). Family court judges often ponder settlement options from the beginning of any case. Abused mothers can disrupt the settlement process. When a parent seeks a civil protection order against another parent, many judges are concerned that a protection order will prevent or prolong resolution because, in part, of the restricted communication between parents that may result. Since most parents seeking a protection order are women, the impression of the mother as obstructionist can be presumed by judges when mothers seek court protection. The mother's safety concerns, and those of her children, become subordinate to the demand of resolution. Domestic abuse cases are more likely to proceed to trial, which may be the only way in which the mother can present compelling evidence of abuse, annoying the court further. Mothers without counsel are at a distinct disadvantage at trial. "As a result, few survivors have access to potentially powerful corroborative evidence. Moreover, they lack the benefit of legal advice about what types of more easily available evidence would be useful to bring to court" (Epstein & Goodman 2019, 399).

Whether she has counsel or not, when a mother raises claims of abuse, particularly child sexual abuse, she is more than likely to lose custody of the children. A study of New York court decisions found that gender bias in custody decision-making was a factor when mothers raised claims of sexual abuse lost custody when alienation claims were alleged against the mother (Milchman 2017). A later study confirmed anti-female bias but for a range of abuse claims raised by mothers, not limited to child sexual abuse. The study showed that mothers were far less likely to be awarded custody when parental alienation claims countered allegations of mother or child abuse (Meier et al. 2020, 3).

Recommendations

Whenever abuse allegations are raised, alienation claims should not be entertained (Meier 2010, 220–221). Safety must be the first line of inquiry without the distractions of claims that the non-abusive parent is vengefully or pathologically interfering with the relationship between the children and the alleged abuser.

Second, judges and other court actors must take a holistic view of domestic abuse. Many criminal and civil statutes define abuse in terms of physical harm. Criminal abuse cases are often brought on the basis of a specific physical act. This narrow view deprives the judge of an appreciation of the repetitive acts of coercion that form the pattern of abuse. Non-physical forms of coercion are in most U.S. jurisdictions insufficient to justify criminal prosecution or to be used as the basis of obtaining a civil protection order. A singular incident of physical abuse is easily minimized by judges and juries. It is only when one can piece together the various forms of abuse, including rages, financial control, mental abuse, and coercion that a court can understand the constant control that an abuser exerts over partners and children. Once so informed, the judge can assess the harm done by the abusive partner in more realistic terms.

Finally, court actors must examine their biases against women, particularly in women's role as mothers. We exist in a world where women are promoted as sex objects rather than CEOs. Movies, music, and other art forms promote many stereotypes of women and deny their competency and autonomy. How likely is it that we are all free of bias toward women, no matter what our gender? The courts often incorporate many of these presumptions and stereotypes into analysis and decision-making without awareness of the harm done to women and children. This is difficult work. The exploration is crucial, however, as a first step toward ensuring fair and impartial hearings and in making safety the primary consideration in the best interests of the child.

When judges and other court personnel understand the persistent coercion and control that constitutes abuse, then they can understand alienation claims as part of an ongoing use of abusive tactics to discredit and harm the abused partner and the children.

References

Alaska, 2021. § 25.24.150. Judgments for Custody; Supervised Visitation.
Arthurs, Maureen Evans. "I'm a Black Woman with a White Husband. People Assume I'm a Prostitute All the Time." *Washington Post*, Nov. 13, 2014. https://www.washingtonpost.com/posteverything/wp/2014/11/13/im-a-beautiful-black-woman-with-a-white-husband-people-assume-im-a-prostitute-all-the-time/

Azzopardi, Corry, et al. 2017. "From Freud to Feminism: Gendered Constructions of Blame Across Theories of Child Sexual Abuse." *Journal of Child Sexual Abuse* 27, no. 3: 254–275.

Bekiempis, Victoria. 2020. "More Immigrant Women Say They Were Abused by Ice Gynecologist." *The Guardian*, Dec. 22, 2020. https://www.theguardian.com/us-news/2020/dec/22/ice-gynecologist-hysterectomies-georgia

Bi, Stephanie and Tobin Klusty. 2015. "Forced Sterilizations of HIV-Positive Women: A Global Ethics and Policy Failure." *American Medical Association Journal of Ethics* 17, no. 10: 952–957. https://journalofethics.ama-assn.org/sites/journalofethics.ama-assn.org/files/2018-05/pfor2-1510.pdf

Calderone, K.L. 1990. "The Influence of Gender on the Frequency of Pain and Sedative Medication Administered to Postoperative Patients." *Sex Roles* 23: 713–725. doi: 10.1007/BF00289259.

Cogley, Fr. James. 2003. "Legacy of Sex Abuse Denial Can Be Traced Back to Freud." *Irish Times*, May 26, 2003. https://www.irishtimes.com/opinion/legacy-of-sex-abuse-denial-can-be-traced-back-to-freud-1.360285

DeCosse, Sarah A. 1992. "Simply Unbelievable: Reasonable Women and Hostile Environment Sexual Harassment." *Law and Inequality: A Journal of Theory and Practice* 10, no. 2: 285–310.

Douthart, Regine, et al. 2021. "U.S. Maternal Mortality Within a Global Context: Historical Trends, Current State, and Future Directions." Journal of Women's Health. https://doi.org/10.1089/jwh.2020.8863.

Drew, Margaret. 2017. "It's Not Complicated: Containing Criminal Law's Influence on the Title IX Process." *Tennessee Journal of Race, Gender, & Social Justice* 6, no. 2: 191–240.

Epstein, Deborah and Lisa Goodman. 2019. "Discounting Women: Doubting Domestic Violence Survivors' Credibility and Dismissing Their Experiences." *University of Pennsylvania Law Review* 167: 399–461.

Everson, Mark D. and Barbara W. Boat. 1989. "False Allegations of Sexual Abuse by Children and Adolescents." *Journal of the American Academy of Child and Adolescent Psychiatry* 28, no. 2: 230–235.

The Federal Assembly – The Swiss Parliament. n.d. "Women's Suffrage in Switzerland: 100 Years of Struggle." https://www.parlament.ch/en/%C3%BCber-das-parlament/political-women/conquest-of-equal-rights/women-suffrage

Fox, Greer L. 1977. "'Nice Girl': Social Control of Women through a Value Construct." *Journal of Women in Culture and Society* 4, no. 2 (Summer): 805–817.

Goodmark, Leigh. 2008. "When is a Battered Woman Not a Battered Woman? When She Fights Back." *Yale Journal of Law and Feminism* 20: 76–129.

Grabe, Maria E. et al. 2006. "Gender in Crime News: A Case Study Test on the Chivalry Hypothesis." *Mass Communication and Society* 9, no.2 (May): 137–163.

Gritz, Jennie Rothenberg and Eleanor Barkhorn. 2012. "Why Are People Still Uncomfortable with Female Rabbis and Pastors?" *The Atlantic*, Dec. 21, 2012. https://www.theatlantic.com/sexes/archive/2012/12/why-are-people-still-uncomfortable-with-female-rabbis-and-pastors/266542/

Grossberg, M. 1983. "Who Gets the Child? Custody, Guardianship, and the Rise of a Judicial Patriarchy in Nineteenth-Century America." *Feminist Studies* 9, no.2: 235–260.

Johnson, M. M. 1988. *Strong Mothers, Weak Wives: The Search for Gender Equality*. Berkeley, CA: University of California Press. https://publishing.cdlib.org/ucpressebooks/view?docId=ft0k40038c;brand=ucpress

Kasten, Patricia. "Why Women Stayed Away from Church After Childbirth." *Catholic News Service*, Feb. 1, 2015. https://www.thecompassnews.org/2015/02/women-stayed-away-church-birth/

Kiesel, Laura. 2017. "Women and Pain: disparities in experiences and treatments." *Harvard Health Blog*, Oct. 9, 2017, https://www.health.harvard.edu/blog/women-and-pain-disparities-in-experience-and-treatment-2017100912562

Kocieniewski, David and Gary Gately. 2006. "Man Shoots 11, Killing 5 Girls, in Amish School." *The New York Times*, Oct. 3, 2006, https://www.nytimes.com/2006/10/03/us/03amish.html

Kohn, Laurie. 2003. "Barriers to Reliable Credibility Assessments: Domestic Violence Victim-Witnesses." *American University Journal Gender Social Policy and Law* 11, 733–748.

Long, Jennifer G. n.d. "Explaining Counterintuitive Victim Behavior in Domestic Violence and Sexual Assault Cases." *The Voice: Helping Prosecutors Give Victims a Voice* 1, no. 4 http://www.ncdsv.org/images/Explaining%20Counterintuitive%20victim%20behavior.pdf

Madeira, Jody L. 2012. "Woman Scorned? Resurrecting Infertile Women's Decision-Making Autonomy." *Maryland Law Review* 71: 339–410. https://www.repository.law.indiana.edu/facpub/1309

Manian, Maya. 2020. "Immigration Detention and Coerced Sterilization: History Tragically Repeats Itself." *American Civil Liberties Union*, Sept. 29, 2020. https://www.aclu.org/news/immigrants-rights/immigration-detention-and-coerced-sterilization-history-tragically-repeats-itself/

Manjeshwar, Sanjana. 2020. "America's Forgotten History of Forced Sterilization." *Berkeley Political Review*, Nov. 4, 2020. https://bpr.berkeley.edu/2020/11/04/americas-forgotten-history-of-forced-sterilization/

Meier, Joan S. 2010. "Getting Real About Abuse and Alienation: A Critique of Drozd and Olesen's Decision Tree." *Journal of Child Custody* 7: 219–252.

Meier, Joan, et al. 2020. "Child Custody Outcomes in Cases Involving Parental Alienation and Abuse Allegations, What Do the Data Show?" *Journal of Social Welfare and Family Law* 42, no. 1: 92–105.

Milchman, M. S., 2017. "Misogynistic Cultural Argument in Parental Alienation versus Child Sexual Abuse Cases." *Journal of Child Custody* 14, no. 4: 211–233.

Mooney, Jane. 2021. "Foreword," in *Women Abuse in Rural Places*, VI – Walter S. DeKeseredy. Abingdon: Routledge.

Moore, Rebecca. 2015. "In the beginning...Eve," in *Women in the Christian Tradition*, 19–26. New York University Press, New York City. Series Editor Catherine Wessinger.

Morris, Anne. 2009. "Gendered Dynamics of Abuse and Violence in Families: Considering the Abusive Household Gender Regime." *Child Abuse Review* 18, no. 6: 414–427.

Newby, Ryan Ellis. 2011. "Evil Women and Innocent Victims: The Effect of Gender on California Sentences for Domestic Homicide." *Hasting's Women's Law Journal* 22, no. 1 (Winter): 113–156.

Niebuhr, Gustav. 1998. "Southern Baptists Declare Wife Should 'Submit' to Her Husband." *New York Times*, June 10, 1998. https://www.nytimes.com/1998/06/10/us/southern-baptists-declare-wife-should-submit-to-her-husband.html

Novak, Nicole, et al. 2018. "Disproportionate Sterilization of Latinos under California's Eugenic Sterilization Program 1920–1945." *American Journal of Public Health*. https://ajph.aphapublications.org/doi/10.2105/AJPH.2018.304369

Patel, Priti. 2017." Forced Sterilization of Women as Discrimination." *Public Health Reviews* 38. https://publichealthreviews.biomedcentral.com/articles/10.1186/s40985-017-0060-9

Robertson, Kate. 2007. "Cleaning Up on Attitude Feminine Hygiene Is Dirty; A Menstruating Woman Is Not Unclean; She's Normal. Here's Yet Another Bizarre Marketing Ploy to Make Us Feel Ashamed." *Toronto Star*, Jan 22, 2007: B.

Rosen, Maggie. 2017. "A Feminist Perspective on the History of Women as Witches." *Dissenting Voices* 6, no. 1. http://digitalcommons.brockport.edu/dissentingvoices/vol6/iss1/5

Rutgers Robert Wood Johnson Medical School. n.d. https://www.rwjms.rutgers.edu/RURWJ_SSLAnmatedPDF_FIN/html5.html

Sandstron, Aleksandra. 2016. "Women Relatively Rare in Top Positions of Religious Leadership." *Pew Research*, March 2, 2016. https://www.pewresearch.org/fact-tank/2016/03/02/women-relatively-rare-in-top-positions-of-religious-leadership/

Sax, Boria. 2000. "The Mermaid and Her Sisters: From Archaic Goddess to Consumer Society." *Interdisciplinary Studies in Literature and Environment* 7, no. 2 (Summer): 43–54.

Schafran, Lynn Hecht. 1997. "Credibility in the Courts: Why Is There a Gender Gap." *Judges Journal* 34, no. 1 (Spring): 40–41.

Schusdek, Alexander. 1966. "Freud's 'Seduction Theory': A Reconstruction." *Journal of the History of Behavioral Sciences* 2, no. 2: 159–166.

Stern, Alexandra Minna. 2005. "Steralized in the Name of Public Health Race, Immigration, and Reproductive Control in Modern California." *American Journal of Public Health* 95, no. 7: 1128–1138.

Taylor, D. J. 2021. "Why Women are Blamed for Everything: Exploring teriVictim-Blaming of Women Subjected to Violence and Trauma." *Lulu.com*.

Ternet, Rachel Scheral. 2016. "A Racist Stereotype Is Shattered: Study Finds White Youth Are More Likely to Abuse Hard Drugs Than Black Youth." *Salon*, Apr. 7, 2016. https://www.salon.com/2016/04/06/this_racist_stereotype_is_shattered_study_finds_white_youth_are_more_likely_to_abuse_hard_drugs_than_black_youth_partner/

U.S. Constitution, amend. 19, sec. 2.

U.S. Department of Health and Human Services. 2016. "Racial Disproportionality and Disparity in Child Welfare." https://www.childwelfare.gov/pubPDFs/racial_disproportionality.pdf

UPI. 1989. "Researchers Say Women Are Less Likely to Receive Pain Medication." https://www.upi.com/Archives/1989/03/11/Researcher-says-women-less-likely-to-get-painkillers/2047605595600/

"Voting Rights Act of 1965." U.S. Congressional Serial Set (1965): 1–90.

Weiser, Dana A. 2017. "Confronting Myths about Sexual Assault: A Feminist Analysis of the False Report Literature." *Special Issue: Feminist Framings of Sexual Violence on College Campuses* 66, no. 1: 46–60.

Winsor, Morgan and James Bwala. 2021. "More Chibok Girls Have Escaped from Boko Haram Almost 7 Years Later, Parents Say." *ABC News*, Jan. 29, 2021. https://abcnews.go.com/International/chibok-girls-escaped-boko-haram-years-parents/story?id=75560018

Woodhouse, Barbara Bennet. 1992. "'Who Owns the Child?': Meyer and Pierce and the Child as Property." *William and Mary Law Review* 33: 995–1122. https://scholarship.law.wm.edu/wmlr/vol33/iss4/2

Chapter 9

Developmental changes in children and adolescents

Relevance for parental alienation discussions

Jean Mercer

It would be impossible to have a case of "parental alienation" without having a child and at least one parent involved. When it is claimed that a parent has encouraged a child to avoid the other parent, there is much discussion of the behavior and personalities of the parents. The child, whose attitude and behavior are presumably the crux of the matter, has received much less research attention. In fact, publications involving the parental alienation belief system have offered almost no information on some of the most obvious questions about children in these cases. What is the age range for children who are avoiding a parent? Are there more boys or more girls in these cases? Is puberty a factor that helps to trigger children's avoidance of a parent? Are children who avoid a parent different from those who do not avoid, in temperament or personality characteristics? Answers to these questions could help us solve the riddle of avoidance in cases where the reason is not obvious, perhaps precluding any unfounded assumptions that a parent had encouraged the child's avoidance. This chapter cannot give the answers but will discuss things we already know about child development that are possibly relevant to these family situations.

Law, psychology, and child development

However much the two fields may interact with each other, law and psychology continue to speak different languages on some issues and to be at occasional cross-purposes. This is evident in the discussion on the parental alienation belief system, a set of ideas that are mentioned far more often in courts than among psychologists. But of all the possible unshared ideas of law and psychology, the one that may show the greatest number of contradictions between the fields is _child development_.

Family court judges have the option of considering developmental differences between older and younger children, and some jurisdictions use guidelines that recognize the growing abilities of adolescents to make good choices for themselves. This situation has resulted in a patchwork of decisions relevant to child custody. In the 40 or 50 years since children's emotional

DOI: 10.4324/9781003095927-11

attachment to caregivers began to be discussed in legal circles, some judges have opined that an infant of 12 months is not old enough to have formed an attachment, whereas others have thought that a 16-year-old would suffer serious attachment-related psychological damage from custody change (Mercer 2006). These decisions involved attempts to consider developmental differences but were distorted by failure to understand developmental change.

Across the board, however, the law regards human beings from birth to age 18 (in most countries) as if they were the same. All are minors and all have the same minimum rights. Efforts to state a further list of rights for minors, like the United Nations Convention on the Rights of the Child, have not been wholly successful, in large part because of the reluctance of the United States to participate. But even that list of rights, desirable as it might be, considers childhood and adolescence as a period of life that is uniformly different from adulthood. This view is not correct; the differences are by no means uniform.

Child development concepts

The study of child development is a field that includes work in psychology, biology, sociology, and medicine. All of these disciplines include specialties that focus on *development*. This term refers to changes that take place over time and which mark the gradual progress of any human being from a fertilized ovum to an adult. Ideally, developmental change is understood through *longitudinal* research. Longitudinal studies examine characteristics of a group of participants repeatedly as they increase in age, allowing each person's measures at any age to be compared with his or her own measures at an earlier stage. This design enables researchers to see developmental patterns over time and avoid being confused by individual differences. Longitudinal studies are time-consuming and expensive, however, so researchers often fall back on *cross-sectional* studies that compare groups of participants of one age with other groups of different ages.

Developmental change depends on two factors, both as they work independently and also as they interact with each other. One important factor driving development is *experience*. Children become more adult-like as they get older, in part because they learn from experience, either spontaneously or because they are instructed and schooled on adult skills. A toddler does not understand how to pay for a purchase as a 12-year-old does—but another 12-year-old from an economy that uses barter will not understand it either (although she could if she were taught). Because adults can often control children's experiences, through schooling, socialization at home, or psychological interventions, we stress the role these events play in development. Sometimes we refer to them as *formative experiences*. Parental alienation advocates place a strong emphasis on childhood experiences as shapers of personality and cognitive ability and consider experiences with parents to have particular formative power. Proponents of the parental alienation belief system are most concerned with the impact of negative experiences, as are researchers who study a range of adverse childhood experiences (ACEs) and connect them with harms to both mental and physical health.

It is not uncommon for authors who are naïve about child development to assume that experiences are the sole, or at least the most important, drivers of developmental change. Parents, teachers, and therapists all like to believe that their actions are the primary causes of children's development. Researchers and theorists of child development, however, place an equal or greater emphasis on a second driver of development: *maturation*. Maturation is a biological factor that causes many of the changes between conception and adulthood, and that shapes even those it does not directly cause. Just as embryo and fetus normally progress through highly predictable changes in size and physical features, human beings after birth progress through predictable *stages* of physical, emotional, and cognitive development. (The term "stage" is given to a period in which some aspect of the individual is qualitatively different from what it was before and will be later, with these changes unfolding in a predictable sequence.) Some of these changes are highly *canalized*, or difficult for experience to change, but others are considerably affected by experience. Thus, for example, the timing of language development is strongly dependent on maturation, but the specific language that develops is a result of experience. In many instances, the ways experience affects an individual depend on the person's maturational level, so, for instance, the impact of divorce or any parental actions on a child will be different for a toddler and for a teenager. It is notable that even a serious adverse experience, however influential it may be, does not cause maturation to stop.

Claims about parental encouragement of child avoidant behavior focus on the role of experience with a parent on a child's development, as do many other developmental questions. Most of the psychological research on this issue has concentrated on infant-caregiver interactions. Some rules have emerged from these studies, and they are of interest, although it must be stressed that it is not clear whether we can generalize from infant-parent interactions to relationships between parents and older children or adolescents.

One important rule about the role of experiences with parents is that the effects are *bidirectional*. This means that children influence parents and change them, just as parents influence children. In cases where parental encouragement of child avoidant behavior is claimed, it is important to determine what, if any, role a child may have played in initiating avoidance of a parent, as well as the roles both parents had. Characteristics of the child may cause anger or exacerbate poor parenting skills in one parent or intensify anxiety and protectiveness in the other.

The effects of experiences with parents are also *transactional* (Sameroff 1983). This term has unfortunately come to be used commonly to refer to commercial exchanges, but it retains a specific meaning in developmental studies. Parent-child effects are transactional when they not only involve mutual impacts but also change over time. Such changes can occur as a result of experience (e.g., a new parent gets better at soothing a crying infant by practice; a baby learns to anticipate parental comforting when it has happened often) or of maturation (e.g., as a baby grows older, her reasons for crying change, and the parent is pushed to do things differently). Again, it is not certain to what extent these rules about infants apply to older children, but it is plausible that a parent's response to a child's distress about divorce will change both as the child gets older and as the length of the experience increases. In the same way, the nature of the child's response to the divorce changes with the child's maturation.

Some developmental topics and parental alienation considerations

What ages or stages are we talking about when we refer to child avoidant behavior and parental encouragement?

Because children's characteristics are qualitatively different at different developmental stages, any discussion of the relations between the parental alienation belief system and development must consider the ages of the children involved. Neither physical, nor emotional, nor cognitive characteristics will remain the same for years at a time, and all these characteristics can influence how divorce or marital conflict will affect a given child.

I have encountered one or two cases in which preschool children were said to display child avoidant behavior and to have avoided one parent because of the actions of the other parent. I believe this is rare in the United States but may be more common in other countries. Published work on parental alienation-related cases suggests that the lower limit of the age range for child avoidant behavior cases is about nine years (and even this may apply only when older siblings are in the picture). The upper limit is normally the 18th birthday, after which the young person is no longer a minor. There are occasional cases in which a parent has a young adult declared incompetent and in need of guardianship and maintains control over a son or daughter more than 18 years of age, but this seems to be quite unusual.

Generally, parental alienation-related cases involve boys or girls from the preteen years through age 17. This fact suggests that developmental information from research on infants, toddlers, and preschoolers is not particularly useful for understanding child avoidant behavior, unless there is in a specific case, some reason to think that earlier developmental events have somehow been the foundation for a current rejection of a parent. Nevertheless, it has been common for parental alienation proponents to use information about much younger children as a rationale for their arguments. It has been less common—in fact quite rare—for such authors to reference developmental phenomena that are likely to belong to the ages of the children involved in parental alienation-related cases.

Social and emotional development and the parental alienation belief system

As child avoidance concerns are most obviously related to social and emotional relationships between parents and children, and to children's emotional attitudes toward their parents, social and emotional development is of particular interest here.

Attachment

The idea of emotional attachment of a young child to a caregiver, as initially described by John Bowlby in the 1940s, is almost universally appealed to in any discussion about children, even though on the whole it is very poorly understood. Briefly, attachment is the term used to describe the attitude and behavior of a toddler toward familiar caregivers. The child seeks to stay near the caregiver when she is hungry, tired, sick, or frightened, avoids close contact with unfamiliar people, and shows distress and anxiety when separated from the familiar person or approached too closely by strangers. Intense grief and distress may last for weeks if the child experiences abrupt, long-term separation from familiar caregivers, but children will recover from such an experience and form new attachments if given sensitive, responsive care by new caregivers. Brief separations are also likely to trigger distress, but children recover from this and adapt to repeated experiences, especially if a temporary caregiver becomes familiar to them. Attachment is a very robust developmental phenomenon and young children readily form attachments if they are with consistent, sensitive, responsive caregivers, even when there are several such people.

As children develop through the preschool and early school years, they become much more able to tolerate separation from familiar people and to develop secondary attachments to teachers, aunts and uncles, babysitters, and so on. They may still have strong preferences for familiar people when injured, sick, or under stress, but they can accept care from others without the intense grief of earlier years. They can maintain an emotional attachment to a parent in spite of separation, although they may also respond with anger to being or feeling abandoned.

By the later elementary school and middle school years, children have advanced still further in being able to maintain attachments when away from a caregiver. At this stage of life, children in many cultures are sent away from home for longer or shorter periods, to boarding schools, to summer camps, or to work for other families. The children may feel homesick or mildly anxious in the new situations, but if their experiences are positive, they adapt and do well. They do not lose emotional attachments and if on good terms with parents are happy to see them from time to time, but they do not require much contact as long as they do not encounter adverse circumstances. They can deal well with non-parent adults who are friendly and helpful and can have excellent peer relationships. Their emotional attachment to familiar caregivers has transmuted into a set of ideas and feelings that shape all their social relationships, not just those with their parents. As Psouni, Breinholst, Esbjorn, and Steele (2020) have pointed out, "the evaluation of the attachment system in middle childhood ought to also include other important individuals, for instance, best friends" (p. 2).

During adolescence, boys and girls may or may not maintain close relationships with their parents, depending on circumstances. They often develop very positive attitudes—even "crushes"—toward teachers, coaches, or non-parent adults in their families. Above all, their emotional attachments begin to turn toward their peers and to include romantic involvements which may come to feel far more important than the parent relationship. Although still benefiting from positive parental guidance, teenagers are focused on leaving their families and moving into adult life. Abrupt separations, like the death of a parent, are of course disturbing and distressing to most adolescents, but their reactions to loss are more like those of adults and do not include the intense, almost existential, sense of threat that seems to be experienced by much younger children when separated from familiar people.

Temperament and personality

Earlier in this chapter, it was remarked that people commonly assume that adult caregivers "shape" children's personality development. That viewpoint fails to take into account biological differences among children and the extent to which these shape both child and caregiver actions.

Temperament is a term used to describe individual, biologically determined ways of responding to the world. Infants, children, adolescents, and adults are all creatures of their own temperaments. To a considerable extent, the personality characteristics of a newborn baby predict certain individual characteristics as they will appear in one, five, ten, and more years. Of course, the way a person responded to the environment at birth or even at one year of age is not going to be the same as the responses seen at age ten or older. A distressed baby cries, but a distressed 15 year old might shout, swear, throw things, or run away. However, a newborn who is calm (compared to other newborns) and easy to comfort (compared to other newborns) grows to be a 15 year old who is calm (compared to other 15 year olds) and easy to reason with and help when troubled (compared to other 15 year olds). These temperamental features stay constant even though the specific behaviors change with age.

The study of temperament has involved various classifications of temperamental types. Briefly, it may be helpful to think about three features of temperament that seem to make a lot of difference to personality over the years (Thomas and Chess 1986). These are *mood quality, adaptability, and threshold of responsiveness.* Mood quality refers to the tendency of an individual to be cheerful, or to be slightly sad, when in an emotionally neutral situation. Adaptability refers to the tendency to adjust slowly or more rapidly to changing conditions, including social and relationship changes. Threshold of responsiveness describes the individual's tendency to respond to slight changes in the environment (for example, small alterations in food temperature or taste) or to fail to notice any but large changes.

Babies are described as difficult in temperament when they have a tendency to negative mood quality, do not adapt easily to change, and are very reactive to slight differences in the environment. These characteristics tend to remain somewhat problematic through childhood and adolescence, but as children become more able to take care of their own needs, a difficult temperament puts less pressure on caregivers, and children themselves may learn "workarounds" that help them deal better with environmental factors.

Resilience is a personality characteristic that may be partly biological and partly learned. Resilient individuals who encounter difficult situations, whether social problems or other adverse events, may be strongly affected by those problems, but they "bounce back" when a problem clears up. Less resilient people may continue to experience the negative effects of an experience even though the event is over, and time has passed.

Relevance of temperament to parental alienation issues

Temperament is an individual factor that helps determine how an experience will affect a person. Resilient children and those with "easy" temperaments may adapt relatively quickly to changes and may recover completely from adverse experiences. Less resilient, "difficult" children are more likely to display negative feelings, to adapt slowly to change, and to be aware of slight differences that someone else might easily ignore.

Divorce involves considerable change in children's lives, from alterations in time with each parent (and grandparent) to changed routines of daily living and lessened financial resources. Children may move to a new house with a parent, and if they attend public schools this may entail transfer to a new school. Neighbors and playmates may be different. In addition, one or both parents may introduce new romantic partners, who often bring their own children into the picture with them. Aspects of life that used to be open to choice, like how holidays are spent, may now be the subject of a parenting plan ordered by a court.

Children who are not resilient or temperamentally comfortable with change can respond with intense protest and negativism to these changed circumstances. Their protest may be general, or it may focus on one parent and be expressed by avoidance of that parent. Such children may demand to stay in one place, with one parent, to avoid the difficulties of change and life disruption that are so hard for them to cope with. Although no child or teenager welcomes divorce unless abuse and domestic violence have been present, the resilient and "easy" child is less likely to protest so vehemently or to express such powerful negative feelings.

Cognitive development and parental alienation concerns

Children's relationships with their parents are by definition associated with their social and emotional lives and the way those lives change developmentally. However, relationships also depend on people's beliefs, attitudes, and cognitive skills. Children's abilities to think and remember have been described as changing in a stage-like manner just as social and emotional characteristics change. That is, rather than simply getting better and better at thinking as they age, children show different ways of thinking at different ages. Much attention has been paid to very early cognitive development, but because most children involved in parental alienation-related cases are older, infant and toddler cognition is not of much interest for the purposes of this chapter. Instead, we need to look at cognitive abilities in later childhood and adolescence.

Older children and concrete operational thought

Children in the preteen years often have an excellent command of language and know many facts, especially about things that interest them. They like to master specialized information (not necessarily about school subjects!) and enjoy their own expertise in some area that interests them—which may be of as little interest to adults as the latest stats on a young celebrity.

The kind of thinking shown most of the time by children in this age group has been described as *concrete operational thought* (Wadsworth 2003). Unlike younger children, preteens are able to work with cognitive operations like decisions to add or subtract or putting items into complex categories. Some of the operations they use have been taught in school, others they have figured out by themselves or learned through observation. They can easily solve class inclusion problems that stump preschoolers. For example, given a dozen wooden beads of which nine are painted white and the others are unpainted, they can correctly answer the question, "are there more wooden beads or more painted beads?", which young children cannot do. Children with concrete operational thinking skills can understand that a painted bead can be a wooden bead at the same time, which they must do in order to solve this problem.

Although preteens can perform many cognitive operations, they are still limited by the *concrete* part of this cognitive stage. It is difficult for them to think about problems that do not involve real things—even though they enjoy fantastic stories. They can solve a lot of concrete problems but are troubled when asked to speculate or predict about something that has never yet happened or seems impossible. They may just guess if asked to do this.

Adolescents and formal operational thought

During adolescence, most (but not all) young people develop into a new cognitive stage. Their ways of thinking are qualitatively different from what they were before, so they are not just quicker to solve problems than younger children, they actually can solve problems in whole new ways. This new stage is called the period of *formal operational thinking* (Wadsworth 2003). Adolescents begin to be able to apply mental operations to information without being concerned about whether something could actually happen. They pay attention to the *form* of a problem or question, not the concrete details. They thus become free to speculate and predict possibilities, although they are not always correct in their conclusions (any more than older people are).

In formal operational thinking, adolescents can mentally hold one or more factors constant while thinking about how other factors can change and what the outcome of those changes could be if they happened. This ability means that they can think in terms of probabilities—how often one thing might occur, and how this compares with alternative occurrences. They are no longer "stuck" with absolutes that must or must not happen, as they were when thinking concretely. They are also able to consider how events might work out differently if some factors were altered. This in turn makes it possible to consider the perspectives of other people in new ways.

Formal operational thinking is fascinating for teenagers but at times overwhelms them. With new ways to consider the world, they may feel they have no source of stability—it seems as if anything could be true. Many adolescents display a powerful and uncomfortable idealism, as they conceive of how much better the world could be than it is but lack the practical experience to do anything but deplore the reality around them, including their parents' behavior. They may also be disturbed by their own new ability to take other people's perspectives, as they mentally experience an "imaginary audience" whose highly critical notional reactions to themselves teenagers often think of as if they were real.

There have not been many studies of continuing cognitive changes as adolescents approach college years, but one (Perry 1970) suggested that college freshmen arrive with the tendency to accept certain ideas presented to them as "right" and others as "wrong", without much analysis. This seems to be in contradiction to the idea that adolescents can consider many factors at once, but it may simply be that developing cognitive skills are most effectively applied to easy or familiar information rather than to anything new or difficult. It is also the case that emotional stress interferes with cognitive skills and can create real difficulties in using newly developed high-level cognitive abilities.

Relevance of cognitive development to child avoidance issues

The effects of cognitive development on attitudes toward one or both parents are clear. Children at the concrete operational stage are limited in their abilities to think how things could be different from what they are and have difficulty taking the perspectives of other people, especially adults who have very different motives and ideas than children do. Concrete operational children may accept what they are told but take little interest in it unless the statements are related to their own interests and desires. Preteens experiencing divorce are likely to be at this cognitive stage, and it is likely that adolescents may revert to concrete operational thinking when stressed and asked to consider unfamiliar issues like adult relationships.

Formal operational thinking in older adolescents offers different challenges to divorcing families and may easily be connected to avoidance of a parent. Adolescent idealism focuses on how different and better a situation could be than it is, causing the adolescent to see his parents' conflict as unnecessary and deplorable. Pressure to side with and have contact with one parent is likely to result in resistance as the teenager struggles for autonomy and the establishment of a separate identity.

One parental alienation advocate (Warshak 2010) has attributed avoidance of a parent to problems of critical thinking brought about in some way by the preferred parent. For example, Warshak described the avoidant teenager as showing unusual polarization of thinking, leading to the view that one parent was good, the other bad, without gray areas. Warshak has praised a treatment program, Family Bridges™, for treating children's critical thinking difficulties and therefore making it possible for them to be reunited with the avoided parent, whom they now accept because they are thinking more realistically. However, the tendencies that Warshak describes as problems of critical thinking are in fact common among adolescents and even among adults, and no empirical work has even attempted to show differences in thinking skills between adolescents who avoid a parent and those who do not. As for the treatment, considering the period of years over which formal operational thinking develops and becomes consolidated, it is difficult to imagine that a few days of a program could quickly and dramatically alter cognitive skills. Warshak has not demonstrated any changes in critical thinking attributable to the treatment program.

Physical development and child avoidance issues

It's easy to concentrate on emotional and social development when we consider children and adolescents in the abstract, but when we look at actual young people we are forced to remember that they *grow* up. Changes in physical size and maturity drive many steps in development as they enable children to function more like adults. Stronger muscles and longer legs and arms give them new physical abilities.

In addition to their new skills, growing children experience along with growth some profound changes in the way they think about themselves—and the way other people perceive them. Peers, teachers, neighbors, doctors, dentists, and policemen all respond differently to a person they see as more adult-like than they do to one who seems more child-like. These different responses are very much a mixed bag, as they may involve wariness or even fear of a large, strong-looking teenager, but may also feature confidence in or respect for someone who appears adult-like. The responses of parents to physical growth and maturation may be even more mixed than those of outsiders because parents have many years of experience of one way of thinking about a child and may have difficulty "shifting gears" to respond appropriately to the same, now physically different, person.

When we add signs of sexual maturation to the physical growth of preteens and adolescents, there is even more room for confusion and more need for changed attitudes in every family member. Physical growth in later childhood and the teen years is organized around the occurrence of puberty or reproductive maturation. Reproductive maturation in girls is marked unmistakably by menarche, the first occurrence of menstruation. Spermarche, the parallel event in boys, is much less visible for obvious reasons.

The impact of puberty is different for boys and for girls not only because of the noticeability of events for the two sexes, but because of differences in timing. On average, boys reach puberty two years later than girls do (roughly age 15, as compared to roughly age 13). But as is so often the case in development, these average differences are very small compared to the large range of individual differences. For example, girls are considered to be in the normal range for menarche if the event occurs when they are anywhere from age 9 to age 16. There are relatively few girls at the earlier and later ends of this range, however, and both their own feelings and others' responses to them are affected by "early timing" and "late timing", with late-timing girls getting more approval from adults. The same situation—a wide range of normal for age at puberty—holds for boys, but adults generally approve more of early-timing boys.

As puberty approaches, there is a physical build-up taking about two years, in which children's bodies undergo the beginnings of transformation from immature to reproductively mature individuals. After many years of slow growth, children experience growth spurts, with rapid growth of arms and legs followed by growth of the torso, and gains in weight and in musculature. Breasts develop in girls (and sometimes, temporarily, in boys), and hair patterns alter, with sex-related patterns of facial, underarm, and pubic hair. These events make it possible to predict menarche and spermarche with some accuracy and to give the developing adolescent guidance about the physical and social changes just ahead.

For the adolescent, the physical changes of puberty can be sources of pride, anxiety, and embarrassment, especially if they think in terms of the imaginary audience mentioned earlier in this chapter. A noticeable degree of irritability tends to proceed and follow puberty but to calm in a year or so.

Relevance of physical development for child avoidance of a parent

The largest number of preteens and teenagers who are said to show child avoidant behavior, attributed to parental encouragement, appear to be in the pubescent age range. In addition to their tendency to irritability around the time of puberty, these children quite involuntarily bring many complicating factors into the divorce situation. Their rapid growth and other developmental changes add to or even multiply the impact of other changes on family members. The children eat more than they did before, and their rapid growth demands new clothes and shoes just when family finances may be the tightest. Their new involvement in sports, the arts, or hobbies can place much pressure on parents' resources of time and money and create scheduling issues and conflict with parenting plans.

Reproductive maturity of teenagers creates the need for shifting social relationships even in well-functioning, intact families. Even girls who are on excellent terms with their fathers may not want the fathers to be told when menarche arrives. Boys may be concerned about the evidence of ejaculations if the mother or a sister changes their sheets. These worries and anxieties can easily become exaggerated with respect to time spent with a divorced opposite-sex parent or with a new stepparent. A girl may not want to try to handle menstrual hygiene at her father's house (what does she do with a used pad or tampon, for example?), and she may be quite unwilling to explain this to him (or perhaps to anyone).

Puberty brings with it an increased awareness of and knowledge about sexuality. Teenagers who might otherwise manage to deny that their parents have sexual lives may be forced to confront adult sexuality when parents divorce. One or both parents may have boyfriends or girlfriends or may even quickly cohabit or remarry; these are situations where it is impossible to hide all of the manifestations of a sexual relationship. Adolescents can find every aspect of parental sexuality so repugnant that they do not want to see a parent in a bathrobe at breakfast or observe a kiss between a parent and a new partner. These attitudes are clearly in conflict with the right of a divorced parent to enter into a new romantic relationship, but it is important for the parent to understand that the attitudes are a real part of a child's thinking and may even cause the child to avoid contact.

Conclusion

This review of child and adolescent development shows the many changing characteristics of young individuals that may influence their responses to divorce and to one or both parents. Emotional, cognitive, and even physical development can influence a child's thoughts and feelings about parents. These normal changes before and during adolescence help to explain situations in which a child avoids one of his or her divorced parents without having been indoctrinated by the preferred parent.

References

Mercer, Jean. *Understanding Attachment.* Westport, CT: Praeger, 2006.

Psouni, Elia, Sonia Breinholst, Barbara Esbjorn, and Howard Steele. "Factor Structure in the *Friends and Family* Interview." *Scandinavian Journal of Psychology,* 61, 2020: 460–469. DOI: 10.1111/sjop.12604.

Sameroff, Arnold. "Factors in Predicting Successful Parenting." In *Minimizing High-risk Parenting,* edited by Valerie Sasserath, 6–24. Skillman, NJ: Johnson & Johnson, 1983.

Sroufe, L. Alan. "Attachment and Development: A Prospective, Longitudinal Study from Birth to Adulthood." *Attachment & Human Development,* 7, 2005: 349–367.

Thomas, Alexander, and Stella Chess. "The New York Longitudinal Study: From Infancy to Early Adulthood." In *The Study of Temperament,* edited by Robert Plomin and Judy Dunn, 39–52. Hillsdale, NJ: Erlbaum, 1986.

Wadsworth, Barry. *Piaget's Theory of Cognitive and Affective development: Foundations of Constructivism.* New York: Pearson, 2003.

Warshak, Richard. "Using Insights from Social Science to Reconnect Parents and Alienated Children." *Family Court Review,* 48, 2010: 48–80.

Part 3

When a child avoids a parent

Scientific and legal analyses

Chapter 10

Parental alienation concepts and the law

An international perspective

Suzanne Zaccour

When parents separate, they often agree on a custody arrangement without needing the involvement of the courts. However, when they cannot agree, a court will have to determine the parents' respective responsibilities regarding caring for children. While terminology varies across jurisdictions, in Western countries, the general idea is the same: the court must determine the custody arrangement that best furthers the child's interest. This criterion of the "best interest of the child" is the cornerstone of decisions involving children; other issues such as the parents' rights, comfort, or interests are not meant to be considered. The child's wish to live with one parent or the other is generally considered – and is more important the older the child is – but it does not bind the court. This means that a court can always impose on the child a decision against their wishes, although this will be unusual if the child is a teenager.

So where does parental alienation come in? Parental alienation is a belief system that purports to inform the courts of what is in the child's best interest. Typically, the father will argue that it is not in the child's best interest to reside with the mother because the mother is alienating.

The parent who wants the court to consider parental alienation will generally ask for the permission to introduce "expert evidence", meaning to have a psychologist or another mental-health professional testify before the judge. The expert will then provide an opinion as to whether the child is alienated and what the court should do. Sometimes, the custody evaluator chosen to help the court decide on custody matters will spontaneously mention parental alienation, without them having been hired to pose a "diagnosis" on this precise issue.

As with the child's wishes, the expert's opinion does not bind the court, but if the expert is credible, it is likely that the judge will follow, or at least seriously consider, their recommendation. Thus, parental alienation is not a formal legislated criterion, but rather an opinion that can be argued in court and that may come up in expert evaluations (despite the lack of credible scientific evidence supporting a "diagnosis" of parental alienation).

DOI: 10.4324/9781003095927-13

In some jurisdictions, judges are directed to consider, in determining custody, the parents' willingness to facilitate contact with the other parent. This criterion is known as the "friendly parent rule." Courts may also be directed to try to facilitate the child's maximum contact with both parents, as long as such contact is consistent with the child's best interest. Evidence that a parent is "alienating" may then be used to argue that it is not in the child's best interest to grant custody to that parent because they will not facilitate contact with the other parent. Because the parental alienation belief system is increasingly normalized in popular and legal discourse, sometimes courts will come to this conclusion even in the absence of any expert testimony proving the child's "alienation."

Once the court has decided on the custody arrangement, parents must follow it. In cases where parental alienation is a concern, courts may order many things in addition to the custody schedule – they may order parents not to denigrate each other, forbid contact with family members, require parents to communicate to each other certain information regarding the child, etc. Parents sometimes refuse to comply with courts' orders: for example, by not bringing the child to the other parent when they are supposed to or by travelling with the child without the other parent's authorization. Courts have the power to sanction non-compliance with what is known as contempt of court. Contempt is an offence that may lead to a fine or, in rare instances, to jail time. In cases where parental alienation is alleged, conflict levels are generally high between the parents and issues of domestic or family violence are common. Mothers sometimes refuse to comply with court orders because they consider the other parent dangerous. Refusing to let the children exercise their "right" to see their father (it is the child who has a right to access, not the parent) may be done to protect the children from harm. However, violent fathers will often threaten to involve the courts and ask them to declare the mother in contempt. This is one way in which courts may be complicit in post-separation violence.

Having seen how allegations of parental alienation generally play out in custody proceedings, we will now explore in more detail the role that the parental alienation belief system plays in these cases (part 1). We will then consider the major concerns that the parental alienation belief system raises (part 2) before turning to possible solutions (part 3). This chapter is not intended as a practical guide for lawyers who confront allegations of parental alienation, but rather as an international overview of how legal systems have responded to the parental alienation belief system. While describing the use of parental alienation in the courts of all the countries of the world would be impossible, effort is made to draw attention to literature from a diversity of European and American jurisdictions when such literature is available.

This chapter provides an overview of the use – and abuse – of parental alienation theory in court cases from an international perspective. Since their invention, the "parental alienation syndrome" and "parental alienation" belief systems have enjoyed increased recognition by the legal system, to the point of becoming a significant threat to women's and children's safety and autonomy. We will explore how this happened and survey the main concerns raised in the literature regarding courts' reliance on the parental alienation belief system.

When parents separate, they often agree on a custody arrangement without needing the involvement of the courts. However, when they cannot agree, a court will have to determine the parents' respective responsibilities regarding caring for children. While terminology varies across jurisdictions, in Western states, the general idea is the same: the court must determine the custody arrangement that best furthers the child's interest. This criterion of the "best interest of the child" is the cornerstone of decisions involving children; other issues such as the parents' rights, comfort or interests are not meant to be considered. The child's wish to live with one parent or the other is generally considered – and is more important the older the child is – but it does not bind the court. This means that a court can always impose on the child a decision against their wishes, although this will be unusual if the child is a teenager.

So where does parental alienation come in? Parental alienation is a belief system that purports to inform the courts of what is in the child's best interest. Typically, the father will argue that it is not in the child's best interest to reside with the mother because the mother is alienating.

The parent who wants the court to consider parental alienation will generally ask for the permission to introduce "expert evidence", meaning to have a psychologist or another mental-health professional testify before the judge. The expert will then provide an opinion as to whether the child is alienated and what the court should do. Sometimes, the custody evaluator chosen to help the court decide on custody matters will spontaneously mention parental alienation, without them having been hired to pose a "diagnosis" on this precise issue.

As with the child's wishes, the expert's opinion does not bind the court, but if the expert is credible, it is likely that the judge will follow, or at least seriously consider, their recommendation. Thus, parental alienation is not a formal legislated criterion, but rather an opinion that can be argued in court and that may come up in expert evaluations (despite the lack of credible scientific evidence supporting a "diagnosis" of parental alienation).

In some jurisdictions, judges are directed to consider, in determining custody, the parents' willingness to facilitate contact with the other parent. This criterion is known as the "friendly parent rule." Courts may also be directed to try to facilitate the child's maximum contact with both parents, as long as such contact is consistent with the child's best interest. Evidence that a parent is "alienating" may then be used to argue that it is not in the child's best interest to grant custody to that parent because they will not facilitate contact with the other parent. Because the parental alienation belief system is increasingly normalized in popular and legal discourse, sometimes courts will come to this conclusion even in the absence of any expert testimony proving the child's "alienation."

Once the court has decided on the custody arrangement, parents must follow it. In cases where parental alienation is a concern, courts may order many things in addition to the custody schedule – they may order parents not to denigrate each other, forbid contact with family members, require parents to communicate to each other certain information regarding the child, etc. Parents sometimes refuse to comply with courts' orders: for example, by not bringing the child to the other parent when they are supposed to or by travelling with the child without the other parent's authorization. Courts have the power to sanction non-compliance with what is known as contempt of court. Contempt is an offence that may lead to a fine or, in rare instances, to jail time. In cases where parental alienation is alleged, conflict levels are generally high between the parents and issues of domestic or family violence are common. Mothers sometimes refuse to comply with court orders because they consider the other parent dangerous. Refusing to let the children exercise their "right" to see their father (it is the child who has a right to access, not the parent) may be done to protect the children from harm. However, violent fathers will often threaten to involve the courts and ask them to declare the mother in contempt. This is one way in which courts may be complicit in post-separation violence.

Having seen how allegations of parental alienation generally play out in custody proceedings, we will now explore in more detail the role that the parental alienation belief system plays in these cases (part 1). We will then consider the major concerns that the parental alienation belief system raises (part 2) before turning to possible solutions (part 3). This chapter is not intended as a practical guide for lawyers who confront allegations of parental alienation, but rather as an international overview of how legal systems have responded to the parental alienation belief system. While describing the use of parental alienation in the courts of all the countries of the world would be impossible, effort is made to draw attention to literature from a diversity of European and American jurisdictions when such literature is available.

Parental alienation's place and role in the legal system

Normalization of shared custody

The parental alienation belief system has infiltrated the courts, the justice system, and the legal discourse very quickly, to the point of becoming ubiquitous in the family courts in many jurisdictions (see e.g., regarding the US, Meier 2009, 240). For example, a random sample of 96 expert reports in Rome, Italy found a diagnosis of severe parental alienation syndrome in 12% of the cases (Lavadera, Ferracuti, and Togliatti 2012, 339)!

Even though the term parental alienation syndrome was invented in the 1980s, it is only in the past few decades that this ideology has become prevalent in the court systems of many countries. In the US, parental alienation emerged in legal cases in the late 1990s and in the 2000s (Meier 2009, 240). Authors from other jurisdictions also note the emergence and popularization of parental alienation claims in the courts in that period (in France: Prigent 2019, 58; in Australia: Rathus 2020, 8). In Spain, an author observes the development of the parental alienation belief system in the law after the promulgation of a law against gender-based violence in 2004; parental alienation then became "a tool to stall the enforcement of gender equality legislation" (Casas Vila 2020, 1). A Quebec study suggests that the parental alienation belief system is much more prevalent since the 2010s, having now become "commonly used in both family court and child protection services" (Lapierre et al. 2020, 34). The authors conclude that "within the last ten years, what was previously a latent discourse has now become legitimized and institutionalized" (Lapierre et al. 2020, 34).

Several factors explain the rise of parental alienation claims. The rise in shared custody, in particular, is a factor that commentators have associated with the propagation of this ideology in Canada, Italy, Spain, and the United States (Casas Vila 2020, 3; Lavadera, Ferracuti, and Togliatti 2012, 340; Meier 2009, 244; Sheehy and Boyd 2020, 81).

How did we get to a societal preference for shared custody? Traditionally, the law in England (as in other patriarchal countries) granted custody of the children to the father, even in cases of neglect or violence against the child. Intervention into the father–child relationship "was exceedingly rare, and termination of the father–child relationship even rarer" (Katz 1992, 125). Paternal rights were only challenged in the 19th century with the emergence of the "tender years doctrine", which afforded judges the discretion to grant custody to the mother for children under the age of seven (from 1839) or 16 (from 1873) years old (Katz 1992, 127). This change in British law influenced other countries, including most of Europe and the United States.

The tender years doctrine is associated in popular imagination with a preference for mothers over fathers, yet as Canadian author Susan Boyd has demonstrated, the assumed "maternal presumption" was anything but absolute. Mothers who did not fulfil traditional expectations or who were blamed for breaking up the marriage, lacking domestic skills or fleeing the marital home still risked losing custody. Boyd concludes that "[t]he tender years doctrine rarely constituted a clear presumption in favour of mothers unless judges chose to emphasize it" (Boyd 2003, 71).

Effective or not, maternal presumptions sit uneasily with current norms of formal gender equality, and so the tender years doctrine has now been replaced with formal equality between the parents and the increasingly popular norm of shared custody. Indeed, shared custody has become in certain jurisdictions – through legislation or simply judicial practices – the dominant or preferable custody arrangement. In the Unites Stated, Joan Meier explains that

> [t]wenty three states have adopted legislative preferences for joint custody regardless of a party's opposition . . ., but any family lawyer will tell you that even in states that lack such legislation, joint custody is still very strongly preferred and overwhelmingly commonly imposed by courts.
>
> (Meier 2009, 244–245)

Belgium has also gone as far as to impose in the law a preference for shared custody: the parent opposed to it bears the burden of convincing the court not to impose it (Bélanger 2019). Rates of shared custody have also risen significantly in other European jurisdictions (e.g. Denmark and the Netherlands: Spruijt and Duindam 2009; Sweden: Swedish Government 2011). The problem is that "equal shared custody" is equal in name only: often the mother continues to assume the majority of the caretaking work after separation even as the shared custody arrangement threatens her entitlement to child support (see Cadolle 2009).

Within the paradigm of shared custody, each parent is equally important and equally responsible for the child – no matter who was the primary caregiver while the parents resided together. The parental alienation belief system has thus greatly benefitted from the empirically dubious idea that fathers' involvement should be increased and that children benefit from frequent and regular contact with both parents (Meier 2009, 244; see also Shaffer 2007), an idea that has gained in traction because of its seemingly egalitarian quality. Fathers' rights groups have adopted the parental alienation vocabulary and managed to convey in popular discourse the myth that fathers are the underdogs in custody litigation and that this is a grave injustice to be redressed. Therefore, judges and professionals have become suspicious of mothers who ask for full custody of their children, even when they have good reasons to do so (such as violence, neglect, or simply lack of previous care work by the father).

The parental alienation belief system is persistent and pernicious. It can appear under different names and seems to resist attempts to cut it off. For example, Boyd and Lindy has found that in British Columbia "[some] cases have read in a 'friendly parent' rule and emphasized 'maximum contact' even though a deliberate decision was made not to include these [federal] norms in the [provincial legislation]" (Boyd and Lindy 2016, 46). Even when cases make no mention of parental alienation, often the same ideas appear under different names, such as "parental gatekeeping" (Neilson 2018, 8) or "loyalty conflict". Unfortunately, parental alienation has now become an important and even unavoidable issue in family law.

The parental alienation concept and determination of the child's best interests

The parental alienation belief system affects both family court and child protection services, although the former is more studied (Lapierre et al. 2020, 41) and is the focus of this chapter.

What role does the parental alienation ideology play in child custody cases? As we have seen, the parental alienation belief system generally comes up in evaluating parental capacities and in determining what is in the child's best interest. Parental alienation advocates propose that alienating behaviour is not good parenting, and even that it is child abuse; thus, it would not be in the child's best interest to reside with the "alienator." Parental alienation thinking is often introduced through experts rather than the parties (Meier 2009, 240 (United States); Casas Vila 2020, 48 (Spain)): experts will testify, for instance, that the mother has deep psychological issues, that she is alienating the child from the father, and that the child's development will be compromised unless the relationship with the father is restored.

Parental alienation ideology seems particularly useful for attacking the parental capacity of good mothers: if the mother were violent or negligent, the father would not need the parental alienation argument to obtain custody of the child. Parental alienation beliefs thus support fathers' and professionals' attempts to paint caring mothers as inadequate. This is increasingly so since parental alienation proponents have begun insisting that alienation can be done unconsciously and can be caused by warm and involved parenting (see Meier 2009, 248). Therefore, mothers can lose custody for being "alienating" even as they are taking good care of the children and the children are thriving, simply because the mothers supposedly unconsciously resent the father or are asking the court to reduce contacts between the father and the child. What is more, parental alienation seems to be claimed not only when the father's relationship with the child has deteriorated, but also in cases where the child never had a positive relationship with their father.

Courts and evaluators often assume that it is in the child's best interest to have frequent contacts with both parents. As seen in the introduction, such assumptions may be embedded in legislation directing courts to allocate as much time as possible with each parent, and to consider each parent's willingness to facilitate contact with the other parent. Yet as a review of the social science literature concludes, the research.

> suggests that children do not necessarily benefit from greater contact with their non-custodial parent – rather it is the type of parenting the non-custodial parent engages in, not the amount of time that parent spends with the children, that is most significant. [The research also] indicates that children do not fare better post-divorce in joint custody

arrangements than they do in sole custody, and some children – including those in high conflict families – may fare worse.

(Shaffer 2007, 287)

Reliance on the child's best interest by proponents of the parental alienation belief system is all the more ironic given that many cases "have resulted in the total estrangement of the child from the mother in the name of [parental alienation syndrome] prevention" (Meier 2009, 243). In other words, courts are preventing children from seeing their mothers under the pretext that children need both parents!

Furthermore, Linda Neilson has demonstrated in a study of Canadian decisions that the logic and discourse of parental alienation centres more around parental rights than children's interest (Neilson 2018), casting further doubt on the proposition that parental alienation ideology serves to protect children. When courts endorse the parental alienation belief system, they tend to neglect factors relevant to the child's best interest

such as parent-child warmth, the closeness of the parent-child relationships, scrutiny of parenting practices, safety, and stability factors ... Instead courts appear ... to be starting from the premise of parental entitlement to equal parenting and to be attributing blame with punishment when children or their primary care parents resist that concept.

(Neilson 2018, 18–19)

In contrast, "when courts [do] engage in thorough analysis of evidence associated with statutory best interest of the child criteria", they are less likely to find that parental alienation is present, to discount the child's views, or to make punitive orders (Neilson 2018, 19). Thus, parental alienation appears to obscure rather than illuminate the quest to determine the child's best interest.

In addition to painting the "alienator" as a bad parent, the parental alienation belief system also attacks the child's wishes and perceptions. Generally, the wishes of a teenager will be given considerable weight or even be determinative in a custody decision. Yet parental alienation ideology asserts that the alienated child or teenager's wishes are not their "true" desires, but rather reflect brainwashing by the preferred parent. The discounting of the child's wishes simply because they are "alienated" is criticized; as Peter Jaffe, Dan Ashbourne, and Alfred Mamo note,

[t]he notion that children's views have to be 'independent' of those of their parents is unrealistic and defies the whole notion of parenting. Everyone's beliefs, and more so children's, are influenced by significant people in their life, especially those in a position of authority.

(Jaffe, Ashbourne, and Mamo 2010, 141)

Some judges respect the wishes of an older teenager simply because contact becomes difficult to enforce, but others do not hesitate to make repeated attempts to force contact even when the child or teenager persists in asking to live with their mother or for the contacts to cease.

Brazil: explicit legislation on parental alienation

As we have seen, parental alienation ideology has insidiously infiltrated the legal culture even without legislative recognition. Matters are even worse in Brazil due to its explicit legislation on parental alienation. Parental alienation legislation further legitimizes parental alienation ideology, marginalizing the child's concerns and prescribing remedies that are harmful to the child's emotional well-being.

Since 2010, in Brazil, a federal law provides for the assessment and punishment of parental alienation. The lei n° 12.318, de 26 de Agosto de 2010 defines an "act of parental alienation" as

> an interference in the psychological development of the child or adolescent promoted or induced by one of the parents, by the grandparents or by people who have authority, custody or supervision over the child or adolescent, in order that the child or adolescent reject a parent or to prejudice the establishment or maintenance of the child or adolescent's bond with that parent.
>
> (art. 2, my translation)

The law presents examples alienating behaviour, notably false accusations of violence:

I   – to conduct a campaign to disqualify the parent's conduct in them exercising their paternity or maternity;

II   – to hinder the exercise of the parental authority;

III – to hinder the child or adolescent's contact with the parent;

IV   – to hinder the exercise of the legislated right to family life;

V   – to deliberately hide from the parent information relevant to the child or adolescent, including information pertaining to school, health, and changes of domicile;

VI   – to file a false report against the parent, against their family members or against grandparents, to hinder or obstruct their custody of the child or adolescent;

VII – to move far away, without justification, in order to hinder the child or adolescent's living together with the other parent, with their family members or with grandparents (art. 2, my translation).

The law states that alienating behaviour interferes with the child's fundamental right to a "healthy family life" (art. 3, my translation), and that an indication of parental alienation gives a case priority status (art. 4). The judge must then declare provisional measures, and the child and "alienated" parent have a right to, at minimum, supervised access, unless there is an imminent risk to the child, attested by a professional (art 4). The law also empowers the judge to demand a psychological or biopsychosocial evaluation and establishes its modalities (art. 5).

The presence of alienating acts empowers the judge to:

I   – declare the presence of parental alienation and give a warning to the alienator;
II   – change the custody regime in favour of the alienated parent;
III   – order the alienator to pay a fine;
IV   – order psychological or biopsychosocial counselling;
V   – change the custody regime to reverse it or order shared custody;
VI   – precautionarily fix the child or adolescent's residence;
VII   – declare the suspension of parental authority. (art 6, my translation)

If shared custody is impossible, custody is to be granted "with preference for the parent who makes possible the effective living together of the child or adolescent with the other parent" (art. 7, my translation), i.e. the "alienated" parent.

Note that mere alienating *conduct* can give rise to these remedies, seemingly without the need to show that the child actually rejects the "alienated" parent. The problem is that "alienating" actions such as denigrating the other parent are the norm in high-conflict custody cases (Johnston 2005). Of further concern is the fact that the law was enacted despite the shortage of scientific studies in that country (Soma et al. 2016). The remedies provided for are damaging to children, and the law does not seem to account for the fact that the "alienated" parent may not provide the healthiest environment for the child.

Mexico City similarly used to have extreme provisions on parental alienation in the Civil Code of the Federal District, which described alienating behaviours as family violence and required extreme remedies such as immediate custody transfers, "treatment" of the child and a complete cut-off of contacts with the "alienating" parent. Thankfully, the provisions were abolished due to concerns that recognizing parental alienation prevented the identification of situations of family violence.

Fathers' rights groups in several jurisdictions are calling for more laws legitimizing parental alienation ideology. This is highly concerning, as it is likely that legislative support would magnify the damages caused by the parental alienation belief system. While no causal link can be assumed, one study found that Brazilian professionals were more likely than U.S. professionals to find that a proposed scenario involved parental alienation and to endorse changes in the custody arrangement (Goldfarb et al. 2019, 336). Brazilian professionals were also "less likely than their U.S. counterparts to refer a case involving child sexual abuse to [child protection services]" (Goldfarb et al. 2019, 337).

Problems with applying the parental alienation belief system in court cases

Admission into evidence despite lack of scientific basis

Expert or scientific evidence is not automatically admissible in court: it must satisfy an admissibility test. The party who wants to have a psychologist or psychiatrist testify must ask the court for permission.

Many legal scholars have demonstrated that "parental alienation" or "parental alienation syndrome" should not be admissible based on the applicable test, especially in the United States where there is much literature on this question (Hoult 2006; Joyce 2019; Walker, Brantley, and Rigsbee 2004; Williams 2001; Zirogiannis 2001). At the federal level, Rule 702 of the Federal Rules of Evidence states conditions to be met for an expert to testify in court. States have comparable rules regarding the admissibility of expert testimony. Without going into the details, the general idea is to ensure that the proposed evidence is relevant and sufficiently reliable.

Yet commentators have observed that evidence regarding "parental alienation" does not reach the level of reliability and scientific acceptability that would be necessary to make it admissible. As Meier noted in the United States, "family courts and even courts of appeal are increasingly accepting the application of [parental alienation syndrome] or [parental alienation] findings while sidestepping the admissibility question" (Meier 2009, 240). Carol Bruch also observed in 2001 that courts that considered the admissibility of parental alienation syndrome evidence mostly concluded that the test for scientific reliability was not met, yet, in the vast majority of cases, it seems that no one thought to question the admissibility of expert evidence (Bruch 2001a, 540). In my study of Quebec cases, similarly, none of the reported cases for 2016 even mentioned admissibility concerns regarding parental alienation evidence (Zaccour 2018, 1086).

Therefore, despite the requirement that expert evidence be admissible in law as a prerequisite to being presented in court, admissibility seems to be rarely questioned in alienation cases, leading to the courts making important decisions based on unreliable theories.

Parental alienation concepts are overbroad and have inconsistent definitions

There is no single agreed-upon definition of parental alienation. As Jaffe et al. observe, "[d]epending on the knowledge, orientation and training of the professionals involved, the term alienation may have different meanings, with variation in diagnosis and intervention" (Jaffe, Ashbourne, and Mamo 2010, 137). This lack of consensus is mirrored in the law. Courts might not distinguish parental alienation from parental alienation syndrome, apply inconsistent tests and definitions, and order remedies that are no longer recommended by alienation researchers.

Because parental alienation has such a flexible meaning, new models have not managed to fully displace Richard Gardner's "parental alienation syndrome". In Quebec, Simon Lapierre, Patrick Ladouceur, Michèle Frenette, and Isabelle Côté found that even though professionals distanced themselves from Gardner's work and the qualification of parental alienation as a syndrome, "parental alienation syndrome", "parental alienation", "alienating behaviours", and even "high conflict" were often used interchangeably in their discourse (Lapierre et al. 2020, 38). Despite the scientific community's strong rejection of parental alienation syndrome, this concept continues to be applied in court cases, for instance in Spain (Martín López 2009) and in Italy 2006 (Lavadera, Ferracuti, and Togliatti 2012). Thus, the possibility that newer models of alienation might be less gender-biased or more precise than their ancestor parental alienation syndrome grants little – or perhaps no – protection against the absurdities of Gardner's model.

I explored this theme in my study of Quebec court cases, where I found an inconsistent use of parental alienation models, theories, and definitions (Zaccour 2018, 1086). I observed that judges rarely chose a model of parental alienation or parental alienation syndrome or even defined the concept. They concluded that children were alienated without considering whether the children could instead be "realistically estranged" (i.e., whether they had sufficient reasons to reject the parent), and sometimes without expert evidence. Judges also found that very young children and children who had a good relationship with both parents were "alienated". We can conclude that while parental alienation gives court decisions an appearance of objectivity and scientific integrity, it is rather a catch-all term that has little to do with what the literature advances.

Another major problem is that judges and experts will sometimes conclude that parental alienation is present because the parent engages in alienating behaviour *or* because the child rejects a parent, without checking that both conditions are met. This means that parents can be chastised because their child appears "alienated" even when they have done nothing to cause this situation. In other words, mothers, not fathers, are held responsible for the quality of the father-child relationship. Mothers can thus be blamed for relationship problem that predates the separation and that is attributable to the father's violence or absence.

In other cases, mothers are punished for engaging in so-called "alienating" behaviour that had no impact. Yet behaviours commonly described as alienating, such as denigrating the other parent, are extremely prevalent on both sides of high-conflict families and rarely affect the child's relationship with their parents (Johnston 2005). Thus, using a purely parent-focused lens is problematic, especially as the behaviours that can be considered alienating are on a broad spectrum. Put simply: pretty much any case can be described as an alienation case. Even when mothers do nothing to "alienate" their child, they are often blamed for "unconscious" alienating behaviour, even when it is rather the father who denigrates them.

Gardner's parental alienation syndrome was highly problematic, but at least it required the child to exhibit "symptoms" of alienation. The move to new theories seems to have made matters worse. Courts and experts no longer try to paint alienators are evil mothers, and instead emphasize the alienation can be done unconsciously. Mothers can then be accused of alienation merely for asking the court to reduce the child's contacts with the father or for having negative feelings toward their violent ex-partner (Zaccour 2018, 1091). As Meier observes,

> evaluators' and courts' tendency to psychoanalyze mothers and to attribute alienating behavior to their unconscious, has made it possible to accuse a mother of alienation – and thereby dismiss abuse claims –even when she has done nothing to alienate the child.
>
> (Meier 2010, 244)

For example, in some cases mothers are framed as alienators simply because they unconsciously transmit their fear of the father to the child. Lapierre et al. also observe that "the move towards a continuum approach and the focus on 'alienating behaviours' may have resulted in a growing number of women being seen as 'alienating' parents without even a thorough assessment of the family dynamics" (Lapierre et al. 2020, 42). To make matters worse, even as alienation is defined very broadly, courts will go as far as to intervene in situations of "quasi-alienation", were they find "clues" of alienation, a situation "close" to parental alienation, or a "risk" of alienation (Martín López 2009, 10; Zaccour 2018, 1100). With the breadth that parental alienation theory is taking, one is left to wonder if there is even one custody court case where a father could *not* try their luck with an allegation of alienation.

Biases against women

One concern of parental alienation critics is gender bias: even though proponents sometimes use gender-neutral language, in practice, it is mothers who are most often accused of alienation. This is also reflected in professionals' discourse about alienation, where examples provided "generally involv[e] an 'alienating' mother and a 'rejected' father" (Lapierre et al. 2020, 39). Empirical studies have shown that professionals are more likely to rate scenarios as involving parental alienation (Meier and Dickson 2017;

Priolo-Filho et al. 2018) or to endorse specific interventions including a change in custody (Goldfarb et al. 2019) when the alleged alienator is female rather than male.

This gender bias is carried in family court. Studies of court cases have shown mothers to be more likely to be accused of parental alienation. In a Brazilian study, 66% of cases had a woman accused of alienation (generally the mother), compared to only 17% of cases with a male alienator (in 11% of the cases, both a man and a woman were accused of alienation) (Andrade 2016, 190). That same study found that men made more unfounded accusations than women (Andrade 2016, 192). Canadian studies have also found that women are more likely to be seen as alienating and that fathers are more likely to make unsubstantiated allegations of alienation (Bala, Hunt, and McCarney 2010, 176; Harris 2014, 43; Sheehy and Boyd 2020, 82; Zaccour 2018, 1084). In a small Australian study, "[w]hile allegations against the mother [were] slightly more common than allegations against the father, only about half of those involving the mother were substantiated, while all of those against the father were substantiated" (Berns 2001). I found only one study, of expert reports in Italy, that found that "alienating parents were equally divided between fathers and mothers" (Lavadera, Ferracuti, and Togliatti 2012, 337).

The consequences of an accusation of parental alienation are also gendered. In a recent U.S. study, Meier found that "when accused of alienation, mothers have twice the odds of losing custody compared to fathers" (Meier 2020, 100), because they are more likely to lose custody when the accusation of alienation is not credited. In Boyd and Sheehy's Canadian study, women declared alienators were penalized through custody changes at a rate of 48%, whereas only 31% of alienating fathers suffered such consequences (Sheehy and Boyd 2020, 83). In Neilson's Canadian study, children were left in the primary care of their mother despite a definitive parental alienation finding in 17% of the cases, compared with a 36% proportion when it was the father who was found alienating (Neilson 2018, 11). In my Quebec study, mothers accused of alienation were more likely to receive ambiguous findings (for example, there is no proof of alienation but there are "signs" of alienation) and to be imposed preventive remedies (Zaccour 2018, 1084).

Some will say that parental alienation is not biased against women: rather, women are more likely to be alienators because they are more likely to be the custodial parent (Bala, Hunt, and McCarney 2010, 176). Yet this explanation does not account for the many ways in which parental alienation is deeply gendered. For instance, the parental alienation belief system plays with the "taken-for-granted gender stereotype of the 'scorned woman'" (Adams 2006, 327), relying on stereotypes that mothers are vindictive, pathological liars. The preference for the alienation narrative in cases that should instead be about domestic violence is also a form of gender bias (Zaccour 2020, 349).

Minimizing of concerns about abuse and domestic violence

One important form of gender bias and the most important concern of parental alienation critics is the way that accusations of parental alienation are used to retaliate for, and detract courts from, allegations of paternal or domestic violence. Note that I prefer the word "violence" to the more euphemistic term "abuse" (see Ricci 2017), but I understand "violence" in its broader sense. Violence does not necessarily involve physical violence; it includes economic, sexual, emotional, or psychologic violence, stalking, harassment, and court-related harassment, as well as other controlling or coercive behaviours.

Despite scholars' assertion that alienation occurs when the child rejects a parent *without reason*, the alienation belief system thrives in the context of domestic and family violence. In an Australian study of 31 cases involving possible parental alienation "syndrome", 17 included allegations of domestic violence (Berns 2001, 197). And among cases in which the mother was the alleged alienator, 8 out of 17 allegations of alienation were made in response to the mother's allegations of sexual violence toward the child (Berns 2001, 202). A French study based on interviews with 13 separated mothers accused of parental alienation found that they all had been victims of domestic violence, including post-separation violence and violence directed at the children (Prigent and Sueur 2020, 62). That same study found that the label of "alienator" was difficult to escape from: years after the "diagnosis", mothers were still considered dangerous for their children (Prigent and Sueur 2020, 62). Several larger studies have found that a high proportion of parental alienation cases involve allegations of intimate partner violence and/or violence against the child (see e.g., Berns 2001, 198; Sheehy and Boyd 2020; Zaccour 2018, 1083). Domestic violence is not the exception, but rather the norm, in alienation cases.

Often protective mothers' healthy responses to violence, such as trying to limit contact with the father or reaching out to professionals to diagnose, treat, and protect the child, are constructed as evidence of alienation (Bruch 2001b, 388). So is fearing or resenting the father: according to a Canadian study, "women's reactions to violence seem to overshadow men's violence such that women become alienators for not suppressing their own fear" (Sheehy and Boyd 2020, 88). As a result, when parental alienation is at play,

> [c]onsiderable onus is placed on mothers to show they can cooperate with fathers even if [intimate partner violence] has been established: mothers are called alienators if they do not coach their children to view their fathers in a positive light, or force contact.
>
> (Sheehy and Boyd 2020, 88)

False allegations of violence are the emblem of parental alienation. Thus parental alienation has amplified gender bias and myths about family violence in family court: "[a]lthough in the past, the credibility of an abuse claim was always an implicit concern in custody litigation, now, such claims are automatically treated as highly suspect" (Meier 2009, 242). Yet the myth that mothers make up false allegations to gain custody is unsupported by empirical evidence (see Romito and Crisma 2009, 33). Family courts already pay insufficient attention to family violence, awarding custody to abusive fathers in a high proportion of the cases – and even perhaps more often than to victim mothers or non-abusive fathers (see Arizona Coalition Against Domestic Violence 2003; Harrison 2008; Meier 2003; Saccuzzo and Johnson 2004; Silverman et al. 2004). The parental alienation belief system only makes matters worse.

Because of its emphasis on false allegations of violence, the parental alienation belief system "deters the legal system from investigating reports of ill-treatment or sexual abuse on behalf of the noncustodial parent as it tends to automatically classify allegations as false" (Clemente and Padilla-Racero 2015, 181). Judicial focus is diverted from the father's violence to the mother's alleged parental alienation (Harris 2014, 54). As a result, allegations of domestic violence are often ignored, minimized, or left unresolved (Sheehy and Boyd 2020). A research study published in 2004 found that, among mothers who reported violence against the child, three quarters lost custody to the alleged abuser and close to half were accused of parental alienation syndrome (Stahly et al. 2004). In another study, "mothers' claims of abuse, especially child physical or sexual abuse, increase[d] their risk of losing custody, and . . . fathers' cross-claims of alienation virtually double that risk" (Meier 2020, 92). These effects are highly gendered: "fathers alleging mothers are abusive are not similarly undermined when mothers cross-claim alienation" (Meier 2020, 92).

The worst part is that parental alienation is weaponized against mothers even when intimate partner violence is proven and confirmed by the court. Indeed in some cases "alienation trumps abuse" (Meier 2020, 99), meaning that mothers can lose custody to violent fathers even when the court believes the mother. Sheehy and Boyd have observed that, in cases where both alienation and intimate partner violence are at play, "[j]udges are more likely to focus on alienating behaviours than [intimate partner violence] when determining custody and access. [Intimate partner violence] is rarely condemned or related to children's best interests in the way that alienation is" (Sheehy and Boyd 2020, 88).

The risk of losing custody to their abuser – and even losing any right of contact – discourages mothers from denouncing domestic violence (Lapierre and Côté 2016; see also Casas Vila 2020, 8). Authors in Australia have observed that mothers are advised not to ask for no-contact orders because they might be perceived as hostile (Chisholm 2009; Laing 2010; Rhoades, Graycar, and Harrison 2001). These deterring effects render women and children more vulnerable to continued violence. They also deter mothers from leaving a violent partner.

Believers in parental alienation often cast aside these concerns by saying that parental alienation does not apply when the child has good reasons to reject the father. Yet as Janet Johnston and Matthew Sullivan admit, "[d]espite universal agreement that family violence and child abuse preclude a finding of PA, virtually no common criteria exist to ensure these distinctions have been made" (Johnston and Sullivan 2020, 273). Barbara Fidler and Nicholas Bala also observe that "there are no valid empirical assessment protocols or tools that can reliably measure or establish the presence of alienation as differentiated from other types of [parent-child contact problems], including realistic estrangement or justified rejection" (Fidler and Bala 2020, 581).

Moreover, actors in the family justice system often ignore or are misinformed about domestic violence, especially post-separation violence (Lapierre et al. 2020, 40), and they still view "domestic violence as a context that fosters the emergence of 'alienating behaviours' and increases the risk of 'parental alienation'" (Lapierre et al. 2020, 40; see also Godbout and Parent 2012; Meier 2010). My study of Quebec appellate decisions on parental alienation shows that even when there is a history of domestic violence in a file, often appellate courts make no mention of it (Zaccour 2020, 319). Therefore, the proposition – not even shared by all parental alienation proponents – that the parental alienation framework does not apply to circumstances of domestic violence solves nothing. The current significance of parental alienation theory "is inseparable from its utility as a means of discrediting claims of abuse" (Meier 2010, 221).

In fact, it is likely that parental alienation has become so popular exactly because it provides an alternative explanation to the difficult realities of domestic and child violence (Meier 2009, 243). Because judges and evaluators are routinely exposed to conflictual cases, among which family violence is particularly prevalent (Bruch 2001a, 529; Jaffe, Lemon, and Poisson 2003), they may resist the knowledge that most men they encounter have been violent and prefer the explanation that allegations of violence are fabricated (Meier 2009, 243).

Overall, parental alienation ideology reinforces the harmful myths that:

> (a) mothers' rejection of shared custody is highly suspect; (b) vengeful mothers often seek to exclude fathers from children's lives; (c) fathers who contest custody do so out of paternal affection and concern; (d) adult abuse allegations are minimally relevant to children's welfare; (e) mothers frequently fabricate or exaggerate other abuse allegations in order to gain an advantage in custody litigation; and (f) child sexual abuse allegations are used by mothers as an outrageous 'bombshell'.
>
> (Meier 2009, 242)

In promoting and exploiting these myths, parental alienation concepts pose a real danger to mothers and children. As I concluded in a recent article on the disappearance of domestic violence from alienation cases, "[p]arental alienation and domestic violence are not separate fields of study" (Zaccour 2020, 357).

Parental alienation interventions may be harmful

Even if courts were correct in labelling children as "alienated", the remedies that are proposed and applied would still be harmful. While Gardner suggested an immediate change in custody to the rejected parent in cases of severe parental alienation syndrome, scholars working on modern iterations of the concept are sometimes more careful in their proposed remedies. For example, Janet Johnston and Joan Kelly caution that

> [o]nly in those relatively rare situations where the aligned parent is found to be psychotic or severely character-disordered, a serious abduction risk, and has corresponding serious parenting deficits do we consider a change of custody warranted. Even then, to obtain custody the rejected parent should be assessed as providing a better alternative.
>
> (Johnston and Kelly 2005, 87)

Despite these words of caution, alienation concepts have often been used to order a change in custody against the child's and the mother's wishes and without proof that the father is a better parent. As Jaffe et al. explain,

> [t]here is a potential danger of a misdiagnosis leading to a change of custody, and children placed at risk if the rejected parent is abusive or neglectful, inadequate, or a virtual stranger to the child. There is also a risk that important attachment relationships with the favored parent are disrupted or severed, resulting in traumatic separations and loss. . ... Furthermore, changes in custody may disrupt children's social and school relationships that were previously important sources of stability and conflict-free zones for them.
>
> (Jaffe, Ashbourne, and Mamo 2010, 138)

Courts have gone as far as to jail children and mothers for resisting court orders responding to findings of alienation (Meier 2009, 238).

In a context where there is "little empirical research evidence to support any specific intervention, such as changing custody" and "no empirical data that indicates whether entrenched alienation and total permanent rejection of a biological parent has long-term deleterious effects on children's psychological development" (Sullivan and Kelly 2001, 313), the drastic interventions recommended by parental alienation "experts" in contested custody cases are truly damaging. Johnston also acknowledges that "[t]he long-term outcomes [of therapeutic work with alienated children and their parents] are a matter of conjecture and currently unknown" (Johnston, Walters, and Friedlander 2001, 329). Anecdotally,

> [i]n more than one case children subjected to these procedures [total cut-off the child's contact with the mother and 'deprogramming' of the child] have become suicidal – and in some cases died – in reaction to court orders to live with the father they believed abused them.
>
> (Meier 2009, 238)

What are possible solutions to the parental alienation problem?

Those whose work is dedicated to highlighting the problems with alienation theory know that offering a fool-proof solution is far from simple. The parental alienation belief system has contaminated the family and child protection systems across many countries, sometimes appearing under a variety of names. Given the pervasiveness of the parental alienation ideology and its many problems, proposed solutions often fall short.

Some proposals target parental alienation's problematic "remedies". We can imagine limiting court interventions to encouraging parents not to denigrate each other and perhaps recommending individual therapy, rather than permitting courts to resort to coercive interventions such as forced therapy, forced contact, or changes in custody.

Some empirical support for a laid-back approach comes from the observation that, in some cases, children spontaneously re-initiate contact with the rejected parent (Darnall and Steinberg 2008). In a study by Johnston and Goldman, "[v]irtually all of the youth who had actively resisted or refused visitation subsequently, on their own accord, initiated reconciliation with the rejected parent some time during their late teens and early twenties" (Johnston and Goldman 2010, 113). Cases where children did not reconnect with their parent mostly "involve[d] a rejected parent with serious parenting deficits" (Johnston and Goldman 2010, 114).

Jaffe et al. suggest that at least in some cases, non-intervention may be the way to go, as a way to first "do no harm" (Jaffe, Ashbourne, and Mamo 2010, 138). They explain that "[t]he negative consequences of some coercive interventions in some cases may be worse than the presenting problems" (Jaffe, Ashbourne, and Mamo 2010, 138) and that "in some cases the benefit of having both relationships may be outweighed by the emotional and financial costs of litigation [and] never ending conflicts" (Jaffe, Ashbourne, and Mamo 2010, 143). Bruch makes similar observations and reasons that:

> Children ought not to be asked to function under circumstances that would challenge or overwhelm even the strongest adults. A child's chance

for healthy development requires that parents, judges, and mental health professionals face the realities of the child's situation. This includes a realistic understanding of the limitations of dispute resolution techniques, therapy, and legal compulsion in high-conflict cases. Overly ambitious efforts with only small chances of success should be shunned in favor of reducing the child's emotional burdens, respecting the child's fears, and enhancing the child's emotional stability.

(Bruch 2001a, 549)

As Judith Wallerstein, Julia Lewis, and Sandra Blakeslee observe:

There is great advantage in allowing natural maturation to take its course and to avoid overzealous intervention to break these alliances, which are usually strengthened by efforts to separate the allies. In this, the alliance may be akin to a moderate case of flu that mobilizes the immune system and generates antibodies. It is not a fulminant cancer requiring radical surgery or limb amputation, especially by poorly trained surgeons.

(Wallerstein, Lewis, and Blakeslee 2001, 116–117)

Certainly, scaling back interventions is an important step toward protecting children's autonomy and emotional safety.

Another angle is to try to prevent parental alienation from being used as a tool of control by violent fathers. Some suggest that parental alienation should not apply in situations of family violence, or, more timidly, in situations where the child's reaction can be explained by the father's violence. Meier develops an interesting proposal. She suggests "limiting the definition of what constitutes alienation so that good faith protective actions cannot be re-framed as alienation" (Meier 2010, 230): "This approach would mean that petitions for protection or taking a child for evaluation or therapy, all of which are routinely pointed to as sinister forms of alienation, could not be considered evidence of 'alienating behaviors'" (Meier 2010, 230). Alienation would be limited to "cases where abuse has been completely ruled out" or to cases "where there is an independent basis for claiming alienation other than the other parent's allegations of abuse and actions consistent with those allegations" (Meier 2010, 230).

I have two caveats to these suggestions. First, we may wonder whether it is possible to use parental alienation concepts without framing protective behaviours as alienation, given how intertwined parental alienation claims are with the idea of false abuse allegations. A second concern is that establishing a domestic violence exception supposes that courts are aware of the context of domestic violence and take it into account. My study of Quebec appellate courts suggests that courts are often unaware or choose to disregard a context of domestic violence in alienation cases (Zaccour 2020).

Another imperative change is to tighten the definition of parental alienation: the concept should not be so broad as to be applicable in all contested cases. Findings of alienation should be ruled out when there is no actual, strong, and consistent rejection by the child, as well as when there is no evidence that the parent engages in conscious, specific, and repeated behaviour to sabotage the parent-child relationship.

Excluding situations of family violence and applying the full definition of alienation (rejection by the child + harmful influence by the parent) could reduce the applicability of the alienation ideology to a handful of cases, thus solving most of its problems. When talking of reforming parental alienation, however, we need to think long and hard about whether and how new definitions will reach the courts and, perhaps most importantly, custody experts. Lapierre et al. have cautioned that

> [a]ttempts to clarify what 'parental alienation' is and when it should or should not be used may . . . have limited impact in practice. [T]hough several documents and key informants noted that 'parental alienation' should not be used in domestic violence situations, abused women are still seen as engaging in 'parental alienation'.
>
> (Lapierre et al. 2020, 42)

The parental alienation belief system is resilient and tends to always find new ways to benefit abusers. However, in conjunction with other steps, limiting interventions, tightening the definition, and excluding cases of domestic and parental violence could help in reducing parental alienation's harmful effects. For example, Meier proposes a seven-step approach that would reduce gender bias and false positives, especially in contexts of family violence:

- "1. Assess abuse first." (Meier 2010, 242)
- "2. Expertise in abuse is required." (Meier 2010, 242)
- "3. Once abuse is found, alienation claims by the accused abuser are not considered" (Meier 2010, 242)
- "4. Where abuse allegations are not confirmed, the allegations themselves may not be treated as evidence of alienation." (Meier 2010, 243)
- "5. Alienation claims are independently evaluated only under limited conditions:" (Meier 2010, 243) ("Only if (1) all possible 'natural' reasons for the child's extreme hostility to the other parent (such as affinity, development, or the disfavored parent's own conduct) have been ruled out; and, (2) there is identifiable intentional alienating behavior by the 'aligned' parent" (Meier 2010, 243)
- "6. Only conscious intent and specific behaviors may constitute alienating conduct." (Meier 2010, 244)
- "7. Remedies for confirmed alienation are limited to healing the child's relationship with the alienated parent" (Meier 2010, 245) rather than undermining the child's relationship with the preferred parent.

Given the difficulties in reforming parental alienation, and its more than questionable origins, perhaps the best way forward is quite simply to abolish the use of parental alienation in the law – maybe through legislation, judicial guidance, and/or professional codes. While this suggestion may seem radical, alienation proponents have not demonstrated that, for all its issues, alienation ideology is worth saving.

Meier observes that "[a]s an objective matter, alienation is, simply, a very minor problem for the courts" (Meier 2010, 239–240), one that is "at issue in only a tiny fraction of cases" (Meier 2010, 244). In these circumstances, why use a psychological label that brings more harm than good? If the deliberate alienating conduct affects the child's well-being, the courts can still make orders to ensure that their best interest is guaranteed. But they should rely on alienation ideology.

Even this radical solution may not succeed given the pervasiveness and the adaptability of the parental alienation belief system. In Spain, "[b]oth the government and the General Council of the Judiciary have taken a stand against the deployment of PAS in the legal system, but the notion of parental alienation is still widely used in family courts" (Casas Vila 2020, 1). Lapierre et al.'s work also suggests

> that drawing attention to the problems associated with Gardner's work on 'parental alienation syndrome', opposing the inclusion of 'parental alienation' in policies and adopting policies that prohibit its use is not sufficient to eradicate reliance on 'parental alienation' in family court and child protection practices.
>
> (Lapierre et al. 2020, 42)

The concept of alienation has already gone through several iterations: "pathological alignment" (Wallerstein and Kelly 1980), "parental alienation syndrome" (Gardner 1992), "parental alienation" (Kelly and Johnston 2001), "access resistance" (Stoltz and Ney 2002), etc. In this context, "professionals may use different terms to designate situations that they still understand as 'parental alienation' and make exactly the same recommendations, making it even more difficult to document the problem" (Lapierre et al. 2020, 42).

This means that to really rid the law of the problems with parental alienation, profound changes must be made. Rules presuming that maximum contact with both parents is in the child's interest and that the custodial parent should be willing to facilitate contact with the non-custodial parent need to be abolished. Preferences for shared custody in contested cases must be clearly rejected, especially in cases of abuse, violence, or negligence. The child and the custodial parent's safety must be given priority above all other concerns. Finally, legal actors and custody evaluators must be trained to understand and recognize domestic violence, especially post-separation violence. As long as domestic violence is minimized, ignored, and misunderstood in custody courts, alienation concepts risk re-sprouting with other names to continue to marginalize women's safety concerns. The vague concept of the best interest of the child also calls for a clearer definition that recognizes the impact of domestic violence on the child's development and on the violent parent's parental capacity. Even the basic functioning of the adversarial justice system is in question and probably needs rethinking (Blank and Ney 2006, 146). Only then will we have addressed the legal context that made it possible for parental alienation ideology to thrive in the first place today.

What is clear is that the use of parental alienation in family courts is not an easy problem, and that bold action must be taken *now*.

Conclusion

This chapter has provided an overview of the use of parental alienation or parental alienation syndrome in custody cases. We have seen that alienation ideology has planted deep roots in legal systems across Europe and America, causing a plethora of problems and putting mothers and children at risk. While the road to a full solution might be hidden from view, what is clear is that radical changes are urgently needed.

While research on alienation concepts often remains situated within one jurisdiction, here I have attempted to gather information from several countries: the United States, Canada, Australia, Mexico, Brazil, Spain, France, and Italy. What has become apparent in the process is how understudied the use of alienation in the courts remains. My hope is to see international collaboration emerge to create robust comparative research contrasting court cases across the world. While the available literature suggests that, to a large extent, problems are shared internationally, digging deeper into different jurisdictions' successes, failures, and challenges would surely enable the development of better strategies to resist the parental alienation belief system.

References

Adams, Michele A. "Framing Contests in Child Custody Disputes: Parental Alienation Syndrome, Child Abuse, Gender, and Fathers' Rights". *Family Law Quarterly* 40, 2006: 315–338.

Andrade, Mariana Cunha de. "Parental Alienation and the Brazilian Justice System: An Empirical Approach". *Brazilian Journal of Empirical Legal Studies* 3, 2016: 184–202.

Arizona Coalition against Domestic Violence. *Battered Mothers' Testimony Project: A Human Rights Approach to Child Custody and Domestic Violence*. Phoenix, AZ: Author, 2003.

Bala, Nicholas, Suzanne Hunt, and Carolyn McCarney. "Parental Alienation: Canadian Court Cases 1989–2008". *Family Court Review* 48, 2010: 164–179.

Bélanger, Marianne. "La garde partagée au Québec, en France et en Belgique : un mode de garde, trois réalités". 28 October 2019. http://www.orfq.inrs.ca/

la-garde-partagee-au-quebec-en-france-et-en-belgique-un-mode-de-garde-trois-realites/.

Berns, Sandra Spelman. "Parents Behaving Badly: Parental Alienation Syndrome in the Family Court—Magic Bullet or Poisoned Chalice". *Australian Journal of Family Law* 15, 2001: 191–214.

Blank, G. Kim, and Tara Ney. 2006. "The (De)construction of Conflict in Divorce Litigation: A Discursive Critique of 'Parental Alienation Syndrome' and 'The Alienated Child'". *Family Court Review* 44, 2006: 135–148.

Boyd, Susan B. *Child Custody, Law, and Women's Work*. Oxford: Oxford University Press, 2003.

Boyd, Susan B., and Ruben Lindy. "Violence against Women and the B.C. Family Law Act: Early Jurisprudence". *Canadian Family Law Quarterly* 35, 2016: 101–138.

Bruch, Carol S. "Parental Alienation Syndrome and Parental Alienation: Getting It Wrong in Child Custody Cases". *Family Law Quarterly* 35, 2001a: 527–552.

Bruch, Carol S. "Parental Alienation Syndrome: Junk Science in Child Custody Determinations". *European Journal of Law Reform* 3, 2001b: 383–404.

Cadolle, Sylvie. "Les points de vue différenciés des pères et des mères sur la résidence alternée". *Spirale*, 1, 2009: 57–77.

Casas Vila, Glòria. "Parental Alienation Syndrome in Spain: Opposed by the Government But Accepted in the Courts". *Journal of Social Welfare and Family Law* 43, 2020: 45–55.

Chisholm, Richard Colin. *Family Courts Violence Review*. Canberra: Attorney-General's Department, 2009.

Clemente, Miguel, and Dolores Padilla-Racero. "Facts Speak Louder Than Words: Science Versus the Pseudoscience of PAS". *Children and Youth Services Review* 56, 2015: 177–184. doi: 10.1016/j.childyouth.2015.07.005.

Darnall, Douglas, and Barbara F. Steinberg. "Motivational Models for Spontaneous Reunification with the Alienated Child: Part I". *The American Journal of Family Therapy* 36, 2008: 107–115.

Fidler, Barbara Jo, and Nicholas Bala. "Concepts, Controversies and Conundrums of 'Alienation': Lessons Learned in a Decade and Reflections on Challenges Ahead". *Family Court Review* 58, 2020: 576–603.

Gardner, Richard A. *True and False Accusations of Child Sex Abuse*. Cresskill, NJ: Creative Therapeutics, 1992. https://www.ncjrs.gov/App/abstractdb/AbstractDB-Details.aspx?id=144770.

Godbout, Elisabeth, and Claudine Parent. "The Life Paths and Lived Experiences of Adults Who Have Experienced Parental Alienation: A Retrospective Study". *Journal of Divorce & Remarriage* 53, 2012: 34–54. doi: 10.1080/10502556.2012.635967.

Goldfarb, Deborah, Sidnei Priolo-Filho, Janelle Sampana, Donna Shestowsky, Samara Wolpe, Lucia C. A. Williams, and Gail S. Goodman. "International Comparison of Family Court Professionals: Perceptions of Parental Alienation and Child Sexual Abuse Allegations". *International Journal on Child Maltreatment: Research, Policy and Practice* 2, 2019: 323–341. doi: 10.1007/s42448-019-00033-6.

Harris, Bryanne M. *Assessing and Responding to Parental Alienation Cases: Does Gender Matter in Canadian Court Decisions?* Master's Thesis, the University of Western Ontario, 2014. Electronic Thesis and Dissertation Repository, 1932. https://ir.lib.uwo.ca/etd/1932.

Harrison, Christine. 2008. "Implacably Hostile or Appropriately Protective? Women Managing Child Contact in the Context of Domestic Violence". *Violence against Women* 14, 2008: 381–405.

Hoult, Jennifer. "The Evidentiary Admissibility of Parental Alienation Syndrome: Science, Law, and Policy". *Children's Legal Rights Journal* 26, 2006: 1–61.

Jaffe, Peter G., Dan Ashbourne, and Alfred A. Mamo. "Early Identification and Prevention of Parent-child Alienation: A Framework for Balancing Risks and Benefits of Intervention". *Family Court Review* 48, 2010: 136–152.

Jaffe, Peter G., Nancy KD Lemon, and Samantha E. Poisson. *Child Custody and Domestic Violence: A Call for Safety and Accountability.* Newbury Park, CA: Sage, 2003.

Johnston, Janet R. "Children of Divorce Who Reject a Parent and Refuse Visitation: Recent Research and Social Policy Implications for the Alienated Child". *Family Law Quarterly* 38, 2005: 757–775.

Johnston, Janet R., and Judith Roth Goldman. "Outcomes of Family Counseling Interventions with Children Who Resist Visitation: An Addendum to Friedlander and Walters (2010)". *Family Court Review* 48, 2010: 12–15.

Johnston, Janet R., and Joan B. Kelly. "Rejoinder to Gardner's 'Commentary on Kelly and Johnston's 'The Alienated Child: A Reformulation of Parental Alienation Syndrome'''. *Sage Family Studies Abstracts* 27, 2005: 0410.

Johnston, Janet R., and Matthew J. Sullivan. "Parental Alienation: In Search of Common Ground for a More Differentiated Theory". *Family Court Review* 58, 2020: 270–292.

Johnston, Janet R., Marjorie Gans Walters, and Steven Friedlander. "Therapeutic Work with Alienated Children and their Families". *Family Court Review* 39, 2001: 316–333.

Joyce, Kimberley J. "Under the Mmicroscope: The Admissibility of Parental Alienation Syndrome". *Journal of the American Academy of Matrimonial Law* 32, 2019: 53–88.

Katz, Sanford N. "'That They May Thrive' Goal of Child Custody: Reflections on the Apparent Erosion of the Tender Years Presumption and the Emergence of the Primary Caretaker Presumptions". *Journal of Contemporary Health Law and Policy* 8, 1992: 123–136.

Kelly, Joan B., and Janet R. Johnston. "The Alienated Child: A Reformulation of Parental Alienation Syndrome". *Family Court Review* 39, 2001: 249–266.

Laing, Lesley. *No Way to Live: Women's Experiences of Negotiating the Family Law System in the Context of Domestic Violence.* Sydney: University of Sydney & Benevolent Society, 2010.

Lapierre, Simon, and Isabelle Côté. "Abused Women and the Threat of Parental Alienation: Shelter Workers' Perspectives". *Children and Youth Services Review* 65, 2016: 120–126.

Lapierre, Simon, Patrick Ladouceur, Michèle Frenette, and Isabelle Côté. "The Legitimization and Institutionalization of 'Parental Alienation' in the Province of Quebec". *Journal of Social Welfare and Family Law* 42, 2020: 30–44. doi: 10.1080/09649069.2019.1701922.

Lavadera, Anna Lubrano, Stefano Ferracuti, and Marisa Malagoli Togliatti. "Parental Alienation Syndrome in Italian Legal Judgments: An Exploratory Study". *International Journal of Law and Psychiatry* 35, 2012: 334–342.

Martín López, Paloma. 'Resistencias a la aplicación de la Ley Integral, el supuesto SAP y su proyección en las resoluciones Jjdiciales'. In *Comunicación Presentada En El III Congreso Del Observatorio de La Violencia de Género*, 1–15, edited by Poder Judicial Espana. Madrid: España, 2009.

Meier, Joan S. "Domestic Violence, Child Custody, and Child Protection: Understanding Judicial Resistance and Imagining the Solutions". *American University Journal of Gender, Social Policy & Law* 11, 2003: 657–732.

Meier, Joan S. "A Historical Perspective on Parental Alienation Syndrome and Parental Alienation". *Journal of Child Custody* 6, 2009: 232–257.

Meier, Joan S. "Getting Real About Abuse and Alienation: A Critique of Drozd and Olesen's Decision Tree". *Journal of Child Custody*, 7, 2010: 219–252.

Meier, Joan S. "US Child Custody Outcomes in Cases Involving Parental Alienation and Abuse Allegations: What Do the Data Show?" *Journal of Social Welfare and Family Law* 42, 2020: 92–105.

Meier, Joan S., and Sean Dickson. "Mapping Gender: Shedding Empirical Light on Family Courts' Treatment of Cases Involving Abuse and Alienation". *Law & Inequality* 35, 2017: 311–334.

Neilson, Linda C. *Parental Alienation Empirical Analysis: Child Best Interests or Parental Rights?* Vancouver: FREDA Centre for Research on Violence Against Women and Children, 2018.

Prigent, Pierre-Guillaume. "'How Is Parental Alienation Used Against Separated and Divorced Mothers in France : Intervention Avec Gwénola Sueur à l'ECDV 2019". Site personnel de Pierre-Guillaume Prigent. 29 September 2019. /29/09/2019/how-is-parental-alienation-used-against-separated-and-divorced-mothers-in-france/.

Prigent, Pierre-Guillaume, and Gwénola Sueur. "À qui profite la pseudo-théorie de l'aliénation parentale ?" *Deliberee* 9, 2020: 57–62.

Priolo-Filho, Sidnei, Deborah Goldfarb, Donna Shestowsky, Janelle Sampana, Lucia C. A. Williams, and Gail S. Goodman. "Judgments Regarding Parental Alienation When Parental Hostility or Child Sexual Abuse is Alleged". *Journal of Child Custody* 15, 2018: 302–329. doi: 10.1080/15379418.2018.1544531.

Rathus, Zoe. "A History of the Use of the Concept of Parental Alienation in the Australian Family Law System: Contradictions, Collisions and their Consequences". *Journal of Social Welfare and Family Law* 42, 2020: 5–17.

Rhoades, Helen, Reg Graycar, and Margaret Harrison. "The Family Law Reform Act 1995: The First Three Years". *Australian Family Lawyer: The Journal of the Family Law Section of the Law Council of Australia* 15, 2001: 1–8.

Ricci, Sandrine. 'Abus'. In *Dictionnaire Critique Du Sexisme Linguistique*, edited by Suzanne Zaccour and Michaël Lessard, 15–21. Montréal: Somme Toute, 2017.

Romito, Patrizia, and Micaela Crisma. "Les violences masculines occultées: Le syndrome d'aliénation parentale". *Empan* 1, 2009: 31–39.

Saccuzzo, Dennis P., and Nancy E. Johnson. "Child Custody Mediation's Failure to Protect: Why Should the Criminal Justice System Care?" *NIJ Journal* 251, 2004: 21–23.

Shaffer, Martha. "Joint Custody, Parental Conflict and Children's Adjustment to Divorce: What the Social Science Literature Does and Does Not Tell Us". *Canadian Family Law Quarterly* 26, 2007: 285–313.

Sheehy, Elizabeth, and Susan B. Boyd. "Penalizing Women's Fear: Intimate Partner Violence and Parental Alienation in Canadian Child Custody Cases". *Journal of Social Welfare and Family Law* 42, 2020: 80–91. doi: 10.1080/09649069.2020.1701940.

Silverman, Jay G., Cynthia M. Mesh, Carrie V. Cuthbert, Kim Slote, and Lundy Bancroft. "Child Custody Determinations in Cases Involving Intimate Partner Violence: A Human Rights Analysis". *American Journal of Public Health* 94, 2004: 951–957.

Soma, Sheila Maria Prado, MSBL de Castro, L. C. A. Williams, and Pedro Magrin Tannús. "Parental Alienation in Brazil: A Review of Scientific Publications". *Psicologia Em Estudo* 21, 2016: 377–388.

Spruijt, Ed, and Vincent Duindam. "Joint Physical Custody in the Netherlands and the Well-being of Children". *Journal of Divorce & Remarriage* 51, 2009: 65–82.

Stahly, Geraldine Butts, Linda Krajewski, Bianca Loya, Kyra Dotter, Kimberly Evans, Wesley Farris, Grace German, et al. "Protective Mothers in Child Custody Disputes: A Study of Judicial Abuse". In *Disorder in the Courts: Mothers and Their Allies Take on the Family Law System*, edited by Helen Grieco, Rachel Allen, and Jennifer Friedlin, 46–62. California: National Organization for Women, 2004.

Stoltz, Jo-Anne M., and Tara Ney. "Resistance to Visitation: Rethinking Parental and Child Alienation". *Family Court Review* 40, 2002: 220–231.

Sullivan, Matthew J., and Joan B. Kelly. "Legal and Psychological Management of Cases with an Alienated Child". *Family Court Review* 39, 2001: 299–315.

Swedish Government. *Continuous Parenthood: Responsibilities, Economy and Cooperation for the Sake of the Child.* Stockholm: Swedish Government Statistics, 2011.

Walker, Lenore E. A., Kristi L. Brantley, and Justin A. Rigsbee. "A Critical Analysis of Parental Alienation Syndrome and its Admissibility in the Family Court". *Journal of Child Custody* 1, 2004: 47–74.

Wallerstein, Judith S., and Joan B. Kelly. "Effects of Divorce on the Visiting Father–child Relationship". *The American Journal of Psychiatry* 137, 1980: 1534–1559.

Wallerstein, Judith S., Julia M. Lewis, and Sandra Blakeslee. *The Unexpected Legacy of Divorce: A 25 Year Landmark Study.* New York: Hyperion, 2001.

Williams, James. "Should Judges Close the Gate on PAS and PA?" *Family Court Review* 39, 2001: 267–281.

Zaccour, Suzanne. "Parental Alienation in Quebec Custody Litigation". *Les Cahiers de Droit* 59, 2018: 1073–1111.

Zaccour, Suzanne. "Does Domestic Violence Disappear from Parental Alienation Cases? Five Lessons from Quebec for Judges, Scholars, and Policymakers". *Canadian Journal of Family Law* 33, 2020: 301–357.

Zirogiannis, Lewis. "Evidentiary Issues with Parental Alienation Syndrome". *Family Court Review* 39, 2001: 334–343.

Chapter 11

Questioning the scientific validity of parental alienation labels in abuse cases

Joan Meier

A judge found that a father had seriously abused his wife and was pursuing custody in part as a means of control. However, when his young daughter reported sexual abuse during subsequent visits with her father, the evaluator suggested that parental alienation might be at work. The judge then concluded that the sexual abuse was not sufficiently proven, and awarded unsupervised visitation (while removing overnights).

– CW v EF (2007)

While parental alienation claims are not limited to cases involving abuse, they are particularly high risk and potentially harmful in those cases. The misuse of alienation to rebut abuse allegations has been extensively described elsewhere (Hunter, Burton and Trinder 2020; Meier 2009; Milchman 2017; Silberg and Dallam 2019). But such abuse-related critiques have not engaged closely with the research, which is routinely propounded in support of the scientific legitimacy of the concept. Yet without meaningful scientific support, alienation is little more than a subjective label. While this chapter aims to educate any professional considering an alienation label in a custody case, the contents may be of particular value to litigants challenging or judges considering the scientific validity and legal admissibility of parental alienation under *Daubert v Merrell Dow Pharmaceuticals, Inc.*, 509 U.S. 579 (1993).

This chapter begins with a brief overview of the concept and its destructive impact on custody and abuse litigation. It then provides an overview of the foundational beliefs driving alienation's use in these cases, and the widely acknowledged lack of objective, scientific support for them. Finally, it addresses some of the strengths and weaknesses of the newer "multi-factorial" approach to children's resistance to one parent.

"Alienation" as a custody weapon

Despite over 20 years of research and scholarship, to this day "parental alienation" still lacks a universal clinical or scientific definition (Johnston

DOI: 10.4324/9781003095927-14

and Sullivan 2020). However, the claim is generally understood to refer to the idea that a child's fear or rejection of one (typically non-custodial) parent stems from the malevolent influence of the preferred (typically custodial) parent. Most alienation writers acknowledge that the "alienation" hypothesis should be considered only if the child's estrangement has no "legitimate" justification, including, but not limited to, abuse (Bernet et al. 2018).

At the heart of the alienation concept is an unquestionable truth: Parents sometimes do try to turn their children against their other parent, perhaps particularly when breaking up. However, before the alienation label became treated as scientific, this kernel of human reality could not and did not imply the dire assertions embedded in "parental alienation." For instance, it was only after parental alienation syndrome ("PAS") and parental alienation ("PA") claims – as scientific constructs – became ubiquitous in court that it became conventional court wisdom that children subjected to such conduct would be permanently and irrevocably scarred, potentially permanently losing their relationship with the "alienated" parent. Prior to the reification of an undesirable parental behavior into a "diagnosis" or scientific condition (Milchman, Geffner and Meier 2020), parents' and children's allegations of paternal abuse were not automatically reframed as evidence of alienation, as they now routinely are (Kansas City Star Editorial Board 2020; Meier 2020). And before the pathologization of parental denigration or exclusion, the reality that parents do sometimes use their children to hurt the other parent did not imply that an "expert" could objectively know when one parent's negative views of the other were legitimate or illegitimate, nor know whether and to what extent those views may have caused a child's estrangement from the other parent. In short, assumptions like these, which are both implicit and explicit in the alienation label, are *not a matter of common sense*. Arguably, they *defy* common sense. Such bold assertions, then, should only be considered plausible if reliable scientific research bears them out. The remainder of this chapter explains why there is no such reliable research to underpin these speculative beliefs.

To be clear, rejecting the scientific legitimacy of parental alienation does not mean that courts should not care about a parent's efforts to turn children against the other parent. It does, however, mean that they should be modest in their assumptions about the impact of such behavior, about a child's reasons for an estrangement from a parent, and about any third party's ability to accurately assess these things. And it does mean that no "treatment" for "parental alienation" can be considered scientifically supported.

How did the alienation label come to be so widely discussed as a form of psychological science, and thus so powerful in custody litigation? Although the concept is viewed by some as a psychological condition, it was invented specifically for litigation. Gardner described PAS as a "syndrome" whereby vengeful mothers employ a variety of strategies including child abuse allegations as a "powerful weapon" to punish the ex and ensure custody to themselves (Gardner 1992a, 1992b; Nichols 2014). PAS, then, was specifically designed to refute court allegations of dangerousness by one parent against the other (primarily mothers against fathers), and to defend or insulate such accused parents in court.

Gardner's PAS caught on widely in courts but was ultimately widely rejected due to its extreme quality and recognized lack of scientific basis as well as the crude sexist explanations for the phenomenon offered by Gardner (Faller 1998; Meier 2013). After years of advocacy by certain proponents for inclusion of the renamed "parental alienation disorder" ("PAD") in the *Diagnostic and Statistical Manual-V*, it was rejected as lacking sufficient scientific support (Crary 2012; Milchman, Geffner and Meier 2020). Nonetheless, the leading advocates for treating parental alienation as a mental health disorder (Bernet, Baker and Morrison 2010) have rolled Gardner's eight criteria for PAS into their criteria for "diagnosing" parental alienation. As has been thoroughly explored by Madelyn Milchman (2019), these criteria are nothing more than subjective interpretations of a child's and parent's attitudes and behaviors toward the other parent, which could just as reflect children and parents seeking to avoid an abusive or otherwise destructive other parent. Moreover, the widespread discrediting of Gardner and PAS (and the *DSM*'s rejection of PAD) (Crary 2012; Meier 2013) should preclude reliance on any alienation expert or construct utilizing the same criteria.

Nonetheless, since Gardner's discrediting, a robust literature has burgeoned, which champions non-syndrome "alienation." The ubiquity of these approaches and the lack of science supporting them as well, are discussed further below.

Because alienation was invented for use in child custody litigation, it necessarily encompasses *both* a child's estrangement from a parent and one parent's criticism or negativity toward the other. If it did not identify a problem for the child, the concept would be irrelevant in custody litigation, and if it did not identify the opposing parent as the problem's source, the claim would not be useful in litigation – at least not to the accusing parent. In fact, if courts were really concerned about a parent-child estrangement on its own merits, an objective inquiry into a child's estrangement would surely focus first on what might have happened between that parent and child to cause it. Unfortunately, however, while this approach might be both efficient and correct from a child's perspective, it is not beneficial to an estranged parent – or professional – who is seeking to blame the other parent for the child's estrangement. The alienation label, then, is *intrinsically* and *necessarily* about blaming one parent for the other's poor relationship with a child. Even if multiple factors are recognized as contributing to a child's estrangement from a parent, the preferred parent is typically held responsible for the problem and for fixing it (Dallam and Silberg, 2016; Lubit, 2019; Milchman, Geffner and Meier 2020).

The harm of alienation labels in custody cases

Scholars including this author have described myriad ways that parental alienation labelling has been used in specific cases to deny or sidestep credible evidence of abuse, with grave consequences (Silberg and Dallam 2019; Meier 2010, 2020). Two examples suffice here:

> A couple divorces after a marriage marked by a "pattern of severe abuse" (as found by the court). During subsequent visits, the 2- and then 4-year-old child accuses her father of putting a "stick in my butt-butt" and "poo-poo" (child's word for vagina). Children's Hospital and County social workers, as well as the child's therapist, suspect sexual abuse and urge the mother to get legal protection for the child. After a civil trial, including an opinion by a forensic evaluator that parental alienation may be at work, the court concludes that the child is fabricating these allegations, possibly because, among other things, she "senses her mother's dislike" for her father. He finds no sexual abuse and orders unsupervised visits to continue – but is reversed on appeal.
>
> (*C.W. v E.F.*, 928 A.2d 655 (2007))

> A woman is periodically yelled at and assaulted by her husband, who also hits and yells at his young sons, while expressing his rage toward their mother. After she flees with the boys to England, later returning after parental kidnapping charges are filed against her, the custody evaluator describes her flight as "shameless alienation." The son's complaints about his father's treatment are pointed to as further evidence of the mother's alienation. Despite finding that the father has twice assaulted the mother, the court switches custody to the father due to the "alienation," and then – after the child reports another incident of paternal abuse, this time substantiated by child protection – the court ends all further visitation with the *mother*.
>
> (Arkansas Coalition Against Domestic Violence et al. 2010)

These cases are not unique; they are emblematic. Numerous scholars and professionals have reported and surveyed the widespread misuse of the alienation label to deny credible reports of domestic violence or child abuse (Bancroft, Silverman and Ritchie 2012; Berg 2011; Dalton, Carbon and Olesen 2003; Meier 2020). For instance, Silberg and Dallam analyzed 27 cases where courts initially rejected abuse allegations against fathers and reversed custody to the abusive parent. Later, new courts reversed the decisions and returned children to their protective mothers. The authors found that allegations of parental alienation were a significant factor in the erroneous initial decisions. Children suffered from ongoing abuse, neglect, loss of their loving and bonded mother, suicidality, depression, and other mental harms, for an average of three years before a second court returned them to their safe and loving home (Silberg and Dallam 2019). Other scholars and professionals have reported courts' and evaluators' routine dismissals of abuse reports when alienation is cross-claimed or raised by an evaluator, litigator, attorney, or judge (Lubit 2019; Hunter et al. 2020; Meier 2020).

The extensive critical literature (Meier, in press) is reinforced by the first-ever national quantitative analysis of U.S. custody courts' responses to abuse and alienation allegations. The *Child Custody Outcomes in Cases Involving Parental Alienation and Abuse Allegations* study reviewed all reported custody cases involving abuse and/or alienation claims during a recent 10-year period in all 50 states. The study found that family courts are generally skeptical of domestic violence allegations (rejecting 55%), and even more skeptical of child abuse allegations (rejecting 73%) (Meier 2020, 96). But when the alleged abuser claims alienation, courts' rejections of abuse claims skyrocket – to 63% for domestic violence, 98% for child sexual abuse, and 82% for child physical abuse allegations (Meier 2020, 97). Mothers lose custody to allegedly abusive fathers approximately ¼ of the time with no alienation crossclaim; that doubles to 50% when the fathers cross-claim alienation (Meier 2020, 96, 98).

These findings have been widely echoed in studies across the globe, including in the United Kingdom, Canada, Italy, Spain, New Zealand, and others (Family Court Review 2020). Each of these country's researchers has concluded that parental alienation is used – successfully – by fathers to negate mothers' and children's abuse allegations. The UK Ministry of Justice's 2019 Harm Panel Report noted that "accusations of parental alienation are often used to threaten and blame victims of domestic abuse who are attempting to protect their children and achieve safer contact arrangements" (Hunter et al. 2020, 159).

While Meier et al.'s empirical study itself does not and cannot verify the truth of any abuse allegations, extensive other independent research has found that allegations of child abuse, even during custody litigation, have historically considered valid 50–72% of the time (Faller 1998; Thoennes and Tjaden 1990). The study's findings that courts reject such allegations at far higher rates thus indicate that many children are being put in harm's way by courts. The harms to children forced into the custody of their abusive fathers can hardly be overstated, given the known harms of child abuse to children (Silberg and Dallam 2019). But even without direct physical or sexual abuse, it is likely that many children removed from loving parents are subjected to emotionally abusive or indifferent, cold, or harsh parenting (DV LEAP et al. 2017), of the sort leading experts report cause children intense suffering (APSAC Guidelines 2019).

Lack of scientific support

The invention of a concept of alienation ("child alienation" or "parental alienation" or just "alienation") *distinct from PAS* was first propounded by a small group of respected forensic experts around the turn of the millennium.

They called for intensive research to explore and support the concept (Johnston 2005, 761 & n. 16). Over the following 10–15 years, a growing number of articles were published about the concept – but to date, there remains no credible scientific evidence underpinning the way the parental alienation concept is understood and used in court.

Exaggerated assertions of scientific support

Before unpacking the literature relied upon by proponents of the alienation concept, this chapter briefly addresses common assertions that alienation is scientifically valid because there are many scholarly publications discussing it (Baker 2013; Bernet et al. 2010; Lorandos 2020). In some instances, these assertions have rested on sources such as "a selection of stories, movies, television shows and non-peer-reviewed books and articles, including citations to only two studies, both dissertations, neither of which proves [the alleged] [parental alienation disorder]" (Pepiton et al. 2012). In asserting that alienation is amply supported by scientific research, Bernet and Baker (2013) typically cite to *qualitative* discussions of estranged children, with no control group, no objective or clinical selection criteria (other than opinion-based labelling) and, most important, *no objective, systematic consideration of alternative reasons for a child's rejection of a parent* (Milchman 2019; Rueda 2004).

Contrary to these assertions, and despite the passage of nearly two decades since Johnston and colleagues' first call for credible research, multiple recent research reviews have convergently concluded that existing alienation studies tend to be small, "methodologically weak," non-random, not generalizable, and based on unreliable applications of the label (Saini et al. 2016, 435). This review was led by several highly regarded scholars and alienation experts and included in a book written to inform the judiciary. They concluded that there was currently *no research* supporting alienation as a scientific construct that could be objectively applied (Saini et al. 2016, 374–376, 419, 423).

Other researchers have also systematically reviewed the scientific status of parental alienation, and similarly concluded that, to date, no scientific validity has been proven (Milchman 2019). Some have pointed out that alienation studies over-rely on retrospective accounts, lack any research controls, and fail to consider or rule out alternative explanations such as abuse or harmful parenting for a child's purported "alienation" (Barnett 2020; Milchman 2019). Moreover, "the use of scales and tests to measure parental alienation in practice lacks a credible evidentiary basis" (Doughty et al. 2020, 72). And one of the first systematic reviews of intensive so-called "treatments" for purported parental alienation, consisting primarily of the removal of children from the parent they trust and care by the parent they dislike or fear (under the guidance of alienation professionals), concluded that "PA advocates have failed to provide empirical support for the safety and effectiveness of their methods" (Mercer 2019, 67).

In short, while the alienation *literature* continues to grow, there remains no objective or reliable measure for identifying and distinguishing alienation from legitimate estrangement (Barnett 2020; Doughty et al. 2020). As long as the alienation label remains subjective and in the eye of the estranged parent (and/or court), alienation labelling fails the most fundamental prerequisite of scientific method: it is not falsifiable (*Daubert v. Merrell Dow Pharm., Inc.*, 1993).

Core beliefs underlying the alienation hypothesis

The quasi-scientific alienation concept packages together three core premises: (i) the causal hypothesis: that a favored parent's criticism, fear, or negative view of the other parent – whether conscious or unconscious – can itself do lasting damage to a child's relationship with the other parent; (ii) that "alienation" can reliably be differentiated from other concededly legitimate causes of a child's estrangement, including, but not limited to, domestic abuse; and (iii) that the harm of alienation to children is so profound as to warrant extreme measures to prevent it, including custody reversal and limited or no contact with the preferred parent. There is virtually no research testing any of these core beliefs; moreover, there is other credible research casting serious doubt on them.

Causation: does one parent's negativity toward the other parent turn a child against the other?

Before proceeding, it should be noted that many parents are labelled hostile or negative when they are merely seeking to keep their children safe or have legitimate concerns about the other's parenting (Hunter et al. 2020). This section, however, questions the asserted impact of a parent's negativity about the other, even when real.

Saini et al., while forthrightly and admirably acknowledging that there is no legitimate scientific evidence or support for the alienation premise, nonetheless assert that there is a broad consensus among forensic psychologists about what constitute "parental alienation behaviors" ("PABs"), which "have the capacity" to harm a child's relationship with the other parent (Saini et al. 2016, 430). But the authors identify no evidence that such behaviors *actually do* result in such harm.

And in fact, the only objective research examining the effect of a parent's denigration of the other to the child, has found that denigration, rather than turning a child against the denigrated parent, turns children *against the denigrator.* Robert Emery, a leading researcher and former Social Science Editor of the *Journal of the Association of Family & Conciliation Courts* (AFCC), the organization most associated with the alienation belief system, with his colleague Jenna Rowen, sought to test the "alienation hypothesis" that when one parent denigrates the other to their child, it can turn the child against the other parent. Stunningly, Rowen and Emery's studies consistently found a "lack of support for the outcomes predicted by the alienation hypothesis": Rather, they found that where one parent denigrates the other, it is usually a reciprocal behavior, and that it "typically backfires" or "boomerangs" against the more aggressively denigrating parent (Rowen and Emery 2018).

This finding helps explain several cases with which this author is familiar in which abused children have complained as much or more about their abusive fathers' nasty comments about their mothers, as about their fathers' direct abuse (*C.W. v E.F.*, 928 A.2d 655, 2007; *Georgia Coalition vs Sexual Assault et al.* 2015). It is, after all, far easier for children to complain about a parent's nasty remarks than about a parent's sexual abuse (Pipe et al. 2007).

In short, there is no objective empirical evidence that even overt denigration of one parent by the other turns children against the denigrated parent, and there is credible research indicating the opposite – that denigration alienates the child from the *denigrator*. As Rowen and Emery state:

> [i]f the parental alienation construct is to stand up to the rigors of science, it will be imperative to provide empirical grounding for such claims. The initial work we have completed on parental denigration calls into question basic suppositions about parental alienation, particularly parental alienation's assumed one-sided nature and the damage done to the denigrated parent's relationship with the child but not to the denigrator's relationship.
> (Rowen and Emery 2019, 207)

The Rowen and Emery studies have, at the time of this writing, received minimal response in the alienation literature.

Is it possible to objectively identify "alienation" and distinguish it from other causes of a parent-child estrangement?

Proponents of both PAS and non-syndrome alienation have acknowledged that a history of family violence, which could itself cause a child's resistance to contact, should preclude an alienation claim (Bernet et al. 2018; Drozd and Olesen 2004). This is eminently reasonable. However, to date, there is still no means of operationalizing a means of differentiating when a parent's own conduct has caused a child to avoid them, as opposed to when a preferred parent has undermined that relationship. Alienation – as a label – facilitates the automatic attribution of a child's avoidance or a parent's concerns about the other's parenting to an illegitimate "alienating" motive without meaningful investigation (Milchman, Geffner, and Meier 2020). For instance, in addition to seeing the label misapplied to children who have been abused or exposed to domestic violence, this author and others have seen children labeled "alienated" when they were simply afraid of a parent's harsh parenting, experiencing developmental changes, having personality clashes, feeling anger about the parental break-up or a parent's lies or refusals to acknowledge their own past behavior, or when they resented a new partner and/or baby (Meier 2021; *Anonymous v. Anonymous* 2019).

Existing research typically fails to differentiate between causes for children's estrangement, simply treating estranged children as presumptively "alienated":

> Until there are scientifically valid studies using independent measures of parenting quality that can distinguish between children who rationally and irrationally reject a parent, PA advocates cannot claim scientific support for identifying alienated children.
>
> (Milchman, 2020, 44)

Moreover, as the UK's Adrienne Barnett points out, "many of the 'typical behaviours' listed in 'checklists' used to identify PA can equally be associated with child adversities other than PA" (Barnett 2020). These include negative or harsh parenting, domestic abuse, extensive parental conflict, excessive litigation, mental health issues, children's realistic fear, lack of parent-child warmth, and weak parental attachments with the allegedly alienated parent (Barnett 2020; Milchman 2019). Yet one of the only existing studies purporting to test a tool for measuring alienation itself fails to screen out abuse or other causes of children's estrangement, simply accepting parents' self-reports, evaluator and court opinions with no verification that alternative causes had been ruled out (which they rarely are) (Rowlands 2018).

Thus, Saini et al.'s comprehensive research review concludes forthrightly that

> there have been no systematic attempts to differentiate a diagnosis of PA or PAS from other conditions that might share similar features . . . [e.g.] realistic estrangement . . . parental abuse, neglect or exposure to intimate partner violence . . . [and] significantly compromised parenting).
>
> (Saini et al. 2016, 423)

The same review states "most importantly, although the majority of researchers purport to exclude from their studies cases where abuse of the child had occurred, few have reported working definitions of child abuse and systematic methods for excluding them from their samples." In fact, several of the studies they reviewed found that, even where one parent was identified as engaging in 'parental alienating behaviors' the other purportedly alienated parent was "more prone to actual abuse of the child" (Saini et al. 2016, 431). Likewise, another respected alienation researcher acknowledges that there is usually a cluster of multiple factors leading to a child's "alienation" (Drozd and Olesen 2004, 67, 73–85). While there may be a consensus among family court professionals about undesirable "parental alienating behaviors" (Saini et al. 2016, 418)), even the alienation research points to the likelihood that harmful parenting or abuse is at least one – if not the dominant – source of many children's "alienation."

In short, there is no research that differentiates, and no validated method for differentiating in individual cases, the reasons why a child might become "alienated" or estranged from one parent (Saini et al. 2016, 431). This means that most if not all alienation "diagnoses" or labels are largely speculative and could be masking legitimate, justifiable estrangements from a destructive parent.

One argument for labelling a child alienated frequently seen in litigation is the peculiar claim that genuinely abused children do not wholly reject a parent without toxic intervention from the other parent (Bernet and Baker 2013, 1010). While it is true that *some* abused children, in *some* contexts such as foster care, continue to love and long for an abusive or neglectful parent's affection, all the children in that study were grateful for having been removed from an unsafe home (Baker et al. 2016). Moreover, children removed from their home and both parents bear little resemblance to children who live with a parent they love and trust while seeking to avoid a parent they experience as abusive or destructive, the normal context of alienation/custody battles.

In fact, contrary to this oft-stated belief, early studies by leading alienation researcher Janet Johnston, found that

> in a large portion of cases, children who reject a parent are not singularly alienated by an angry, vindictive ex-spouse, rather they are also often young, emotionally vulnerable children who are simultaneously enmeshed with the preferred parent and *realistically estranged by inadequate, problematic, or abusive parenting on the part of the rejected parent.*
>
> (Johnston and Goldman 2010, 13) (emphasis added;
> citations omitted)

Johnston and her colleagues concluded that a child's estrangement post-separation is usually the product of multiple factors, *almost always including the estranged parent's own behaviors.* Thus, only "a multi-factor explanation of children's rejection of a parent after divorce," including *both* parent's behaviors, is supportable (Johnston et al. 2005, 206).

In short, there is no scientific support for "parental alienation behaviors" by themselves explaining a child's estrangement from a parent, particularly parents to whom children are bonded and with whom they feel safe. While it is surely possible for one parent to deliberately undermine a child's relationship with the other, the research indicates that children's actual estrangements are often – if not always – at least partly a reaction to their direct experiences with that parent. Therefore, interventions aimed at repairing a parent–child relationship – as opposed to favoring one parent at the expense of the other – should examine and address *both* parents' behaviors and should recognize that abuse and destructive parenting are often the real cause of a child's estrangement.

With regard to scientific validity and admissibility, the failure of alienation research to even begin the process of developing objective methods for differentiating children's reasons for their estrangement from a parent, let alone to scientifically validate such a method, underlines that alienation is not a known, validated, or objective construct. It is, at best, a widely used, *subjective label*, which cannot support particular interventions or responses.

Do parental alienating behaviors cause long-term or significant harm?

As is described in Chapter 7 of this volume, "remedies" for children labelled alienated can be extreme and harmful themselves. Some children have disappeared entirely after being forcibly removed from their bonded and loving parents (Darrell Riley, Electronic Mail 2020). Others have been cut off from their loving parents for months or years, while forced to live with abusive parents (Bundy 2019; Dallam and Silberg 2016). Despite early thoughtful criticism by leading researcher Johnston and colleague, who called the emphasis on custody reversals a "license for tyranny" (Johnston and Kelly 2004, 85), courts today often order coercive "reunification" programs which require such removals (while costing tens of thousands of dollars), (Bundy 2019) and a troubling number of children are removed temporarily or permanently from the care of – and sometimes from all contact with – the parent they love and trust (Electronic Mail 2020; Meier 2020; Reveal 2019). Such draconian interventions are justified by the assertion that parental alienation is irrevocably and profoundly harmful for children, akin to child abuse (Harman et al. 2018). Yet no credible evidence supports either the belief that a parent's alienating behaviors can cause such harm, or that such behaviors are as harmful as direct child abuse.

The only reported evidence of the harms of purported alienation consists of retrospective self-reports from now-adults (Baker 2013). Small studies have asserted that adults who reported that one parent turned them against the other when they were a child suffered from a "range of adverse outcomes, including: lower self-esteem; depression; manipulative behaviour; attachment and identity issues; and relationship problems" (Doughty et al. 2020, 72, citations omitted). But because these studies take self-reports at face value and are incapable of excluding other possible causes of these outcomes, which may not have been known to the individuals when they were children, they "do not allow a causal relationship between adverse outcomes and alienation to be established" (Doughty et al. 2020, 72). Moreover, Saini et al.'s research review concluded that "there is a lack of clear, empirical evidence that children who resist or refuse contact with one of their parents are universally emotionally disturbed or necessarily at risk for long-term negative outcomes," rendering any long-term effects of alienation "inconclusive" (Saini et al. 2016, 436–437).

In fact, as noted above, the only systematic research into how "parental alienating behaviors" affect children has found that they turn them against the *alienating parent*, not the other (Rowen and Emery 2018). Two other studies have similarly contradicted the assumption of lifelong harm: One longitudinal study by leading researcher Johnston found that young "non-alienated" adults who had been the subject of custody disputes scored similarly to their "alienated" counterparts on a scale of emotional distress and attachment insecurity (Johnston and Goldman 2010). Another, by Judith Wallerstein, the first researcher to coin the term "alienation" and to identify parent-child "alliances" during divorce, found in her 25-year follow-up that all the children who had been alienated at divorce reconnected with the disfavored parent, most within one or two years (Wallerstein and Lewis 2004).

Consistent with Wallerstein's finding, Johnston's longitudinal, in-depth study of children in counseling treatment who were involved in custody litigation and developed an estrangement from one parent, found that

> an alienated stance that emerges for the first time during the early teenage years is a common hazard in high-conflict divorced families, but it is unlikely to last (in most cases it ranges from a few months to a couple of years).
>
> (Johnston and Goldman 2010, 113)

"Virtually all of the youth who had actively resisted or refused visitation subsequently, on their own accord, initiated reconciliation with the rejected parent some time during their late teens and early twenties, often after they reached 18 years..." (Johnston and Goldman 2010, 113).

Moreover, Johnston's team found that those young adults who remained estranged from their parent chose to do so for *healthy* reasons. Among the approximately 19% of the program's young clients who remained deeply estranged, these rifts were a product of deficits in that parent:

> [A]n enduring rejection of a parent seems to be rooted in earlier, more chronic family dysfunction and realistic concerns the child has about that parent. . . For these individuals, attempts at reconciling with the rejected parent during their late teens or early twenties had ended in disappointment. They were estranged by a parent's violent, alcoholic, or abusive behavior, or alternatively, provided convincing accounts of the parent's more subtle forms of emotional manipulation and control or lack of empathy and respect for them as a person....
>
> (113)

Finally, and equally significantly, Johnston and team found that the long-term harms of such estrangements were by no means exceptional. They concluded that, while many

> grown children of custody disputes suffered high levels of emotional distress and had difficulties forming secure attachments . . . *those who refused*

contact with one of their parents were not among the most poorly functioning and their capacity for attachments with intimate adult partners ranged over the spectrum. Amongst those with poor outcomes in terms of our goals, *most involve a rejected parent with serious parenting deficits* . . . under these conditions the children, especially the teenagers, should be invited to "get on with life" with help from a supportive therapist if useful, and make the choice of contact at a later date.

(Johnston and Goldman 2010, 114) (emphasis added)

Thus, without evidence that alleged "parental alienating behaviors" are particularly harmful, or any more harmful than myriad other forms of sub-optimal parenting, the draconian and traumatic interventions impelled by alienation labeling are unsupportable. Such custody reversals impose both known and potentially unknown injuries to children (at minimum, the sudden loss of a bonded and primary parent and the forced custody of one they fear) to prevent unknown and potentially lesser harms, with no objective or valid basis.

The multifactorial approach to children's contact resistance or refusal

Contrary to early assertions that if there was abuse, then there was no alienation (Bernet et al. 2018; Drozd and Olesen 2004), in recent years, a number of alienation proponents now assert that both abuse and alienation, and potentially other factors, can convergently explain a child's resistance to contact with a parent (Johnston and Sullivan 2020; Drozd, Olesen and Saini 2013). In part, the "multifactorial" approach, often dubbed "contact resistance/refusal", is a response to growing discomfort of leading scholars with the blame-based single-factor notion of parental alienation which attributes a child's alienation entirely to the preferred parent or the multi-factorial or contact resistance/refusal approach therefore urges that evaluators and courts assess *all* relevant factors – including the estranged parent's own contributions to the problem – in responding to children's resistance to contact with a parent. As will be explained below, in this author's view, while the multi-factorial approach is certainly more realistic about what happens in families that leads to estrangements, it does not remedy – and may even intensify – the undermining of appropriate responses to family abuse. Moreover, some proposed visions of interventions that should flow from a multi-factorial analysis appear both unrealistic and potentially as or more dangerous than the "single-factor" approach for children at risk of abuse.

A leading and recent example of the multi-factorial argument and approach is found in a co-authored article by early leading alienation researcher Janet Johnston and alienation expert Matthew Sullivan. In *Parental alienation: in search of common ground for a more differentiated theory*, the authors emphatically reject the "either/or" approach of earlier thinking that asserted children's contact resistance stems from *either* alienation *or* abuse, insisting instead that there are many "legitimate" reasons for contact resistance, which can operate at once, including developmental stage, situational factors, and poor parenting by the avoided parent (Johnston and Sullivan 2020). The authors conclude that there are "many cases with mixed features" of illegitimate alienation and legitimate estrangement (280), arguing cogently that courts should not ignore abuse or poor parenting just because the other parent has been found to be alienating (Johnston and Sullivan 2020, 273). The article offers several articulate critiques of the single-factor "blame-the-preferred-parent" approach to children's contact resistance, asserting that parentally alienating behaviors are "neither necessary nor sufficient" causes of a child's contact resistance (281). They also wisely point out that there are many cases in which abuse is difficult to prove to a court's satisfaction yet may still legitimately affect children's feelings toward a parent (273, 274). Ultimately, the authors argue that the practical reality is that it is next to impossible to "rule out all legitimate reasons for contact resistance" (277).

While in the abstract, this recognition of the multiple *legitimate* as well as illegitimate reasons a child may avoid one parent, seems sensible as a descriptive and theoretical matter, there are serious problems with application of a multi-factorial approach in practice. First, there is no objective, non-discretionary, bias-precluding way for evaluators or clinicians to make the determination of what factors are affecting the child, let alone which factors are dominant or more deserving of prioritization. Numerous empirical studies have confirmed the presence of common biases among custody evaluators against mothers reporting family abuse, turning such allegations into indicia of alienation, and favoring accused fathers, as well as a widespread lack of essential knowledge about family abuse (Connors 2019; Haselschwerdt, Hardesty, and Hans 2010; Saunders et al. 2011). One New York appeals court reversed a trial decision which relied on another evaluator's "pervasive and manifest bias against the mother" (*Montoya v. Davis*, 156 A.D.3d 132 (N.Y. 3d Dep't 2017)). And the Family Court Outcomes study found that the presence of evaluators in custody cases virtually doubles the rates of unfavorable outcomes for mothers alleging abuse (Meier 2019). Given that custody evaluators' ability to objectively or accurately assess abuse has already been found to be deeply inadequate, there is little reason to believe that inviting evaluators to address abuse, alienation, and many more factors will improve their objectivity or accuracy.

Moreover, it is difficult to imagine how even the best, most expert, and open-minded evaluator can accurately and reliably assess all the factors and craft trustworthy interventions which respond appropriately to varying and potentially contradictory factors. The fact is that these matters are inherently subjective, complex, mercurial, and *psychologically internal*, and no outside evaluator can ever really know for sure the exact causes and proportional contributions of multiple factors that may lead to a child's contact resistance (Emery et al. 2005). Expecting outside observers to accurately analyze all the causes of a child's contact-resistance, let alone "cure" it without causing harm, is unrealistic, to say the least. In fact, Johnston and Sullivan acknowledge the difficulty of applying a multi-factorial approach, stating that it is "less useful" to courts than what they call the single-factor (or blame-driven) approach, which many evaluators "revert to" in court (Johnston and Sullivan 2020, 282).

Second, the multi-factorial approach, at least without stronger and clearer prescriptions for responding to abusive or other harmful behavior by the avoided parent, risks leading to even more sidelining by courts of family abuse and destructive parenting. The very assertion that *both* abuse and alienation can both contribute to contact-resistance (i.e., "hybrid" cases) facilitates the marginalization and dismissal of abuse concerns in favor of alienation concerns, to the great detriment of at-risk children. Even if courts and evaluators acknowledge a parent has abused the children or their mother and has caused the children to fear and avoid him, the multi-factorial approach permits courts to treat a safe parent's supposed alienation behaviors as more problematic. In one case with which this author is familiar, the evaluator reported the allegations of domestic violence, including the children's corroboration and partial victimization, characterized the children's contact resistance as "hybrid," but nonetheless, without more, asserted that the mother's alienation must be prevented, and recommended a custody reversal, using the approach described in Polak (2020). Indeed, it is common for evaluators and courts to treat a preferred parent's actions or words in reaction to abuse or aimed at protecting the child as evidence of "alienation." It is doubtful that a coherent response can be reliably crafted that somehow merges these deeply opposing sensibilities: Whereas a child's reactions to abusive behavior by a parent should generate protective and sympathetic responses by a custody court, interventions against so-called alienation by a preferred parent often leads to harsh and non-sympathetic responses to *the same traumatized children*. In short, these two responses and problems are not easily melded into one holistic response. In contrast, at least the "single-factor" approach theoretically rejects blame on a safe parent for "alienation" when abuse is validated. Johnston and Sullivan do acknowledge that there are diametrically opposed best practices for responding to alienation and to abuse (279 & n. 10).

A chilling example of how the multi-factorial approach can be used to harm children and benefit abusers is apparent in another article in the special issue in which Johnston and Sullivan's piece is published. In *Responding to Severe Parent-Child Rejection Cases Without a Parentectomy: a Blended Sequential Intervention Model and the Role of Courts*, Shely Polak and colleagues start by endorsing the multi-factorial perspective, while noting that it is nearly impossible to adequately assess all the different potential causes of a child's resistance (Polak, Altobelli, and Popielarczyk 2020). They then offer a chart of options for using their blended-sequential model. Stunningly, even "hybrid" and "justified rejection" cases are included among the "moderate to severe" cases for which the chart calls for removal of children from their bonded parent and forced custody with the parent they reject. In other words, even where children *justifiably* fear or resist contact with a parent, this approach mandates at minimum a temporary cut-off from the safe and bonded parent, and forced custody and legal control by that very frightening or harmful parent. This model also recommends treatment for the preferred parent but not the parent who has *caused their own child's estrangement by their own destructive behavior* (512, Figure 2, 518).

The same set of prescriptions/options is also provided for the "most severe" "hybrid" cases, i.e., those in which there are a mix of justified estrangement and alienating behaviors by the preferred parent. Notably, while describing the most severe cases as those with "high levels of anger, hostility, distrust, discordant co-parenting, personality disorders in one or both of the parents, strained parent-child/familial relationships and involvement in protracted litigation," (Polak, Altobelli, and Popielarcyzyk 2020, 508) neglect to mention adult or child abuse by one parent as contributing to such high levels of anger, hostility, and distrust, etc. And since "severity" is often measured based on checklists of children's attitudes toward a parent (Polak, Altobelli and Popielarcyzyk 2020), these "severe" hybrid cases may well be cases of very severe abuse which have led to extreme avoidance and potentially emotional hatred or fear of the parent – that is, the "severity" of the relationship rift may not measure *illegitimate* estrangement, but *legitimate, even healthy* responses to a very destructive parent.

That a multi-factorial approach can lead to such recommendations is a measure of the dangerousness of even the multi-factorial approach. And while Polak et al. mention in passing that their recommendations are "contra-indicated where there is an assessed risk of domestic violence or child abuse" (518), many cases involving past family abuse are not "assessed" as presenting future risk, yet there can be severe *re-traumatization* – even if not repeat abuse – by forced contact with the perpetrator of *past* traumatic abuse.

While abuse is certainly referenced in these articles, and Johnston and Sullivan offer many valuable observations about abuse while constructively criticizing the simplistic approach to alienation, their discussion nonetheless obscures fundamental realities of abuse in custody cases. For instance, their discussion of familial abuse focuses almost entirely on parental *responses* to a child's rejection or "disrespect" (Johnston and Sullivan 2020, 280, 278). Despite the high rates of family abuse allegations in contested custody filings, the article offers little mention of abusive parenting which *precedes* a child's rejection or disrespect, and which may in fact have caused the dissolution. The authors' failure to wrestle with this far more common paradigm of abusive parents in family court is consistent with their approach, which treats both parents as capable of loving, decent parenting. Such a paradigm is surely problematic given the reality that many abusive partners pursue custody – and may harm their children precisely in order – to hurt their ex, and not because they want to be good parents (Bancroft, Silverman and Ritchie 2012).

Finally, two odd lacunae appear in Johnston and Sullivan's discussion of whether and when courts can be expected to identify actual past abuse. For instance, they state (without citation) that "a clear finding of abuse or violence in criminal or dependency court is generally considered definitive evidence of child abuse or serious domestic violence, and there is unlikely to be a later family court trial" (274). This assertion is not accurate: It is actually not unusual for cases with sexual assault or domestic violence convictions or findings to be followed by custody battles and even parental alienation findings against the adult victim (*In re Marriage of Crystal and Shawn H.*, 2013 WL 2940952, (Cal. Ct. App. June 17, 2013); *C.W. v. E.F.*, 928 A.2d 655 (2007)). The authors also observe that, by "emphasizing collaboration and cooperation" family courts do not reliably adjudicate allegations of abuse, as do criminal or dependency courts (Johnston and Sullivan 2020, 279). While this description of family courts is fair enough, the lack of comment on family courts' failures to adjudicate abuse seems to condone a practice that is both contrary to law – every state requires custody courts to consider abuse – and harmful to children (Meier 2020; Silberg and Dallam 2019). Ultimately, despite the paper's many valid and valuable points about abuse and alienation, references like these, along with the article's recommendation for an emphatically forward-looking, co-parenting-prioritizing intervention, are likely to reinforce family courts' minimization or overlooking of abuse.

Conclusion

The above review describes the lack of scientific support for parental alienation as a label administered in custody cases. It also preliminarily raises related but specific concerns about the multi-factorial approach, which sidesteps the difficulties of scientific proof. Alienating *behaviors* are, of course, admissible when presented as facts. But packaging such behaviors into a quasi-scientific concept with particular diagnostic or treatment implications is not scientifically supported, and nor are many of the dire predictions often attached to the term. At the same time, alienation approaches, even multi-factorial ones, are easily used to thwart abuse allegations and even to award custody to allegedly or known abusive parents, with profoundly destructive impacts on children (Silberg and Dallam 2019). In short, parental alienation's use in court to reject or minimize evidence of abusive or poor parenting by an estranged parent is not only unscientific and unsupported, but deeply harmful to many children.

References

Arkansas Coalition Against Domestic Violence et al. Brief Amicus Curiae on Behalf of Petitioner, *O. v. O.*, 2010 Ark. App. 346, 2010 WL 1609411. https://drive.google.com/file/d/1kkENJxL78w0xDNj28eeipcNMhmTduryv/view.

APSAC Task Force. *The Investigation and Determination of Suspected Psychological Maltreatment in Children and Adolescents* (The American Professional Society on the Abuse of Children (APSAC)), 2019. https://www.apsac.org/guidelines.

Baker, Amy, Alyssa Creegan, Alexa Quinones, and Laura Rozelle. "Foster Children's Views of Their Birth Parents: A Review of the Literature." Children & Youth Services Review 67, 2016: 177–183.

Baker, Amy J. L. "Parental Alienation Research and the Daubert standards." In *Parental Alienation: The Handbook for Mental Health and Legal Professionals*, edited by Demosthenes Lorandos, William Bernet and S. Richard Sauber, 322–347. Springfield, IL: Charles C. Thomas, 2013.

Bancroft, Lundy, Jay G. Silverman, and Daniel Ritchie. *The Batterer as Parent: Addressing the Impact of Domestic Violence on Family Dynamics*. California: SAGE, 2012.

Berg, Rita. "Parental Alienation Analysis, Domestic Violence, and Gender Bias in Minnesota Courts." *Minnesota Journal of Law and Inequality* 29, 2011: 5–31.

Bernet, W. and A.J.L. Baker. "Parental alienation, DSM-5, and ICD-11: Response to Critics." *Journal of the American Academy of Psychiatry and the Law* 41, 2013: 98–104.

Bernet, William, Nilgun Gregory, Kathleen M. Reay, and Ronald P Rohner. "An Objective Measure of Splitting in Parental Alienation: The Parental Acceptance–Rejection Questionnaire." *Journal of Forensic Sciences* 63, 2018: 776–783.

Bernet, William, Wilfrid von Boch-Galhau, Amy Baker, and Stephen L. Morrison. "Parental Alienation, DSM-V, and ICD-11." *The American Journal of Family Therapy* 38, 2010: 76–187.

Bundy, Trey, host. "Bitter Custody." Reveal (podcast), 2019. https://revealnews.org/episodes/bitter-custody/.

Crary, D. (2012). *American Psychiatric Association: Parental Alienation is not Mental Disorder*, Associated Press, https://www.timesnews.net/news/local-news/american-psychiatric-association-parental-alienation-is-not-mental-disorder/article_41d93374-1bb3-5230-9803-73e734580aea.html

Dallam, Stephanie, and Joyanna Silberg. "Recommended Treatments for 'Parental Alienation Syndrome' (PAS) May Cause Children Foreseeable and Lasting Psychological Harm." *Journal of Child Custody* 13, 2016: 134–143.

Dalton, Clare, Susan Carbon, and Nancy Olesen. "High Conflict Divorce, Violence, and Abuse: Implications for Custody and Visitation Decisions." *Juvenile & Family Court Journal* 54, 2003: 11–33.

Darrel, Riley, email message to author, September 22, 2020.

Doughty, Julie, Nina Maxwell, and Tom Slater. "Professional Responses to 'Parental Alienation': Research-informed Practice." *The Journal of Social Welfare & Family Law* 42, 2020: 68–79.

Drozd, Leslie, and Nancy Olesen. "Is It Abuse, Alienation, and/or Estrangement? A decision tree." *Journal of Child Custody* 1, 2004: 65–106.

Drozd, Leslie, Nancy Olesen, and Michael Saini. *Parenting Plan and Child Custody Evaluations: Using Decision Trees to Increase Evaluator Competence & Avoid Preventable Errors*. Florida: Professional Resource Press, 2013.

DV LEAP et al. Brief Amici Curiae in support of Plaintiff-Appellant-Respondent, *Anonymous v. Anonymous*, 2017 N.Y. Ct. App. 2d Dept. 2017. https://drive.google.com/file/d/1Lrgioo7JRXG2bT_TiAx3yPbHmCnEBSIc/view.

Emery, Robert E., Randy K. Otto, and William O'Donohue. "A Critical Assessment of Child Custody Evaluations: Limited Science and a Flawed System." *Psychological Science in the Public Interest* 6, 2005: 1–29.

Faller, Kathleen D. "The Parental Alienation Syndrome: What Is It and What Data Support It?" *Child Maltreatment* 3, 1998: 100–115.

Gardner, Richard A. *The Parental Alienation Syndrome: A Guide for Mental Health and Legal Professionals.* Creskill, NJ: Creative Therapeutics, 1992a.

Gardner, Richard A. *True and False Accusations of Child Sex Abuse.* Creskill, NJ: Creative Therapeutics. 1992b.

Georgia Network to End Sexual Assault et al. Brief *Amicus Curiae* in support of Petitioner, *K.D. v. M.D.*, Available at https://drive.google.com/file/d/1pGgbECKRTK7eHSI21fyljNaSTQU5ehJ7/view.

Haselschwerdt, Megan L., Jennifer Hardesty, and Jason D. Hans. "Custody Evaluators' Beliefs About Domestic Violence Allegations During Divorce: Feminist and Family Violence Perspectives." *Journal of Interpersonal Violence* 26, 2011: 1694–1719.

Harman, Jennifer J., Edward Kruk, and Denise Hines. "Parental Alienating Behaviors: An Unacknowledged Form of Family Violence." *Psychological Bulletin* 144, 2018: 1275–1299.

Hunter, Rosemary, Mandy Burton, and Liz Trinder. *Assessing Risk of Harm to Children and Parents in Private Law Custody Cases.* United Kingdom: Ministry of Justice, 2020.

Johnston, Janet R. "Children of Divorce Who Reject a Parent and Refuse Visitation: Recent Research and Social Policy Implications for the Alienated Child." *Family Law Quarterly* 38, 2005: 757–775.

Johnston, Janet R., and Judith Goldman. "Outcomes of Family Counseling Interventions with Children Who Resist Visitation: An Addendum to Friedlander and Walters (2010)." *Family Court Review* 48, 2010: 112–115.

Johnston, Janet R., Marjorie G. Walters, Nancy W. Olesen. "Is It Alienating Parenting, Role Reversal or Child Abuse? A Study of Children's Rejection of a Parent in Child Custody Disputes." *Journal of Emotional Abuse* 5, 2005: 191–218.

Johnston, Janet R., and Matthew Sullivan. "Parental Alienation: In Search of Common Ground for a More Differentiated Theory." *Family Court Review* 58, 2020: 270–292.

Kansas City Star Editorial Board. "Abuse Allegations Should Disqualify Candidate for Missouri House." *Kansas City Star*, 2020. https://www.pressreader.com/usa/the-kansas-city-star/20201016/281651077585122.

Lorandos, Demosthenes. "Parental Alienation in U.S. Courts, 1985 to 2018." *Family Court Review* 58, 2020: 322–339.

Lubit, Roy. "Valid and Invalid Ways to Assess the Reason a Child Rejects a Parent: The Continued Malignant Role of 'Parental Alienation Syndrome'." *Journal of Child Custody* 15, 2019: 42–66.

Meier, Joan S. "Getting Real about Abuse and Alienation: A Critique of Drozd and Olesen's Decision Tree." *Journal of Child Custody* 7, 2010: 219–252.

Meier, Joan S. "Parental Alienation Syndrome and Parental Alienation: A Research Review." *VAWnet, a Project of the National Resource Center on Domestic Violence*, 2013. Available at https://vawnet.org/sites/default/files/materials/files/2016-09/AR_PASUpdate.pdf

Meier, Joan S. "U.S. Child Custody Outcomes in Cases Involving Parental Alienation and Abuse Allegations: What Do the Data Show?" *The Journal of Social Welfare & Family Law* 42, 2020: 92–105

Meier, J. (in press). Denial of Family Violence in Court: An Empirical Analysis and Path Forward for Family Law, 110:4 Georgetown L.J. available at https://papers. ssrn.com/sol3/papers.cfm?abstract_id=3805955.

Mercer, Jean. "Are Intensive Parental Alienation Treatments Effective and Safe for Children and Adolescents?" *Journal of Child Custody* 16, 2019: 67–113.

Milchman, M.S. "Misogynistic Cultural Argument in Parental Alienation Versus Child Sexual Abuse Cases." *Journal of Child Custody* 14(4), 2017: 211–233. DOI: 10.1080/15379418.2017.1416722.

Milchman, Madelyn. "Is a Critique of Parental Alienation Syndrome/Parental Alienation Disorder (PAS/PAD) Timely? A Response to Geffner and Sandoval. APSAC Advisor 32, 2020:43–46.

Milchman, M.S., Robert Geffner, and Joan S. Meier. "Ideology and Rhetoric Replace Science in Some Parental Alienation Literature and Advocacy: A Critique." *Family Court Review* 58, 2020: 340–361.

Nichols, Alison M. "Toward a Child-centered Approach to Evaluating Claims of Alienation in High-conflict Custody Disputes." *Michigan Law Review* 12, 2014: 663–688.

Pepiton, M. Brianna, Lindsey Alvis, Kenneth Allen, and Gregory Logid. "Is Parental Alienation Disorder a Valid Concept? Not According to Scientific Evidence. A Review of 'Parental Alienation, DSM-5 and ICD-11' by William Bernet." *Journal of Child Sexual Abuse* 21, 2012: 244–253.

Polak, Shely, Tom Altobelli, and Linda Popielarczyk. "Responding to Severe Parent–child Rejection Cases without a Parentectomy: A Blended Sequential Intervention Model and the Role of Courts." *Family Court Review* 58, 2020: 507–524.

Rowen, Jenna, and Robert E. Emery. "Parental Denigration: A Form of Conflict that Typically Backfires." *Family Court Review* 56, 2018: 258–268.

Rowen, Jenna, and Robert E. Emery. "Parental Denigration Reports Across Parent–Child Dyads: Divorced Parents Underreport Denigration Behaviors Compared to Children." *Journal of Child Custody* 16, 2019: 197–208.

Rowlands, Gena A. "Parental Alienation: A Measurement Tool." *Journal of Divorce & Remarriage* 60, 2018: 316–331.

Saini, Michael, Janet Johnston, Barbara Fidler, and Nicholas Bala. "Empirical Studies of Alienation," in *Parenting Plan Evaluations: Applied Research for Family Court*, edited by Leslie Drozd, Michael Saini, and Nancy Olesen, 347–430. New York: Oxford University Press, 2016.

Saunders, Daniel G., Kathleen C. Faller, and Richard Tolman. *Child Custody Evaluators' Beliefs about Domestic Abuse Allegations: Their Relationship to Evaluator Demographics, Background, Domestic Violence Knowledge and Custody-visitation Recommendations*. Final Technical Report submitted to the National Institute of Justice, 2011, https://www.ncjrs.gov/pdffiles1/nij/grants/238891.pdf

Silberg, Joyanna, and Stephanie Dallam. "Abusers Gaining Custody in Family Courts: A Case Series of Overturned Decisions." *Journal of Child Custody* 16, 2019: 140–169.

Thoennes, Nancy, and Patricia G. Tjaden. "The Extent, Nature and Validity of Child Sexual Abuse Allegations in Custody/visitation Disputes." *Child Abuse & Neglect* 14, 1990: 151–163.

Wallerstein, Judith. S., and Julia M. Lewis. "The Unexpected Legacy of Divorce: Report of a 25-year Study." *Psychoanalytic Psychology* 21, 2004: 353–370.

Chapter 12

Parental alienation, science, and pseudoscience

Jean Mercer

Science has been defined as "an objective, logical, and systematic method of analysis of phenomena, devised to permit the accumulation of reliable knowledge" (Lastrucci, 1963, 6). With respect to psychology and social science, the most important words here may be "systematic" (following a plan that helps to assure accuracy), "phenomena" (focusing to a considerable extent on observable events), and "accumulation" (considering events in the developing context of other information). All of these require empirical work of observation and analysis of differences between individuals and groups.

Claims of empirical work on parental alienation

Baker (2020) reported results from a long list of empirical studies that she felt supported the parental alienation concept. Some of these were highly relevant to the issue and appeared to be correctly described. In some cases, however, Baker attempted to bring in peripheral work and failed to report or interpret it correctly. For example, in an effort to argue that abused children retain their attachment to and wish to be with the abusive parent, Baker cited a study by Rosenblum and Harlow (1963). She stated that this study had demonstrated that baby rhesus monkeys who were reared by abusive mothers nevertheless clung to the mothers more than non-abused infants, and that this finding supported the idea that children who reject a parent do not do so because that parent has been abusive. However, even ignoring the fact that findings on mother-infant behavior are different for different primate species, Baker was mistaken about the basics of this study. All the infants were being reared with "surrogate" mothers who were either large soft cloth dolls or wire frames with bottles of milk incorporated in them. The question in the study was about the approach-avoidance gradient. Two baby monkeys were blasted with a strong air current from time to time when they were clinging to the cloth "mother" (which they frequently did. A comparison group did not receive the air blast. The babies who received the air blast subsequently clung to the cloth "mothers" more than the comparison group did. Thus, there was in this study none of the parent-infant interaction that normally is

DOI: 10.4324/9781003095927-15

art of a relationship between human or monkey mothers and babies, nor was there any abuse by the "surrogate", but simply an unpleasant experience that occurred only near the "mother". Rather than being comparable to child abuse, this situation might be compared with the presence of a parent when a child has repeated painful medical treatment that leads to increased anxiety and clinging afterward. Failing to read this study carefully makes it seem supportive of the claim that children do not reject abusive parents. Careful reading shows that the study is in fact irrelevant to that issue.

Some empirical work about parental alienation

Baker (2020) listed a series of empirical studies she felt were supportive of the parental alienation concept. She did not include any of the outcome studies that have purported to show the value of parental alienation treatments like Family Bridges (Warshak, 2010). Those studies have been examined elsewhere (Mercer, 2019) and will be further discussed later in this chapter.

A small number of empirical studies are usually presented as evidence of scientific support for the parental alienation concept. Each of them, unfortunately, has major flaws of design or implementation.

Clawar and Rivlin

A study by Clawar and Rivlin (2013), published by the American Bar Association, is frequently held up as evidence for the parental alienation concept. Clawar and Rivlin examined cases of child avoidance of a parent as they appeared in the records of the Chicago courts, accumulating over a thousand cases. The study is sometimes described as having a thousand participants, but it is in fact quite different from research that seeks a thousand participants, treats all in the same way, makes systematic measurements of some factor, and (ideally) compares the group with another which received different treatment. The Clawar and Rivlin study is in fact a case series comprising a thousand cases, and as such cannot be replicated. Case studies are often used to try to establish a pattern, but because the single data points cannot be handled statistically, this is difficult (Yin, 1984). Clawar and Rivlin described a long list of "syndromes" or behaviors of the preferred parent but did not provide operational definitions or indicate how often each of the behaviors occurred. The study was essentially a case series rather than work that could show how rejecting children and their preferred parents differed from others; a very extensive case series is still a case series. Notably, although Clawar and Rivlin presented in tabular form many characteristics of the parents, such as educational background, little information about the children was supplied. In spite of the obvious contributions of age and developmental status to children's attitudes and behavior (see Chapter 9), the group of children was simply described as ranging from infancy to age 20 years. These flaws in the study and reporting made it impossible to generalize from Clawar and Rivlin's data to any larger population.

Baker's questionnaire studies

Baker's (2020) discussion of empirical work on the parental alienation concept included extensive material on her own work which attempted to establish a questionnaire that would help identify cases of parental alienation. The efforts on this project followed a predictable and appropriate line of thinking but were badly marred by conceptual errors.

Baker (2005) interviewed 40 adults who self-identified as having been alienated by one parent during childhood. This community sample was achieved by flyers and word of mouth. Baker used the interview material to establish a list of 12 parental alienating behaviors (that is, behaviors of the preferred parent, not of the child), each of which was mentioned by at least 20% of the sample, suggesting that there was at least one that was not mentioned by about 80% but was included in the list.

Curiously, self-identification would appear to be at odds with important points about the parental alienation concept. Alienated children are said to display the "independent thinker" phenomenon, in which they assert that their opinions are their own and could not be influenced by those of the preferred parent. Perhaps Baker posits that this view changes with maturation so that adults recognize that there were once attempts to change their thinking. Otherwise, it would seem that this sample did not involve people who had been alienated from a parent, but people whom one parent had unsuccessfully attempted to alienate, resulting not in a change of attitude toward the "targeted" parent, but instead in considerable annoyance with the parent who was trying to manipulate opinions, a result in line with the findings of Rowen and Emery (2018) but irrelevant to the issue of establishing how alienating parents behave.

Baker and Darnall (2006) used a similar approach in studying 97 people who self-identified as parents whose children had been caused to become alienated. The authors asked the participants to list all of the behaviors they believed the other parent had carried out that contributed to the child's alienation and unjustified rejection. Baker and Darnall classified the responses into eight categories and reported that the inter-rater reliability on the classifications was high. They did not, however, apparently attempt to find evidence of what the parents had actually done in the way of alienating behaviors, nor what evidence showed that the children did avoid or reject the interviewed parents.

In a later step toward creating a checklist or survey for assessment of alienating behaviors, Baker and Chambers (2011) operationalized the items on their list and explored the usefulness of the list by administering it to a community sample of adults who reported having experienced alienating behaviors as children. The final question on the list of possible alienating behaviors was whether one of the respondent's parents had tried to turn the child against the other. People who replied "yes" to this had significantly higher scores than those who answered "no" suggesting that perhaps that single question summarized all the other questions, which would not be surprising considering that the participants had identified themselves as having experienced alienating behaviors. In fact, it is difficult to see how people could have identified themselves as having experienced alienating behaviors if they did not think one parent had tried to turn them against the other. Alienating behaviors would appear to be, by definition, attempts to turn a child against a parent.

Baker herself (2020) acknowledged the design problems of these studies, noting that the approach was both retrospective and self-reporting. Retrospective studies can be problematic if there is no available objective evidence of the events being considered, as participants may forget, experience changes in memory over time, and be biased to report what the investigators are looking for or to give socially acceptable responses. Research on school performance or physical injury can be done well retrospectively because school and medical records exist, but there may be few or no records of family events.

Self-report also presents potential problems. Baker noted, arguing in favor of self-report, that it is "unlikely that the vast majority of people who participated in all of these different research studies misrepresented their experience in a way that consistently produced the same result" (2020, 243). However, the issue is not so much of misrepresentation but of memory lapses or of misapprehensions of events during childhood that are now recalled in nonveridical fashion. These sources of bias or error suggest that Baker's questionnaire, however well it may capture the participants' recall of childhood events, has not been shown to provide any evidence about what the childhood events actually were.

Applying Rohner's work

Bernet, Gregory, Reay, and Rohner (2020) reported that a sample of children who were in programs intended to correct parental alienation answered a questionnaire differently than a comparison group obtained through a commercial service. The questionnaire was the Parental Acceptance-Rejection Questionnaire (PARQ: Rohner, 2004). The PARQ asks children for statements about whether their parents are accepting or rejecting of them (the children). Bernet et al. found that the children in parental alienation programs gave more polarized responses than the comparison group, which it was argued, supported the idea of "splitting" or exaggeration of differences in the thinking of children alleged to have been exposed to parental alienating behaviors (as proposed by Warshak, 2010). Clearly, however, the PARQ examines children's beliefs about their parents' attitudes toward them, not the children's own attitudes, and it is quite reasonable that children taken from the preferred parent's custody and placed in a program against their own wishes might think of the preferred parent as liking them "just the way they are" and the other parent as disliking and wanting to change them. Demonstration that they show cognitive "splitting" would be done more suitably with questions about attitudes of persons outside the custody conflict such as siblings, friends, or teachers. If those people were also seen as polarized in acceptance or rejection, that could be taken as better evidence for the PARQ claim.

The use of a commercially established comparison group in this study is quite unusual and should have been discussed in the article, but was not. It was left unclear in what way the comparison group was matched with the parental alienation group. The Bernet et al. study thus is as questionable in terms of research design as the other work described in this section.

Measurement and analysis in parental alienation discussions

In considering whether parental alienation concepts and methods can be called scientific, a look at measurement is an important step. Is there an established protocol for identifying cases where a child's avoidant behavior is influenced by a parent's encouragement? (The reader should note that we do not speak of this as diagnosis, as there is no diagnostic category equivalent to the problems described by parental alienation proponents.) Some authors who are proponents of the parental alienation system assert that they make the identification by searching for behavior meeting the criteria described by Gardner decades ago (and discussed elsewhere in this book). Gardner's criteria include the child's denigration of the nonpreferred parent, reasons for rejection of the parent stated by the child but considered by the evaluator to be frivolous or trivial, and the statement of reasons considered by the evaluator to be "borrowed scenarios" that are not typical of children's thinking. Parental encouragement is usually inferred from the existence of these child behaviors, although specific items like emails to a third party may be included in the mix. Published work on this topic does not provide any detailed protocol for identifying parent encouragement of child avoidant behavior. There are some points that are conspicuously left unconsidered in the discussion on identification methods. One is that although Gardner and other parental alienation advocates considered interpersonal violence and abuse to be non-frivolous, acceptable reasons for a child's rejection of a parent, there appears to be no established method for ruling out these events in the course of identifying parent encouragement of child avoidant behavior. Second, the criteria as they are described are based on retrospective accounts given by adults who recall behaviors of their own parents that they felt were intended to damage the child's relationship with the other parent; there are no criteria based on empirical studies of parent behaviors in the present. Third, behaviors asserted to encourage child avoidant behavior are considered outside the context of all parent or child behaviors. Rather than looking for positive or encouraging statements and comparing their frequency to that of disparaging statements or actions, identification cherry-picks negative behaviors that discourage children from contact with one parent.

As a result of these problems of measurement, it is fair to say that there is no established protocol for identifying situations where parents encourage children to avoid the other parent, nor is there any standard evaluation method for supplying information to family courts. In the absence of standardized forms of measurement or identification, no further scientific work is possible. However, researchers are currently making efforts to create systems of identification of parental alienation (see, e.g., Milchman's work in Chapter 6).

A parental alienation advocate's detailed protocols

The previous section emphasized the idea that identification of parent encouragement of child avoidant behavior is poorly operationalized and involves vague and ambiguous methods and decisions. This is quite generally the case, and, again, it militates against meaningful scientific analysis. However, the existence of standardized assessment measures alone cannot guarantee that scientific work will follow. One parental alienation proponent, who has not published this work in professional journals but has presented it in reports and testimony to courts, describes in some detail two protocols that he uses to support the assertion that one parent has encouraged a child to reject the other parent (Childress, 2018).

The first identification method proposed by Childress is referred to as the "ABAB single case research design." Such a design exists and has been used extensively for tasks like determining whether one of several possible treatments is helpful to a child. Problems of mood or behavior are measured in four situations: Condition A is a period of time when the child's usual conditions are experienced, and problem behaviors are measured. Condition B is a period of time when a treatment is given, and problem behaviors are again measured. The last two conditions replicate the first, with an eye to being sure that any differences seen between A and B are due to the effects of the treatment and not simply to the passage of time. In cases where a treatment is already known to work well for certain problems, the effect of the treatment may also help in the identification of the problem's cause.

Childress proposed that the ABAB method could be used with a treatment called High Rad to Reunification (described later in this chapter). In the A (no treatment) condition, a child's rejection of one parent would be assessed. The B condition would be the High Road program, with a second assessment of rejection. Childress's view was that if a child rejected a parent less following the High Road program, this was evidence that the other parent had encouraged the child's avoidant behavior. However, there are serious problems with this approach. The usual use of the ABAB design requires that all factors will be held constant except the treatment itself; if this is not done, it is impossible to know whether the treatment or some other factor caused any apparent differences. The High Road program entails changes in a number of possible causal factors. For example, before attending the program, children are court-ordered to leave the custody of the preferred parent and to go to that of the nonpreferred parent, altering at a stroke a number of factors that can influence mood and behavior.

Childress has also proposed the use of what he calls the Custody Resolution Method, as employed by his colleague, the life coach, Dorcy Pruter. According to Childress, when Pruter is working on a case where a child's avoidance is attributed to parental encouragement, she collects documents that can provide information about the preferred parent's conduct. Childress has not said what these documents are, in any particular case. Pruter then has her staff peruse the documents and note occurrence of statements or behaviors that fit the criteria for parent encouragement of child avoidance as listed by Childress. (He does not describe any consideration of unrelated behaviors, such as might give a broader picture of parent attitude.) The staff-counted material is then passed on to Childress for assessment. His report to the court does not involve any corollary material or interviews with parent or child.

Science and experimentation in psychology: evidence-based treatment

As other chapters of this book have discussed, methods of identifying a child's negative attitude toward a parent as due to parental alienation behavior are without acceptable empirical support. There is no established protocol for objective identification of child avoidant behavior linked to parent encouragement. Treatments intended to change the child's attitude are also without adequate empirical support. The work referenced by parental alienation proponents as support for their methods does not meet the standards required of *evidence-based treatments* (EBTs), practices shown to be effective at a high level (or quality) of evidence. Professional organizations and governmental agencies encourage the use of treatments that have been shown to be effective by randomized controlled trials (RCTs) or clinical controlled trials (CCTs). These EBTs do not include any of the self-styled parental alienation treatments. Neither are parental alienation-related treatments listed on websites that evaluate psychological treatments for children, like effectivetherapy.org or cebce4cw.org. As of the present writing, there are published claims of effectiveness for the treatments Family Bridges (Warshak, 2010, 2019), Overcoming Barriers (Saini, 2019), and Turning Points (Gottlieb, 2012), but none of these meet standards for EBTs. High Road to Reunification has also been said to be evidence-based (Childress, 2015), but no supporting data have been published.

As much as EBT use is encouraged, it would be far from accurate to say that all psychotherapies in current use meet EBT standards. In fact, if a treatment were not used until it could be called an EBT, the logical outcome would be that it could never be an EBT. Treatments must be used experimentally for some time before empirical evidence about their effectiveness can be collected. Psychological treatments are time-consuming on the whole, so trials of safety and effectiveness make take years to do. Treatments that are under systematic study are called *experimental* treatments until an evidence basis is established.

Experimental treatments

Before a treatment gets to the experimental stage of investigation, a lot of thought and observation are required. Systematic trials cost money to carry out. That money will not be made available by foundations or government sources unless the treatment is a *plausible* one. Plausibility means that the assumptions and logic of the treatment make sense in terms of other known information. A treatment that invents a brand-new mechanism of psychological change will probably not be seen as plausible unless there is some supportive evidence to show that it might work as predicted. A treatment that does not involve some reliable way to measure changes would also be considered implausible. Treatments for problems of childhood and adolescence must be in line with established evidence about childhood development or they are lacking in plausibility.

Before psychological treatments can be part of systematic investigations, they must also be carefully described and taught to practitioners in such a way that the treatment is done in the same way in every case. This requires *manualization* of the treatment rather than simple instruction or learning by observation. Continued supervision of therapists is needed to assure *intervention fidelity*—that treatment is done in the same way for every participant in a study. Without intervention fidelity, it makes no sense to claim that a treatment was effective or even that it was safe.

When clients are going to receive experimental treatments, they must be informed that this is the case. This is true for psychology just as well as for medicine, although the ways people could be harmed by experimental medical treatments are generally more obvious than is the case for psychological treatment. Informed consent is needed for all psychological treatment except that ordered by courts, and informed consent includes being informed about the research that supports the treatment. When psychological treatments are well-established as evidence-based, informed consent documents need to include information about both benefits and risks of the treatment. Practitioners of experimental treatments do not have such information to give, so they need to be clear in communicating that risks and benefits are not well understood. Parental alienation treatments and other reunification therapies do not seem to have been accompanied by this kind of information or designated as experimental interventions. As they are often used following a court order, questions about information and consent are not the usual ones.

The very idea that a psychological treatment could be associated with risks is unfamiliar to many people who might receive an experimental treatment. Somehow, we imagine that an intervention that has the power to make positive changes for us does not also have the power to make potential negative changes. If something is called a therapy, we expect it to be beneficial. Because this mistake is so common, information about experimental (and other) psychological interventions needs to include material about possible *adverse events* following a treatment. These can include direct harms like intensification of existing negative feelings or behaviors, or like the beginning of new problems like depression or even suicidality. Adverse events can also be indirect harms such as the waste of a family's resources of time and money when a treatment is ineffective, or "opportunity costs" when resources poured into a treatment mean that family members miss unrelated benefits like music lessons or vacations. Some psychologists have argued that treatments that make a person feel upset, cry, or be angry or frightened are also displaying adverse events and should not be used unless it is clear that a treatment helps, and no other treatment is possible.

Psychological treatments that are pseudoscientific

The issues discussed so far are complicated by the fact that there is a third possible category to add to "scientific" and "unscientific". This is the category of *pseudoscience*. Pseudoscientific material involves a sort of sham science, with a pretense of following scientific practices, but none of the actual work of scientific investigation, measurement, hypothesis-testing, and transparent reporting that characterize acceptable science. Understanding the pseudoscientific nature of the parental alienation belief system is especially important because scientific background can strongly influence whether evidence is accepted in the courtroom.

What if a psychological treatment is not evidence-based and its practitioners do not say it is experimental? It might be a brand-new, innovative therapy that has not even reached the stage of systematic investigation but is plausible, logical, and in line with known facts about human development, personality, and mental illness. But it might also be a pseudoscientific *alternative psychotherapy*.

The term "alternative psychotherapy" (Mercer, 2014) is derived from the medical term complementary-and-alternative medicine (CAM). CAM treatments are not evidence-based, nor are they plausible enough to be receiving systematic investigation as experimental treatments. If they were supported by acceptable evidence, they would be ordinary medicine rather than CAM and the same distinction applies to psychological interventions. There is a difference between CAM and alternative psychotherapies, though. The difference is that CAM methods are sometimes used in a complementary fashion—that is, in addition to evidence-based medicine—rather than as an alternative to evidence-based medicine. This is not usually the case for psychological interventions. Alternative psychological treatments are used as their name suggests, instead of, rather than together with, evidence-based or genuinely experimental interventions.

Alternative psychotherapies are sometimes presented as if they are evidence-based when they are not supported by acceptable evidence. Alternative practitioners of various kinds have sometimes claimed that the term EBT simply means that a treatment is a good one; one even told a large audience that an evidence-based treatment was any treatment that had been the subject of a publication in a peer-reviewed journal. In some cases, proponents of alternative psychotherapies cite research that is genuine but not actually relevant to the safety or effectiveness of the treatment in question; they may reference animal studies because these are "scientific", even though generalizing from animals to humans may be difficult.

What is pseudoscience?

When proponents of an alternative psychotherapy claim that the treatment has scientific support, but it is clear that it does not have any record of adequate systematic investigation, it may be appropriate to call the treatment *pseudoscientific*. Pseudoscientific assertions claim the support of systematic investigations following scientific guidelines, but do not actually have such support. There is more wrong here than the simple inadequacy of the claims; the claims about the treatment are disguised as something they are not, for the purpose of attracting purchasers of the treatment. Pseudoscience thus involves an element of commercial fraud as well as of false claims made for their own sake.

Thinkers have been struggling to define "science" for a century and more, with limited success. If it were possible to have a clear, valid, absolute list of characteristics of science, it would be easy to argue that pseudoscience is material that claims those characteristics but does not really have them. But although there are some traits that all scientific endeavors share, such as hypothesis-testing, the ways researchers "do science" depend in part on the topics they study. Astronomers and epidemiologists cannot do experiments, but chemists must do them. Psychologists sometimes can and sometimes can't, depending on the topic they are studying. Thus, pseudoscience cannot be defined just by looking at what characteristics are missing in a general way— though careful examination of the support for pseudoscientific claims shows whether their evidence has not met the highest standards of related disciplines.

Pseudoscientific material can differ in its specifics, just as scientific work can, but there are some traits that have been described as helping to identify pseudoscience (Grimes and Bishop, 2018; Hupp, Mercer, Thyer, and Pignotti, 2019). Here are some that are especially relevant to the parental alienation belief system:

- The research that is reported has no outside source of funding, so the researchers have a financial interest in showing that they have safe, effective methods. (Outside funding is not reported in published research related to parental alienation cases.)
- Exaggerated claims of effectiveness are made without support by adequate research and may involve publication in journals with low standards. (The research claimed to support the parental alienation belief system does not meet the criteria for evidence-based treatments.)
- Findings are misrepresented. (For example, studies of adults' reports of their parents' behavior are said to provide clear evidence that children who avoid a parent have had similar experiences.)
- The way a treatment is said to work is not congruent with well-established existing knowledge. (For example, attitude change does not necessarily result from new information or from intense motivators like threats.)
- Treatments have not been shown to work by a discipline's usual standards of evidence but are claimed to be effective anyway. (Evidence for parental alienation treatments does not meet usual standards.)
- Treatments have not only not been tested but are also based on implausible ideas. (As there is no evidence that children who avoid a parent have been "brainwashed", it is implausible that they can be "deprogrammed" by the methods used.)
- Treatments are potentially harmful, either directly or in terms of side effects. (It is plausible that experiences with the treatments could be harmful, and there is anecdotal evidence that they have been harmful.)
- Technical terminology is used to obfuscate rather than to clarify the discussion. (Esoteric terms such as "targeted parent" and "aftercare professional" imply a body of knowledge that does not exist.)

Conclusion

The material in this chapter demonstrates that empirical work related to parental alienation is weak in design and implementation, and assertions about that work are pseudoscientific in nature. This conclusion has rarely been brought into court proceedings but may have the potential for arguing more strongly against the parental alienation belief system than do present attempts to exclude parental alienation authors' research reports as admissible evidence, as discussed in Chapter 13.

References

Baker, Amy. "The Long-term Effects of Parental Alienation on Adult Children: A Qualitative Research Study." *American Journal of Family Therapy* 33, 2005: 289–302.

Baker, Amy. "Mounting Evidence Supports Reliability and Validity of Parental Alienation." Accessed March 30, 2020 at https://psychplogytoday.com/us/blog/caught-between-parents-/201107/mounting-evidence-supports-reliability-and-validity-parental

Baker, Amy. "Parental Alienation and Empirical Research." In *Parental Alienation: Science and Law*, edited by Demosthenes Lorandos and William Bernet, 207–253. Springfield, IL: Charles C. Thomas, 2020.

Baker, Amy, and Jaclyn Chambers. "Adult Recall of Childhood Exposure to Parental Conflict: Unpacking the Black Box of Parental Alienation." *Journal of Divorce and Remarriage* 52, 2011: 55–76.

Baker, Amy, and Douglas Darnall. "Behaviors and Strategies Used in Parental Alienation: A Survey of Parental Experiences." *Journal of Divorce and Remarriage* 45, 2006: 97–124.

Bernet, William, Nilhun Gregory, Kathleen Reay, and Ronald Rohner. "Measuring the Difference between Parental Alienation and Parental Estrangement: The PARQ-gap." *Journal of Forensic Sciences* 65, 2020: 1225–1234. doi:10.1111/1556-4029.14300.

Childress, Craig. *An Attachment-based Model of Parental Alienation: Foundations.* Claremont, CA: Oaksong, 2015.

Childress, Craig. *An Attachment-based Model of Parental Alienation: Single Case ABAB Assessment & Remedy.* Claremont, CA: Oaksong, 2018.

Clawar, Stanley, and Brynne Rivlin. *Children Held Hostage: Dealing With Programmed and Brainwashed Children.* Chicago: American Bar Association, 1991, 2013.

Conscious Co-parenting Institute "Overview of High Road to Reunification." Unpublished Paper, n.d..

Gottlieb, Linda. *The Parental Alienation Syndrome: A Family Therapy and Collaborative Systems Approach to Alienation.* Springfield, IL: Charles C. Thomas, 2012.

Grimes, David, and Dorothy Bishop. "Distinguishing Polemic from Commentary in Science: Some Guidelines Illustrated with the Case of Sage and Burgio (2017)." *Child Development* 89, 2018: 141–147.

Hupp, Stephen, Jean Mercer, Bruce Thyer, and Monica Pignotti. "Critical Thinking about Psychotherapy." In *Pseudoscience in Child and Adolescent Psychotherapy*, edited by Stephen Hupp, 1–13. New York: Cambridge University Press, 2019.

Lastrucci, Carlo. *The Scientific Approach: Basic Principles of the Scientific Method.* Cambridge, MA: Schenkman, 1963.

Mercer, Jean. "Are Intensive Parental Alienation Treatments Safe or Effective for Children and Adolescents?" Journal of Child Custody 16, 2019:67–113.

Mercer, Jean. *Alternative Psychotherapies.* Lanham, MD: Rowman & Littlefield, 2014.

Rohner, Ronald. "The Parental 'Acceptance-rejection Syndrome': Universal Correlates of Perceived Rejection." *American Psychologist* 59, 2004: 830–840.

Rosenblum, Leon, and Harry Harlow. "Approach-avoidance Conflict in the Mother-surrogate Situation." *Psychological Reports* 12, 1963: 83–85.

Rowen, Jenna, and Robert Emery. "Parental Denigration: A Form of Conflict That Typically Backfires." *Family Court Review* 56, 2018: 258–268.

Saini, Michael. "Strengthening Coparenting Relationships to Improve Strained Parent-child Relationships: A Follow-up Study of Parents' Experiences of Attending the Overcoming Barriers Family Camp." *Family Court Review* 57, 2019: 217–230.

Warshak, Richard. "Family Bridges: Using Insights from Social Sciences to Reconnect Parents and Alienated Children." *Family Court Review* 48, 2010: 48–80.

Warshak, Richard. "Reclaiming Parent-child Relationships: Outcomes of Family Bridges with Alienated Children." *Journal of Divorce and Remarriage* 60, 2019: 645–667.

Yin, Robert. *Case Study Research*. Beverly Hills, CA: Sage, 1984.

Chapter 13

Conclusion

The current issues about parental alienation

Jean Mercer and Margaret Drew

In our original editorial planning for this volume, we did not propose to deny the possible existence of cases in which a divorced parent encouraged a child to reject and avoid the other parent. It is clear that some children do reject a divorced parent, and it would be foolhardy to attempt to claim that this phenomenon does not exist or that it is never associated with parent encouragement.

Our concern about these cases of child avoidance was the serious lack of nuance with which the parental alienation belief system has been and is being applied by family courts. We see multiple problems in the use of parental alienation concepts in child custody decisions, as discussed earlier in this book. Here are some of the difficulties:

- The lack of an established protocol for identification of cases in which a parent has encouraged a child's avoidance of the other parent.
- Weaponization of parental alienation allegations, with increased levels of stress and conflict within separating families, even in cases where judicial decisions do not order custody change.
- Increases in stress and conflict due to unsupported claims that parent encouragement of child avoidance is a form of family violence.
- Incorrect assertions that the parental alienation belief system has a strong scientific foundation, used in arguments for custody decisions.
- Use of allegations that a parent has encouraged a child's avoidance to counter allegations of child abuse, potentially placing children in contact with abusers.
- Orders by courts for parental alienation treatments that lack an acceptable evidence basis, to the probable financial and personal harm of family members.
- Allegations that a parent has encouraged a child's avoidance of the other parent that give additional leverage to the parent with financial advantages, who can bring in parental alienation proponents as expert witnesses and can afford lengthy litigation.

DOI: 10.4324/9781003095927-16

- The incorporation of the parental alienation belief system into legal decisions and even into legislation in countries around the world, making the problems noted here of broad concern.

The authors of chapters in this book have discussed these concerns in detail and confirmed that these and other difficulties are very real. How these problems are to be solved remains an unanswered question. In the remainder of this concluding chapter, we will discuss steps that need to be taken. We will consider these in two categories: directions for research by psychologists and social scientists, and legal issues.

Important directions in child avoidance research

Very little of the research related to the parental alienation belief system meets high scientific standards, and very few attempts have been made to answer obvious basic questions. The interdisciplinary nature of the topic is one of the barriers researchers must overcome, but the identification of fruitful research topics is also a major issue. What should researchers be doing to give us useful information about child avoidance of a parent, with or without the encouragement of the other parent?

Establishing a protocol for identification

As we noted earlier, there is presently no established protocol for identification of cases where child avoidance of a parent is caused by the encouragement of the other parent outlined a possible approach to this problem. Parental alienation advocates have not presented a description of their methods or described how they rule out previous abuse or domestic violence on the part of the avoided parent. No published description suggests that there are methods of identifying these cases that are both reliable (would yield the same results when used by different practitioners) and valid (would yield results that are equivalent to other known methods).

The essential first step for study of any phenomenon is the development of a capacity to operationally define and to identify the phenomenon. A second step would be to quantify the phenomenon so it would be possible to measure whether circumstances increased or lessened it. In the present case, these steps would involve identification of both child avoidant behavior and of any parent encouragement of that behavior. It would appear from statements of involved families that evidence brought to discussions of child avoidant behavior can vary from adamant refusal of contact, with physical reactions like vomiting when it is forced, to requests for scheduling changes. What these have in common is that one parent is displeased and seeks legal help to force child obedience. It would also appear that in most cases, parent encouragement is not only ill-defined, varying from an occasional negative remark or facial expression to abduction of the child, but is also usually inferred rather than observed. Published parental alienation-related material does not indicate methods for identifying parent encouragement nor does it outline methods for ruling out child abuse or domestic violence as causes of the child's avoidance. Without established protocols for identifying the behaviors of the child and the preferred parent, no systematic investigation or independent confirmation of results can take place. To be genuinely useful, such protocols would need to be supported by evidence of validity and reliability. They would also accurately discriminate between children who avoided a parent because of past experiences with that parent, and those who avoided a parent because of persuasion by the other parent or any other reason.

The lack of an identification protocol substantially weakens existing research on parental alienation treatments. Children who have received these treatments appear to have been identified as parental alienation cases because of judges' decisions, whose basis remains unclear. Post-treatment assessments have not compared the pre- and post-treatment attitudes of the children and could not do so because there was no standard pre-treatment evaluation.

Incidence and prevalence

Establishment of a protocol for the identification of parental alienation cases would be an essential step toward a scientific understanding of some children's avoidance of divorced parents. Such a protocol would make it possible to study the incidence (number of cases) and prevalence (proportion of cases) of families in which a parent encourages a child's avoidance. Presently, without such a protocol, estimates of the occurrence of parental alienation cases is entirely based on judicial decisions, and as such decisions may not be made public, the estimates can only be very rough. In any case, such estimates completely miss cases in which parental disagreements are settled out of court, as well as those that do not enter the court system but receive treatment by private mental health professionals, or those in which the avoided parent makes no effort at reunification. Research on this issue needs to follow the methods of epidemiology in order to ascertain whether parental alienation cases are rare or common, but again, without an established identification protocol, this cannot be done. It should be noted that such a protocol would be independent of any issue about a diagnosis of parental alienation as a mental health disorder.

Is parent encouragement of child avoidance actually harmful?

Proponents of the parental alienation belief system argue that child avoidance of a parent following encouragement by the other parent is harmful to the child. The degree of harm has been compared to that of child psychological abuse and other adverse childhood experiences (Harman, Kruk, and Hines

2018). However, no empirical evidence exists to show that this is so. There is evidence of psychological harm experienced by some but not all children of divorce, and there is at this juncture no evidence that discriminates harm in parental alienation cases from other harms of divorce. For a scientific under-standing of child avoidance cases, it would be essential to determine whether children who had been encouraged to avoid a parent later showed more psycho-logical problems than children of divorce who had not avoided a parent, or even than children of intact marriages. This information is not presently available.

Judicial decisions based on the parental alienation belief system present a curious contrast to other positions society takes about contacts between parents and children. Despite some evidence of psychological harm done by divorce, we do not forbid parents to divorce. Although poor social and par-enting skills are problematic factors in children's lives, we do not require parents to improve their skills or prohibit contact with their children until they do so. Divorced parents may move away from their children and may re-marry freely even though these events are less than optimal for the children. When some parents voluntarily remove themselves from contact with their children, an action that might be expected to be harmful, courts do not order them to act in the children's best interests by cultivating good relationships. Even imprisoned criminals have the right but not the obligation to have contact with their children. These facts suggest that the harms to children asserted by parental alienation advocates are exaggerated and prioritized for reasons other than the children's best interests.

Characteristics of the children: an essential research topic

Some authors (Fidler and Bala 2010; Friedlander and Walters 2010) have de-scribed characteristics of preferred and of nonpreferred parents, sometimes citing behavioral weaknesses or even mental health disorders as aspects of each of these groups. Much less has been said about the avoidant children, although age ranges have been reported for children in parental alienation treatments. Because one child in a family may avoid a parent while another does not, it is reasonable to think that some basic or even constitutional child characteristics may help to determine whether a child will avoid a parent (whether encouraged by the other parent or not). The agency of children in shaping their own development is a concept that has received far too little attention in parental alienation-related work.

Roles of stepparents and stepsiblings

Parental alienation proponents have noted that remarriage of one parent may be followed by a child avoiding that parent. However, there has been little or no work about the roles played by new spouses and the children of those spouses in triggering a child's avoidance of the remarried parent. Although it is possible that remarriage could create jealousy in the other parent and could cause that parent to encourage a child to avoid the remarried person, it is also possible that a new spouse could be either unwelcoming or overly welcoming to a visiting child, or that reactions of new stepsiblings could be aversive for a child who would want to avoid visits. None of these issues have received careful research investigation at this point.

The shared delusional disorder issue

Although the term parental alienation does not refer to an established diagnosis, it has been used over a couple of decades to suggest that there is psychopathology in cases where child avoidant behavior is argued to have resulted from parent encouragement. In the past few years, arguments in such cases have begun to refer to an established diagnosis, Shared Delusional Disorder. The proposal is that the preferred parent suffers from the delusion that the nonpreferred parent is reasonably to be feared or hated, and this delusion has become shared with the child as a result of interactions with the preferred parent, with the result that the child now avoids the nonpreferred parent. The present authors have seen documents in three ongoing custody cases in which a psychologist has diagnosed the preferred parent and the child as showing Shared Delusional Disorder. As the prevalence of Delusional Disorder has been estimated at 0.18% (Suvisaari et al. 2009), and as none of these diagnoses were based on extensive interviews or psychological testing, these conclusions seem questionable. They raise an important issue, however. The influence of the parental alienation approach to child avoidant behavior has been somewhat weakened by the fact that there is no "official" parental alienation diagnosis, but use of the Shared Delusional Disorder diagnosis would solve that problem and permit what is essentially the parental alienation belief system view, retrofitted with a legitimate diagnostic label. This suggests that research on child avoidant behavior with parental encouragement needs to include investigation of the frequency with which Shared Delusional Disorder is claimed and the methods that are being used to provide this diagnosis.

Arguing the admissibility of parental alienation concepts in courts

Parental alienation advocates such as Baker (2013) and Lorandos (2020) have argued that parental alienation principles and practices are admissible in courts as scientific evidence. We reject this position and encourage lawyers and mental health professionals to challenge and counter it.

Meeting the Daubert standards

In federal courts in the United States, evidence presented as science-based should meet the standards set in *Daubert v. Merrell Dow Pharmaceuticals* in 1993.

State courts increasingly use the same standards, which include five factors: 1. Whether a theory or technique can be or has been tested, 2. Whether the topic has received peer review and publication, 3. The known or potential error rate of a method, 4. The existence and maintenance of standards controlling the operation of a method, and 5. Whether there is widespread acceptance within a relevant scientific community. The parental alienation belief system meets some but by no means all these standards.

Testability

The parental alienation belief system would be testable if there were an established protocol for identifying cases where parents had encouraged child avoidance and discriminating them from other child avoidance cases. Testing the predictions of parental alienation concepts would still be expensive and time-consuming, but there would be no unusual difficulties in carrying out this process—if parental alienation cases could be identified with accuracy. However, no protocol for identification has been established on the basis of empirical support. As a result, there has been no test of the parental alienation belief system, and there can be no such test until there is an empirically supported identification method.

Peer review and publication

A number of professional journals that claim to be peer-reviewed have accepted and published articles that take the parental alienation approach. It appears that none of these publications has thoroughly described identification, treatment, and later assessment of parental alienation cases. As some of the methods are proprietary (for example, Family Bridges™), this is not entirely surprising. Also unsurprising is that articles rebutting the parental alienation belief system have been published in peer-reviewed professional journals.

Known or potential error rate

Today, scientific evidence is characterized by an awareness of the potential for error. In some cases, this awareness is shown by statistical work that indicates the amount of variation in measurements used. In other cases, reports include information about false negatives (cases where a problem was present but not detected) and false positives (cases where a problem was thought to be detected although it did not exist). Reports of outcomes of parental alienation treatments have not usually included statistical analyses. Warshak (2019), a prominent parental alienation advocate, has noted the lack of available information about false positive and false negative identifications of parental alienation cases. There is thus no estimate of an error rate that can be associated with parental alienation concepts or practices.

Standards controlling the operation of a method

There appears to be no organization that oversees all methods that apply parental alienation concepts. As mentioned earlier, the use of proprietary methods and treatments may be responsible for this. People may seek to be trained to carry out parental alienation-related methods by individuals who are well-known as proponents of the parental alienation belief system. In one case, the Conscious Co-Parenting Institute (www.consciouscoparent-ing.com) offers training through remote as well as face-to-face methods and charges fees for these experiences but provides no information about standards of performance. The operation of Family Bridges™ is not based in an office or institution, but uses hotel rooms as venues for treatment, reducing the possibility of oversight. There is no certification or licensure in the field of parental alienation that is approved or overseen by any educational or clinical institution.

Widespread acceptance in scientific community

Applying the *Daubert* standard of widespread acceptance in the relevant scientific community requires us to decide which that community might be. We suggest that the scientific communities of greatest relevance are those that study child development and developmental psychopathology, these being the fields that focus most on outcomes of childhood experiences like those posited by parental alienation proponents. No articles on child avoidance encouraged by a parent have appeared in the major journals in these fields, suggesting that there is little acceptance of the parental alienation belief system in the relevant scientific communities.

Specific community standards

The *Daubert* standards refer to the views of relevant scientific communities without describing those views or suggesting how a relevant community might be identified. Philosophers of science have focused on such issues to a far greater extent than the courts have as of this writing. For example, the philosopher Paul Feyerabend stated as a thesis that "the events, procedures, and results that constitute the sciences have no common structure; there are no elements that occur in every scientific investigation but are missing elsewhere" (2010, xix). Feyerabend also gave the opinion that a

> theory of science that devises standards and structural methods for all scientific activities and authorizes them by reference to 'Reason' or 'Rationality' may impress outsiders—but it is much too crude an instrument for the people on the spot, that is, for scientists facing some concrete research problem.
> (2010 xix)

The Supreme Court of the United States is not in the business of creating a theory of science and did not do so in listing the *Daubert* standards, which are so general that they can be broadly applied and still leave open for discussion the concerns and standards of relevant scientific communities.

The most relevant scientific community for the study of child avoidance of a parent is that of psychology. Psychologists have made a specialty of studying and critiquing research methods, to a point where mental and behavioral health professionals of many disciplines look to work in psychology to provide research standards. From the mid-1990s, psychologists have followed the lead of the evidence-based medicine movement and have developed standards for defining methods as empirically supported. Those standards were discussed in the introductory chapter of this book, and later chapters made it clear that empirical research by parental alienation proponents has never met the standards established by psychologists as a scientific community. Arguments presented by parental alienation advocates have never referenced those community standards, and it is time that litigation about child custody did include reference to the community standards.

In addition to features of research design that provide a reliable evidence basis for conclusions, standards of the psychological community also include both qualitative and quantitative analysis of measured factors. Such analyses have not been characteristic of parental alienation proponents' research. Where attempts at statistical analysis exist, they have often failed to consider the established criteria for using specific tests, a problem shown in a study by Baker and Verrocchio (2016), for just one example. Readers who are interested in this issue can find an excellent discussion of community standards about statistical analysis in an article by Morris, Grice, and Cox (2016) as well as elsewhere. Morris et al. correctly called the failure to meet community standards about the use of statistics a matter of "quantitative alchemy".

Parental alienation practices as an alternative psychotherapy

In the medical sphere, non-evidence-based diagnoses and treatments are often referred to as CAM (complementary and alternative) practices. Complementary treatments are administered together with conventional therapies, while alternative treatments, as the name suggests, are chosen instead of conventional, evidence-based methods. It is highly unusual to have patients choose to use non-evidence-based mental health interventions as well as conventional treatments, so the "complementary" term does not usually apply. However, there are a number of alternative psychotherapies that clients may choose for themselves or for their children (Mercer 2013).

Interventions for children who avoid a parent (parental alienation treatments or PATs) have much in common with alternative psychotherapies, over and above the lack of evidence basis. Comparing PATs with the well-known alternative psychotherapy for children, Holding Therapy (see Chaffin et al. 2006), we see a number of similarities in their histories. Both forms of treatment:

- Proposed a problem category without a clear evidence basis
- Claimed that diagnostic manuals would later contain the proposed diagnosis
- Made alarming but unsubstantiated claims about the effects of lack of treatment
- Claimed that conventional methods of treatment were ineffective or exacerbated problems
- Used coercive treatments
- Were associated with harm to some children
- Were associated with suicidality in some children
- Were marked by surrender of professional licenses by some practitioners
- Sought support from parent groups rather than from the professional community

This list of similarities suggests that parental alienation principles and practices may well deserve to be categorized as alternative psychotherapy. Of course, this categorization could be strongly challenged if adequate work were presented to support the parental alienation belief system.

Conclusion

In closing, we caution parents of children who resist contact with one parent, and professionals who work with parents and with children, to exercise great care in their thinking about causes of this behavior. Children's behavior is as complex and many-factored as that of adults, perhaps even more so as children move through developmental transitions. That a complicated behavior could have a single, simple cause is a remote possibility. Experiences with parenting are only one of many sources of child mood and behavior. If we assume otherwise, we risk serious mistakes that can be harmful to children and to other family members as well.

Two mantras of child development are applicable here. One is: "don't just do something; stand there and watch"—that is, observe what is actually happening in a family before rushing to correct it. The other is: "this isn't rocket science, it's a lot more complicated than that". Anyone who presents a simple explanation and solution to a child's concerning behavior is more likely than not to be wrong.

Finally, one topic that has not been addressed is the ethics of using the parental alienation belief system in child custody disputes. The belief system, as shown, is not a scientifically supported "theory" or even concept. Alienation is a litigation tool. For mental health professionals to advance unsupported beliefs to lead a court to minimize abuse allegations is ethically, if not morally, wrong. Hiding behind "expert" opinions is not permitted when a lawyer knows that the information presented to the court is not sound. Lawyers have a duty of candor to the court as well as a duty to investigate (American Bar Association 2021). In civil matters, such as those in family court, legal ethics requires that the lawyer not mislead the court. While lawyers can debate whether testimony of the alienation belief system should be permitted in court, the more that alienation is promoted as a "scientifically supported theory" and the science proves otherwise, the more risk lawyers run in violating ethics rules on their duty of candor to the court and their duty not to advance frivolous claims.

While the tide seems to be turning against the unquestioned promotion of the parental alienation belief system (Chapter 2), courts must demand that those lawyers advancing this system present solid evidence of validity or non-validity of their statements. Unfortunately, lawyers are hired by parents and not by children. Were it otherwise, children's safety might be prioritized over parent access and the best interest of the child standard might be paramount in custody contested cases.

References

American Bar Association. *Model Rules of Professional Conduct.* (2021). https://www.americanbar.org/groups/professional_responsibility/publications/model_rules_of_professional_conduct/model_rules_of_professional_conduct_table_of_contents/

Baker, Amy. "Parental Alienation Research and the *Daubert* Standards." In *Parental Alienation: The Handbook for Mental Health and Legal Professionals*, edited by Demosthenes Lorandos, William Bernet, and Richard Sauber, 322–347. Springfield, IL: Charles C. Thomas, 2013.

Baker, Amy, and Maria Verrocchio. "Exposure to Parental Alienation and Subsequent Anxiety and Depression in Italian Adults." *American Journal of Family Therapy* 44, 2016: 255–271.

Chaffin, Mark, Rochele Hanson, Benjamin Saunders, Todd Nichols, Douglas Barnett, Charles Zeanah… Cindy Miller-Perrin. "Report of the APSAC Task Force on Attachment Therapy, Reactive Attachment Disorder, and Attachment Problems." *Child Maltreatment* 11, 2006: 76–89.

Feyerabend, Paul. *Against Method* (4th edition). New York: Verso, 2010.

Fidler, Barbara, and Nicholas Bala. "Children Resisting Post-separation Contact with a Parent: Concepts, Controversies, and Conundrums." *Family Court Review* 48, 2010: 10–47.

Friedlander, Steven, and Marjorie Walters. "When a Child Rejects a Parent: Tailoring the Intervention to Fit the Problem." *Family Court Review* 48, 2010: 98–111.

Harman, Jennifer, Edward Kruk, and Denise Hines. "Parental Alienating Behaviors: An Unacknowledged Form of Family Violence." *Psychological Bulletin* 144, 2018: 1275–1299.

Lorandos, Demosthenes. "Admissibility of the Construct—Parental Alienation." In *Parental Alienation—Science and Law*, edited by Demosthenes Lorandos and William Bernet, 324–364. Springfield, IL: Charles C. Thomas, 2020.

Mercer, Jean. *Alternative Psychotherapies*. Lanham, MD: Rowman & Littlefield, 2013.

Morris, Stefanie, James Grice, and Ryan Cox. "Scale Imposition as Quantitative Alchemy: Studies in the Transitivity of Neuroticism Ratings." *Basic and Applied Social Psychology* 39, 2016: 1–18.

Suvisaari, Janna, Jonna Perala, Samuli Saami, Hannu Juvonen, Annamari Tuulio-Henriksson, and Jouko Lonnqvist. "The Epidemiology and Descriptive and Predictive Validity of DSM-IV Delusional Disorder and Subtypes of Schizophrenia." *Clinical Schizophrenia & Related Psychoses* 2, 2009: 289–297.

Warshak, R. "Reclaiming Parent-child Relationships: Outcomes of Family Bridges with Alienated Children." *Journal of Divorce and Remarriage* 60, 2019: 645–667.

Index

Note: *Italic* page numbers refer to figures.